Chicano Poetry: A Response to Chaos

CHICANO POETRY
A Response to Chaos

by Bruce-Novoa, 1944-

University of Texas Press
Austin

Para Juan Carlos y mis Padres

Copyright © 1982 by the University of Texas Press
All rights reserved
Printed in the United States of America
First edition, 1982

Requests for permission to reproduce material
from this work should be sent to:
Permissions
University of Texas Press
Box 7819
Austin, Texas 78712

Library of Congress Cataloging in Publication Data
Bruce-Novoa, 1944–
    Chicano poetry.
    Bibliography: p.
    Includes index.
    1. American poetry—Mexican American authors—History
and criticism. 2. American poetry—20th century—History and criticism.
I. Title.
PS153.M4B73   811'.54'0986872073   81–23129
ISBN 0–292–71075–5   AACR2

Because this page cannot legibly accommodate all the copyright
notices, page 238 constitutes an extension of the copyright page.

CONTENTS

Preface   vii

1. Introduction   3
2. Rescuing the World Center:
   Montoya, Navarro, Delgado, Salinas   14
3. The Heroics of Sacrifice: *I Am Joaquín*   48
4. The Teachings of Alurista:
   A Chicano Way of Knowledge   69
5. The Heroics of Self-Love: Sergio Elizondo   96
6. The Voice of Silence: Miguel Méndez, Poet   116
7. Time, Death, and the Other Voice of Silence:
   Tino Villanueva   131
8. A Voice against Silence: Ricardo Sánchez   151
9. Rituals of Devastation and Resurrection:
   Bernice Zamora   160
10. Patricide and Resurrection: Gary Soto   185
11. Conclusion   212

Notes   217

Selected Bibliography   229

Index   233

PREFACE

"Chicano literature, as treated here, is a recent phenomenon." "Admittedly, this literature, or at least its publication, was a by-product of the Chicano Movement, the socio-political civil rights struggle begun in the mid-1960's, by and on behalf of people of Mexican descent living in the United States." Thus begin the first two paragraphs of the introduction to my *Chicano Authors: Inquiry by Interview* (1980), and nothing has happened to change these and the other opinions therein. For background information on the Movement, the term *Chicano*, and the literature, see that book. Here I will assume knowledge of some basic facts about Chicanos.

The literature treated in the previous book and this one is the same, albeit seen from a different perspective. The main section of *Chicano Authors* is dedicated to the authors' opinions; while in the present book, the authors retreat to a secondary position to allow us to concentrate on their work. Another way to state it might be that, here, my opinions are featured; but that is not really the point. The texts are the primary material; all interpretation is secondary to the reading itself. It has always been my purpose to lead readers back to texts, with an increased ability to enjoy and understand them. My method is to read the texts as literature, reacting to them as subjects with their own life, and endeavoring to let them speak through yet another voice. Not that I ignore the social context of literature; *Chicano Authors* is dedicated to exactly that. Rather, as a critic, or artist, one must work according to one's talents, training, and predilections. Mine led me to choose textual analysis. Texts have certain qualities as subjects and objects in the world, and can be studied from different perspectives; they will yield surprising and joyful varieties of versions of themselves. Variety within sameness is one of the beauties of life. Hunter S. Thompson warns that a writer should start to worry when she or he begins to auto-plagiarize, but I would risk reminding the reader that in 1974 I called for many approaches to Chicano literature; Chicano criticism should be a dynamic interplay of many readings, none of which can presume to be absolute. The sum of all readings—always open to increase—will make up the expanding space of Chicano criticism. I certainly would not now claim preemptive rights for my readings, as some critics have for theirs. This book is one possibility in the space of many; may it prove helpful.

The seminal lectures and articles for this book date from 1974–1975. The essence of the interpretations was introduced in the fall of 1974 in a lecture, "The Space of Chicano Literature," published in 1975 with a slightly different version in Spanish, "Literatura chicana: La respuesta al caos." My subsequent work has been a development of this material. Since the beginning my reading has been guided by certain writers: Juan García Ponce, Octavio Paz, Georges Bataille, Maurice Blanchot, and Mircea Eliade. Of the Chicano authors, José Montoya has been a constant inspiration, and the discussions of my ideas with Bernice Zamora have been illuminating. But if this book has a primary source, it is teaching. All my analyses were developed for, if not in, the classrooms at Yale University. Therefore, much credit must go to my students. The text and notes bespeak their contributions. A special expression of thanks is due to Margarita Vargas, who proofread the manuscript.

I am grateful to the National Chicano Council for Higher Education, the Rockefeller Foundation, and Yale University for granting me leave time and funds to complete this study.

Chicano Poetry: A Response to Chaos

Many heroes lived before Agamemnon,
but all unwept . . .

Horace

1. INTRODUCTION

Man cannot live except in . . . sacred space. And when there is no hierophany to reveal it to him, he constructs it for himself.
—Mircea Eliade, *Patterns in Comparative Religion*, p. 382.

The poetry studied here was written by authors of Mexican heritage residing permanently in the United States and is further identifiable as "Chicano" in that it coincides with the civil rights struggle by and for that group in the mid-1960's—the Chicano Movement. Not that people of Mexican extraction living in the U.S.A. did not write poetry before the 1960's; they did.[1] However, *Chicano literature*, as most people use the term, is that which is associated with a new consciousness of political, social, and cultural identity linked to the Chicano Movement. Some works sprang directly from the struggle, written by political activists like Rodolfo Gonzales, the leader of the Denver-based Crusade for Justice. Other works may have been written before the Movement, like José Montoya's "El Louie" or some of Bernice Zamora's poems, but publication was brought about by the cultural fervor of the Movement, which stimulated the founding of journals and publishing houses specializing in Chicano writing. Moreover, the literature quickly became part of the Movement's ideological material, giving it the particular tone we know today. How much was the ideology of a mythological homeland called Aztlán a product of Alurista's poetry or vice versa? *I Am Joaquín* probably turned more young Chicanos toward cultural nationalism than any political essay. The exact relationship between political activism and Chicano literature is yet to be properly evaluated, however;[2] I leave the task to social scientists trained to do it. This study concerns itself with literary texts, those which form the heart of Chicano literature during its first decade and a half.

From the material published since 1965, we can distinguish works that have established themselves as the essential core of Chicano poetry. Other poems, books, and authors exist, and in great variety. Criticism, however, must attempt to identify those works which best characterize a literature. The selection reflects what the majority of critics and teachers consider the most significant Chicano poetry to date. Some exclusions may be questioned, but no serious objection can be raised to those included. Any comprehensive study of Chicano poetry will utilize these texts.

Methodology and Model

Transformational grammar provides terminology useful for literary analysis: *surface structure*, the distribution of grammatical elements as experienced by the speaker, listener, or reader of a sentence; and *deep structure*, the underlying distribution of the essential elements. The essential elements of a deep structure, before arrangement, are known as the *chosen elements*, while in their distributional order they are referred to as the *underlying string*. Deep structures become surface structures through a series of transformations, often attributable to the context in which the transformations are carried out.[3] This is not a book of linguistic analysis; I simply wish to define some terms basic to this study.

Literature can be studied as surface in order to understand and enjoy how a piece is organized and presented. The surface cannot be ignored; it is the primary level of encounter and, in most cases, the readers' first and last level of encounter with the work. If it does not seduce them, the work will be of no interest to the general public, though it may be an aesthetic marvel for the specialist. So surface design is the first consideration. The critic, however, can trace the elements to the deep structure to discover what the surface metaphorically and essentially represents. Works can then be compared in their deep structure and the transformations they pass through.

The deep structure's elements are the basic universal antinomies. Speaking of the level equivalent to deep structure in his model of narrative analysis, Floyd Merrel explains it in the following manner:

> This axiological component constitutes an abstract representation of the fundamental "existential" antinomies of human thought common to all peoples in all societies; and therein lies its universal nature. These antinomies are analogous to the basic antinomies of thought found in the structure of myths according to the theory of Claude Lévi-Strauss. A system of primitive irreconcilable tensions struggling for resolution, they are manifested in a text in the form of

binary oppositions such as life vs. death, individual vs. group, freedom vs. necessity.[4]

One could add others, such as sacred versus profane, order versus chaos, power versus weakness, but the archetypal antinomy is life versus death—Eros versus Thanatos. All other formulations are already transformations of that one basic antinomy—life itself in its duality.

In the distribution into the underlying string, however, there can be varying degrees of predominance by one pole over the other. The surface structure will represent the dynamics of the underlying string in its metaphors and themes. The works of one author, or a group, may vary greatly in their surface structures, but if the deep structures share the same elements in the same underlying string, that configuration is the world view of the writer or writers in question.

If Chicano literature is more than an arbitrary conglomeration, one might expect the deep structure of its major works to share elements and their distribution; that is the case. The great variety of Chicano literature derives from one deep structure arranged in the same underlying string:

$$\frac{\text{DEATH}}{\text{LIFE}} \longrightarrow \begin{matrix} R \\ E \\ S \\ C \\ U \\ E \end{matrix} \ \text{OF} \ \begin{matrix} I \\ M \\ A \\ G \\ E \\ S \end{matrix} \longrightarrow \frac{\text{LIFE}}{\text{DEATH}}$$

Written out, the deep structure passes through the following process: threat of disappearance to an *axis mundi* object[5] → rescue of the threatened object's images from disappearance → response to the threat in the form of the work of art as a new object. The underlying string moves from one imbalance, that of imminent death threatening to destroy life, to the affirmation of life over death. The paradigm chart is seen below:

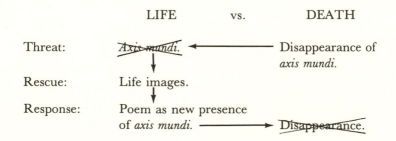

	LIFE	vs.	DEATH
Threat:	~~Axis mundi.~~ ←———		Disappearance of *axis mundi.*
Rescue:	Life images. ↓		
Response:	Poem as new presence of *axis mundi.* ———→		~~Disappearance.~~

The work passes through the diachronic sequence of reading to arrive at the new imbalance. However, the paradigm exists synchronically in the work as a whole; therefore, the antinomy of LIFE and DEATH actually is held in dynamic equilibrium. Essentially, Chicano literature's deep paradigm calls for a coming to terms with death as a necessary factor in life, but not as the predominant presence in it. Life should determine death; not death, life.

The terms ~~axis mundi~~ and ~~disappearance~~ are placed "under erasure" in the sense that Jacques Derrida utilizes the Heideggerian technique.[6] The terms are not eliminated, which would dismiss them altogether; but their particular significance has been checked, the effect canceled by the power of the opposing presence. The canceled term remains because its presence is necessary to the poem's dynamics. Moreover, this technique also implies that the sign cannot bring forth the presence of its signified; hence, the sign is an object itself, other than the represented object. Under erasure the sign is a surface object in which "the completely other is announced as such—without any simplicity, and identity, any resemblance or continuity—in that which is not it."[7] The *axis mundi*, threatened by disappearance in the world's real order, is named as Other, as a word whose represented object, its signified, is absent. The Other takes on the poem's body, the language, until its presence is the poem itself as an image. This gives the *axis mundi* a new surface, actually a new signified; the poem signifies itself as a presence there, visible to the reader. The object named is now the poem. Therefore, the term appears without erasure. *Disappearance* is the absence of the signified *axis mundi*. When the *axis mundi* reappears as the poem, *disappearance* goes under erasure to signify that the original threat is still real—the object in the world's real order is still threatened. In terms of the rescued and transformed *axis mundi*, disappearance is now checked and effectively canceled. The threat remains, though under erasure, because it is necessary to maintain the dynamics of the paradigm.

Thus it can be seen that Chicano literature does not simply posit escapist panaceas. The threat remains present, though checked, in the literature. Moreover, if the reader does not activate the process—an action often demanding commitment and involvement much beyond casual reading—the disappearance will dominate the poem's surface image, resulting in a misreading. An active reading that eventually reaches the last element of the deep structure can be compared to the pilgrimage to the sacred center. Like the journey from profane space to sacred space, it is difficult, and for those directly involved in the life-and-death venture it is a rite of passage. The reward is renewed cultural life.[8]

This paradigm was not imposed on the literature, but sprang from it. Close textual analysis revealed it. This is not to say that it must remain this way. The literature may change; the social context may cease to create the world view mirrored in the paradigm. Those are not our concerns at the moment. The purpose is to share these findings vis-à-vis the major Chicano works whose existence defines the literature better than any abstract, critical, or socio-political ideal.

Elegy as Paradigm

I have considered calling elegy the paradigmatic model of Chicano literature, hesitating because the term is often misinterpreted. I may be accused of claiming that Chicano literature laments a dead culture. However, elegy should be understood as "A lyric . . . suggested either by death of an actual person or by the poet's contemplation of the tragic aspects of life. In either case, the emotion, originally expressed as a lament, finds consolation in the contemplation of some permanent principle."[9]

Much of Chicano literature is elegiac in that it treats the death or disappearance of a person, a group, an area, the traditional ways, or some period of time. Yet it also seeks some transcendent presence—permanence may be too absolute a word for our times—which would enable the writer, the reader, and the community to survive and project themselves into the future.[10] The threat of disappearance alone, before actual death, can raise a fearful exclamation, a call for unity, an evocation of history and traditions upon which to perpetuate the status quo. This is closer to epic, of course, but at the heart of the epic lies the poet's intuition that the status quo is slipping into oblivion. While the elegy is a lyrical lament for a disappeared object, the epic can be seen as a narrative, an a priori anti-lament, a shamanistic prayer of protection, a drawing of the magic circle around one's own in hopes of delaying the disaster until past glories can be reactivated; at the same time it is a hopeful eulogy.

The elegy itself is less a lament for the dead than consolation for the survivors, who must go on living in spite of the loss of a societal structuring element, the *axis mundi*, be it person or thing. One does not, except ironically, compose elegies to meaningless characters; they are sung to kings, leaders, heroes, mothers, lovers, home, country—and again we enter the realm of epic. The dead disappear, but their presence was and is indispensable; momentarily death shakes life to its roots. "It is like 'the end of the world,' a reversion to chaos," Mircea Eliade says about the disappearance of an *axis mundi*.[11] How can one survive such a loss? By magic, by the sacred invocation of a transcendent principle, by the cosmicization[12] of alien space—in short, through ritual.

Very likely elegy began as a spontaneous lament for the dead and was incorporated into funeral ritual; or perhaps the elegy was the basis for the funeral ritual. Though modern society has lost much of the primitive ritualistic sense, one can still recognize the prayer within the elegy. This prayer relies on the word's power to evoke the presence of a signified—a power denied by Derrida and others, but still assumed by traditional, or what Eliade would call primitive people. The prayer evokes the deceased in a transmuted form, the word, created by the living. Those who depended on the *axis mundi* invert the causal relationship and create that presence to console themselves through a revelation of transcendence. The revelation, as a ritual, itself becomes an *axis mundi*, and the group recuperates its coherence. Chaos is avoided by renewing the order of the home space. This is a defensive interpretation of the arbitrary, absurd, menacing reality of the unknown. It is *Homo poeta* reasserting the fiction of the cultural explanation of life. The disappeared figure returns as the center of the ritual, through which the heroic virtues or special qualities are displayed and offered to the people as their common inheritance. The model is held up for imitation and guidance; at times, as in tragedy, it is used to caution the people against straying from the accepted code of behavior. Danger is forestalled by recalling the dead, transformed into an image, and thus into a transcendent being; this provides a basis for future projection. In effect, life itself is revealed as the transcendent reality in which particular deaths only serve to demonstrate and affirm the process. The funeral ritual proves the group's transcendence of death's menace in that as an activity, a presence in itself, it displays the group in the coherent, orderly process of living its cultural plan. Lament proves communal purpose, modulating into joy.

In the case of Chicano literature, the threat takes on various images, from death itself to such metaphors as urban renewal, schools, technological change, written culture, or simply time. In whatever form, it represents the imminent disappearance of the culture as we know it, for the *axis mundi* which radiates order may cease to function completely or in part.

Assimilation into another culture is a form of death for those who fear losing their own culture. True, it can be seen as a necessary process for entering the receiving society, but those forced to change may not be convinced. The melting-pot ideal is fine for those who have forgotten the excruciating pain of being melted down and repoured into a different mold. Nor does it make it easier to be told by others that their ancestors endured the same thing. It has never been easy, and at a time of crisis, when the final product—American society in this case, but actually modern society in general—is under attack by those who inhabit its inner circle, the rites of passage appear to be an absurd death in and of themselves. For over a century philosophers have been telling us that modern society is in disintegration; the individual's state is alienation, anomie. Those who should know best warn of the futility of the passage into modern society. Even if the end were not chaos, the passage itself is chaotic, at any time. The loss of self, the abandonment of familiar customs, and insecurity are necessary tolls, or so it seems. We revert back to the image—melting, destruction, loss of form and definition. For what? To emerge into the unknown. From all indications the passage is inevitable for the immigrant to the United States. To those who must suffer it, despite resistance, the elegy serves, at its most pessimistic (optimistic?), to soothe the pain and provide a link to what is left behind, a token memory, a touchstone to the past; at its optimistic best (worst?), it becomes a shamanistic fetish around which the faithful may rally to resist the process, to influence its outcome, and, perhaps, to sabotage the foundry. Either way, the paradigm functions.

One's ethnic culture, especially if the source culture is a traditional one, operates much like what traditional—and many modern—people call *our world*. According to Eliade, "One of the outstanding characteristics of traditional societies is the opposition that they assume between their inhabited territory and the unknown and indeterminate space that surrounds it. The former is the world (more precisely, our world), the cosmos; everything outside it is no longer a cosmos but a sort of 'other world,' a foreign, chaotic space, peopled by ghosts, demons, 'foreigners' (who are assimilated to demons and the souls of the dead)." Eliade adds another relevant comment: "An unknown, foreign, and unoccupied territory (which often means, 'unoccupied by our people') still shares in the fluid and larval modality of chaos."[13] This explains the determination to salvage barrios from urban renewal and Chicano children from monolingual schools. Yet in our time the "foreigners" may live next door or in the same household. Space is no longer strictly a geographic matter, but one of psychology. In mobile, pluralistic societies, culture and ethnicity become *our world* space; to stray from it is to venture into a chaos where *our* rules no longer apply, *our* values no longer are secure.

Homo Poeta or Culture as Heroics

The philosopher Ernest Becker dedicated his life to the study of the modern spiritual impasse. In *The Structure of Evil*, he traced the development of alienation and, correlatively, that of the response to it: *Homo poeta*, a person who creates self-meaning through language, play, work, ritual, and art; a seeker of the ideal of, in Kant's words, achieving maximum individuality within maximum community. That few societies, if any, can provide *Homo poeta* a salutary environment does not change the fact that people desire secure meaning through the fullest combination of their spiritual and physical faculties. A culture may not be perfect, may even be oppressive, but to those who live in it, who have been socialized according to its customs, it seems the most logical and ample field of self-expression. In other words, if *Homo poeta* cannot create a totally spontaneous way of life, then he finds the most fulfilling one possible, which is usually the nurturing one, because it offers significance and security without demanding new behavior patterns. "The basic stimulus to group exclusiveness is that it signifies a protest against the impoverishment of meaning," Becker explains. "The exclusive group stages its own ideal dream, which all members live in unison. It draws on the combined personalities of all its members, including ancestors with whom the group feels intimate ties. . . . the outsider represents an immediate impoverishment in a joint drama."[14] The outsider's ideal dream may be highly ordered, but its being another's space makes it chaotic to *us*. To move from one group to another bodes the loss of meaning, a type of death. It is like moving out of one's sacred space and into the surrounding chaos. "If, by some evil chance," Eliade states, "one strays into it, he feels emptied of his ontic substance, as if he were dissolving in Chaos, and he finally dies."[15]

In *The Denial of Death* (which could subtitle this book), Becker convincingly argues that those exclusive stagings of ideal dreams—Eliade's cosmicizing and consecrating of space—comprise codes of heroic action.

> Society is and always has been: a symbolic action system, a structure of statuses and roles, customs and rules for behavior, designed to serve as a vehicle for earthly heroism.
> . . . What the anthropologists call 'cultural relativity' is thus

really the relativity of hero-systems. . . . But each cultural
system is a dramatization of earthly heroics; each system cuts
out roles for performances of various degrees of heroism:
from the ''high'' . . . to the ''low'' . . . the plain, everyday,
earthly heroism wrought by gnarled working hands guiding a
family through hunger and disease.
    It doesn't matter whether the cultural hero-system is
frankly magical, religious, and primitive or secular, scientific, and civilized. It is still a mythical hero-system in which
people serve in order to earn a feeling of primary value, of
cosmic specialness, of ultimate usefulness to creation, of unshakable meaning. They earn this feeling by carving out a
place in nature, by building an edifice that reflects human
value: a temple, a cathedral, a totem pole, a skyscraper, a
family that spans three generations. The hope and belief is
that the things that man creates in society are of lasting
worth and meaning, that they outlive or outshine death and
decay, that man and his products count.[16]

In religious societies, those places, buildings, tribal histories
and the act of creating them are hierophanies, things in which the
sacred manifests itself. Hierophanies make places sacred, but they
also ''ensure that sacredness will continue there. There in that place
[cultural ritual], the hierophany repeats itself. In this way the place
becomes an inexhaustible source of power and sacredness and
enables man, simply by entering it, to have a share in the power, to
hold communion with the sacredness.''[17] In contemporary, profane
society, heroics are crypto-religious rituals that evoke veiled
hierophanies.
    Assimilation, deculturation, or acculturation can be seen as the
struggle between exclusive codes of heroics, two cosmic orders that
consider one another the Chaotic Other. What gives people personal
worth, a knowledge of usefulness and meaning, is their own heroic
system, played out within the space they call ''our world.'' To cross
over to another system signifies the renunciation of the old system, a
venture into profane chaos, a death trauma. Yet the irony of the
situation is that even those already in the receiving culture feel
deprived of secure meaning. Becker summarizes the matter from
both the insider's and the outsider's perspective. ''The minority
groups in present-day industrial society, who shout for freedom and
human dignity, are really clumsily asking that they be given a sense
of primary heroism of which they have been cheated historically.
This is why their insistent claims are so troublesome and upsetting:

how do we do such an 'unreasonable' thing within the ways in which society is now set up? 'They are asking for the impossible' is the way we usually put our bafflement.''[18]

Chicano literature is an elegy to a "symbolic action system" endangered by the threat of change or disappearance. It is *Homo poeta Chicanus*' effort to stage a personal heroic dream. It is a life-and-death struggle, a denial of death if you will, a response to the chaos of ceasing to be, demanded of one in becoming another—or in becoming, even, ourselves.

Chicanos

Yes, ourselves. (This seems to demand a definition of the term *Chicano*, but I will avoid that labyrinth of etymologies, connotations, private illusions or public prejudice, for which Tino Villanueva has spun the best Ariadnean string.[19] For my purposes Chicano literature is that which is accepted as Chicano by the readers, or claimed to be by Chicano authors. And Chicanos are all people of Mexican descent living permanently in the United States.) Ourselves because much of what we nostalgically recall and fear will be lost in transition to the U.S. system is actually Mexican, and we are Chicano. We are that intercultural, interlingual reality formed over a century or more of confrontation between Mexico and the United States. But we are neither one, exclusively; nor are we totally both. To be one or the other is not to be Chicano. We continually expand a space between the two, claiming from both sides a larger area for our own reality. At the same time, we create interlocking tensions that bind the two, forcing them into a new relationship. Neither of them welcomes the Chicano presence nor what it demands vis-à-vis the other, because it produces changes in them, synthesizing them into a new and different reality, a different cosmic center, which logically should be the future of both. But human beings and nations still resist change, not just Chicanos.

Language is the best example of this intercultural space. I will not repeat arguments made in the introduction to *Chicano Authors: Inquiry by Interview*. Suffice it to say that Chicanos inhabit a linguistic area in constant flux between English and Spanish. The two languages inform one another at every level. There are certain grammatical usages, words, connotations, spellings which to a native speaker of Spanish or English, or to the true bilingual, appear to be mistakes, cases of code switching or interference in linguistic terms, but which to the Chicano native speaker are common usages, the living reality of an interlingual space.

That Mexicans abhor what they call our deterioration of their language and culture explains the pain involved in becoming ourselves. Part of us is Mexican, the part most often forced to change; the heroic system under pressure is the Mexican one. Yet the Chicano image posited as a response and alternative to total assimilation implies a change from the Mexican image. The new image continually synthesizes the Mexican and U.S. systems. This responds to the complete loss involved in traveling from one to another, and a pragmatic acceptance of the impossibility of remaining strictly Mexican within the United States. (It is a good possibility that complete separation is futile even within Mexico, where U.S. influence produces rapid and radical changes.)

Will Chicanismo prove a lasting, viable synthesis or a watering post on the road to assimilation? Perhaps someday we will study a new intralingual, intracultural reality of Chicanismo, a new identity for Mexican-U.S. unity. Its citizens would then fear the trauma of becoming again only one or the other. Dreams! For the present, however, we speak of a culture of synthesis in constant dynamic tension, flux, and uncertainty, and of the literature it produces. That literature acknowledges the stress and the danger of the situation and responds. The literature's existence is already a synthesis, arrived at through the process explained as the paradigmatic deep structure of Chicano literature.

2. RESCUING THE WORLD CENTER
Montoya, Navarro, Delgado, Salinas

Yace en tinieblas dormida su fama,
dañada de olvido por falta de autores.
—Juan Mena, *El laberinto de la fortuna*[1]

When leaders disappear and the home space is threatened, society totters at the brink of the abyss; if the poet is also repressed, its fate seems sealed. One might assume, from the poems studied in this chapter, that this was the Chicano situation. These often-anthologized classics of early Chicano writing attempt to rescue a self-created, separatist hero—the Pachuco[2]—and the barrio, or Chicano neighborhood, as sources of cultural signification. In so doing, the poet's role in restoring communal well-being is treated as essential. Moreover, each poem exemplifies the paradigm as it will be found in the book-length works to be studied later.

José Montoya's "El Louie"

The clearest expression of the paradigm of Chicano literature is "El Louie,"[3] José Montoya's elegy to a dead Pachuco. It centers the expanding space of that literature, informing its development while incarnating its essence.

Louie Rodríguez was the leader of a Pachuco group in a small northern California town during the 1940's and 1950's. His death threatens to strip the group of their symbolic center. "Hoy enterraron al Louie" [Today they buried Louie], the poem begins, initiating its presence with the absence of the central figure, not specifically his death, but the final disappearance of his visible form; and one purpose of the poem is to restore a visible presence to Louie, a new body, which will be the text itself. The poet seems unable to treat death at this point, because, as the reader finds out eventually, it was a death that the poet judges unworthy of Louie's life, a death the cold facts of which might overshadow the positive elements of his life. So all the reader is told in the beginning is that Louie has been buried today.

The second stanza establishes Louie's representational significance, as well as his anti-hero image equally at odds with good and evil poles of socio-religious standards.

> And San Pedro o sanpinche   [St. Peter or saintdamned]
> are in for it. And those
> times of the forties
> and early fifties
> lost un vato de atolle.   [a great dude]

Montoya's language can be misleadingly simple; more is happening in this stanza than it seems at first glance.

While the poem's opening word, *Hoy*, concentrates it in the present moment dominated by disappearance, the second stanza expands temporally forward and backward. The future is implied by reference to the guardians of afterlife; but both are simultaneously relegated to the realm of the dubious. By a simple *o* [or] which can be read as *it makes no difference*, the two are equated in their opposition to Louie. Their equation is underscored by the phonological similarity of *San Pedro* and *sanpinche*. The substitution of *pinche* for *Pedro* creates a metonymic link which cancels the efficacy of religious codes for evaluating life's worth. Louie can go to either one, for they are the same with respect to him; therefore, behavior cannot be judged by established moral codes, which make the difference clear. Only existential and situational ethics are left. The poem then looks back into the period which Louie represented. Finally, death reappears euphemistically in the verb *lost*, which also reintroduces Louie himself with a slang reference to his grandeur; but nonetheless, he is absent.

The poem's pattern of movement has been established by this point: a centrifugal expansion from the center, Louie, then a withdrawal to the point of origin. It will be repeated throughout in an effort to reclaim worldly space for Louie. As a unit, the poem follows the same movement, expanding from absence, to verbal and violent presence in the middle, to a fading and eventual centering on Louie alone. The difference between beginning and end is what the poem intends to establish. The result is a rescued, transformed *axis mundi*.

Stanza 3 refocuses on the end of Louie's life, and the image is not positive.

kind of slim and drawn
there towards the end,
aging fast from too much
booze y la vida dura. But   [the hard life]
class to the end.

The *end* that occupies the greater part of the space is that of wasting away, degradation. The combination of English and Spanish causal factors represents mutually dependent, though potentially conflictive, forces in Louie's life; at the end they are both negative and feed off of each other. The repetition of *end* sets up a contrast essential to the poem. Louie's disappearance cannot be denied; it is the poem's primary fact. In stanza 3 the significance of the end is put into question. Will it fix Louie in the negative imagery of degradation, or can the *end* be redefined?[4] The *But* hangs like a hesitant objection at the end of almost overwhelming negativity; and if there can be no alternative, then the group, the period, and by extension Chicano culture are stigmatized. Which *end*? Or, more accurately stated, will the reader focus on the *end* or on the life of class prior to degradation? If the poem accomplishes the latter, which is its purpose, then Louie's *end* will be defined as the poem itself—life as permanent visibility —instead of opprobrious death and disappearance.

The last line of stanza 3 also defines the existential values to be utilized to determine significance. Life is to be judged in terms of class, not what is done but how, which equals life as an aesthetic act. This reflects perfectly the poem's irony and lyricized prose. Though much of Louie's experience is that of negation and denial, it was also one of creative, signifying fantasy that transformed the prosaic, normal world into something more exciting. While the poem appears to be narrative prose, its determining factors are not grammatical or logical, but affective, phonological.[5] In short, the poem proposes to save what appears negative or insignificant to the logical, objective—outsider's—eye by rendering it aesthetic. The poem's wager is that class is a superior morality. If the poem succeeds on the level of beauty, of art, then the prosaic details are transcended. This is not a frivolous level of the work, but primary, because if the poem fails, Louie fails; and the poem is only imitating Louie.

From the statement of its thesis, which refers to the reader's future judgment, the poem shifts into the past. The next eighty-one lines cover Louie's fantasy-reality life as it followed an outward path only to retreat and finally return to the beginning. We encounter Louie in Sanjo [San Jose], California, in line 12, playing, poker this time. Lines 91–92 return us to the slim-and-drawn Louie of stanza 3, and line 93 is a reprise of the opening verse. Thus between lines 12 and 92 lies Louie's life, framed by the *end* and the geographic location of Sanjo, which in truth is the spatial sign corresponding to Louie as a life center in expansion; the town of Fowler, which also frames the central portion, but appearing a few lines after Sanjo (17 and 94), represents Louie's center at its most reduced. The movement will spin out and back around this center. Moreover, Sanjo is metonymically linked to San Pedro and sanpinche, perhaps as a neutral ground between them, neither one nor the other, emphasizing in this way the suspension of life in the existential world only.

In stanza 4 Louie, in a topcoat, plays "the role of Bogard, Cagney, or Raft." Montoya calls on Hollywood lore to depict his central character, setting up a contrast and interplay between the unrealizable celluloid dreams and Louie's life, which follows in the next thirteen stanzas. It is important to remember that these actors were archetypical anti-heroes, who often played characters from ethnic minorities of the lower economic class. At the same time, they cannot be separated from their reality as stars, who realized the American Dream of wealth and fame by playing, among others, criminal roles. Montoya achieves a multiple irony, for though the "role" is Hollywoodesque, it corresponds, in a sense, to Louie's reality—he is like the characters and he uses costumes and roles to achieve his goals. The frustration comes in that the actors distinguished themselves on a plane where rewards were forthcoming, an aesthetic plane unavailable to Louie, though he, too, lived aesthetically.

Stanzas 5–10 (lines 17–60) focus on Louie as a Pachuco leader, his life merging again with media images in stanza 11, after which Louie is seen outside the immediate peer group, with another film reference appearing at the end of the poem. Thus his supposed reality is framed and toned by film legends, though it is firmly set in particularity. Louie is located in a specific place, Fowler, and within an extended family, the Rodríguez, whose fame is said to have reached beyond their town to the surrounding area. Small, coinciding circles open in the world, with Fowler as its geographical center and the Rodríguez as its emotive, human center; and Louie is the common axis of both. The circles are activated by the symbols of the subculture—the car, music, women, and clothes (stanza 6):

48 Fleetline, two-tone—
buenas garras and always   [good clothes]

rucas—como la Mary y   [women—like Mary and
la Helen . . . siempre con   Helen . . . always with
liras bien afinadas   well-tuned guitars]

Montoya creates an image of motion and joy, providing enough specific details to anchor it in the mind. *Fleetline* epitomizes youth; the rhythm underscores it, and the finely tuned instruments sum it up. Yet, as the guitar image implies, the beauty of harmony can go out of tune. Dualities ring with the imagery: *two-tone*, the harmonizing of two colors in one object; the English names with Spanish articles. As Orlando Ramírez has observed,[6] at this point in the poem the languages harmonize well and do not demand our attention—at least if one is interlingual—but the forces they represent will eventually split, producing death in the character who is both their creator and their creation. Montoya's task is to convey those forces faithfully, even their negative aspects, while at the same time harmonizing them on the level of class, to salvage life.

With the circle populated and activated, a much vaster expansion follows in stanza 7. Louie thinks up the *idea* for tailor-made zoot suits, linking his small-town group to the legendary Pachuco cities of Los Angeles and El Paso. Louie's imaginative powers, emphasized by the repetition of the word *idea*, inscribe the group within a wider code of significance. Note that it is the same imaginative role-playing as in Louie's Hollywood imitations, and both are realized through clothing, disguises. Louie could alter reality by taking it to the aesthetic. His process involves the changing of surface imagery through imagination applied to ordinary materials, altering their representational value to approximate a higher realm of existence, in reality beyond his reach; in both cases that realm is an aesthetic reality.[7] Montoya does the same thing with words to reopen Louie's absence into a presence.

Louie's genius for transforming surfaces catalyzes a corresponding internal transformation: the first *we* appears (line 35). Group identity crystallizes around an idea rendered visible as a surface image. Simultaneously, the poem's perspective crystallizes around this *we*, assuming an insider's view, which underscores the endeavor's urgency. Louie equals *we*.

When the group's expansive movement collides with outsiders, violence threatens, and a call goes out for Louie. The poem's central verses are a dialogue of danger, resolved by Louie's mere presence, without violence ever appearing in the stanza. (Again the poem mirrors itself, for violence menaces the group at the poem's outset, and only recalling Louie can prevent group disintegration.) The poem now performs a Hollywood transformation learned from Louie, projecting Louie's role in the incident into the code of film heroics. Stanza 11 replays the scene as if it were a B-movie, with "melodramatic music,"[8] and Louie is compared to three movie stars, two Mexicans and Bogart again,[9] leading us back into the fantasy world from which the memory images began in stanza 4.

> And Louie would come through—
> melodramatic music, like in the
> mono—tan tan taran!—Cruz   [movies]
> Diablo, El Charro Negro! Bogard
> smile (his smile is deadly as
> his vaisas!) He dug roles, man,   [fists]
> and names—like blackie, little
> Louie . . .

The juxtaposition of the smile and fists captures Louie's duality, not only of surface image and reality, but, again, of language codes. The fists seem to represent the frustration with the contradiction between fantasy and reality, and perhaps this explains the parenthesis within which the image is framed. For a split second the poem opens a breach in Louie's façade to reveal him, as in a well-timed, stop-action close-up of the character in essence, one of those pauses in a movie when the scene freezes for emphasis—an epiphany of contradiction.

Immediately, the poem spins out of the parenthesis into Louie's roles, as if we had seen too much, penetrated too far, and were being forced to retreat. The flash of insight is not easily forgotten, however, and the roles meant to distract us are, at first, feeble, and thus the more telling, as though they still fall under the revealing radiance of the parenthesis: *blackie, little Louie*. They refer to media characters, but the names function also as words with broader connotations. The first is racially disparaging, and both are diminutives which reduce Louie's image to the pitiful. Even the placement of *little* emphasizes it with a line stop.

The poem then addresses Louie by name, only to draw a direct denial of the name from Louie and an affirmation of another role: "call me Diamonds." The nickname, a reference to the criminal Legs Diamonds, reveals a fantasy of extreme monetary value and affluence, pure whiteness, and an impenetrable aesthetic object. A diamond's faceted surface is capable of dazzling reflections, but the stone depends on exterior sources for its brilliance and tones; and thus, like Louie, it transforms prosaic reality into beauty by reflecting it in a precious center. Louie's chosen identity counterposes a radically different image to that of the *vaisas*,[10] those strong, practical, prosaic tools of work and violence—though the word *vaisas* is more aesthetic than the common *puños*, *manos*, *fists*, or *hands*.

On the first reading, of course, the poem's rhythm sweeps the reader past all of these considerations; in addition, as though realizing how tenuous Louie's self-image is, the poet does not allow it to stand as a stanza as we might expect. Instead, he joins it to what really should be a separate unit, thus rapidly pushing us into the more believable subject of Louie's military service in Korea. The positive-negative duality of it mirrors what Montoya has said would happen in the afterlife: "heroism and the stockade!" When he comes home, his clothes and medals attract attention and admiration. Although his heroism was real, what Louie—and the reader—discover is a reaffirmation of the effectiveness of the same process of disguises he had developed in stanzas 4 and 7. It might be noted in passing that Louie's Hollywood heroes also donned uniforms during war years to sell the public the role that he plays here. However, Louie reaps none of the rewards, and he hocks his medals for liquor. Louie's circle of expansion had reached its maximum and has begun a rapid retreat back into game-playing within his familiar home space. The liquor reference is ominous, because it begins to reestablish the booze-y-la-vida-dura image of the *end*. The poem is moving toward its end as well.

Montoya concentrates our attention once more on the contradiction between the roles and the hands. Before this, the poem has focused on, among other things, guitar playing, knife wielding, fists, and alluded to Louie's skill with a rifle. Now, Louie's fists open into dexterous hands to win honors in barber college; and as always he surpasses the norm of performance to achieve excellence in aesthetic expression. But instead of dressing the part of a barber, he hocks his "velardo de la peluca," the barber's briefcase, which not only held the tools of the trade, but represented the position.

Louie rejects two avenues of escape traditionally open to ethnic minorities, the military and the career of barber. The hocking of the objects that proved his successful mastery of those professions underscores the conclusion that Louie rejected society, and was not rejected by it. He could not adapt to discipline or to prosaic routine; he preferred the excitement of the game, his hands playing cards in search of quick money.

The poem's main section (lines 12–92) closes back around Louie, first in one frame, Sanjo; then it slips to another, the image of a down-and-out, fading Louie. The "slim and drawn / there towards the end" of stanza 3 echoes in the "Lean times . . ." of stanza 18, with the suspension points of the latter silently repeating the "there towards the end" of the former. Everything is pointing toward the end and the question of which meaning it will assume.

The end comes when the first verse is repeated, apparently bringing a closure by returning to the very beginning, beyond which there seems to be nowhere to go. Montoya has been avoiding that *end* of disappearance in exactly an attempt to go beyond to something else. But he still does not seem ready and refuses to confront death, evasively evoking the image of Louie as a legendary figure living on in the collective memory of the younger generation of "baby chukes." Stanza 20 begins back at the spatial epicenter, Fowler, to try to spin outward once again into life.

Y en Fowler at Nesei's	[And in Fowler]
pool parlor los baby chukes	[the]
se acuerdan de Louie, el carnal	[remember Louie, the relative
del Candi y el Ponchi—la vez	of Candi and Ponchi—the time
que lo fileriaron en el Casa	they knifed him in the Casa
Dome y cuando se catio con	Dome and when he went to blows with
La Chiva.	The Goat.]

Expansion, however, is ominously contradicted by the spatial imagery. From the epicenter of Fowler, the poem does not spin out to the surrounding towns, as before, but constricts to one building, probably with one rectangular room, in which groups of Chukes revolve around smaller rectangles, on which a set of fifteen balls is fragmented down into particular spheres. One can well imagine focusing on the tip of a cue stick about to strike the cue ball to begin a game, an image of another opening effort, but now severely restricted within the playing area. Ironically the image is one of isolating the balls and dropping them below the playing surface, as Louie has been buried below a surface. The game image here is a metaphor for sublimated macho violence. Louie's memory lingers in it.

Quickly, the poem runs out of new material to feed on; Louie is not acting but being evoked as a memory by younger actors in the game. So the poem resorts to old material, repeating word for word line 18 and part of 19: "carnal del Candi y el / Ponchi—" Thus the text suddenly falls into the trap; it, too, is recalling the past, going backward, closing down. For the poem, as for the Chukes, Louie has no future, only past. The relatives' names feed into a dash, which in line 19 introduced the extended family, Los Rodríguez; now the dash leads only to sad memories of Louie's "lean times." The knifing contrasts strikingly with the fight scene in the center of Louie's life. Whereas before he had resolved conflict with his mere presence, now he is trapped, surrounded, and pierced. *Casa* [House] *Dome* is a double enclosure, rendered more sinister because *casa* also means home; Louie is knifed in his own home area. Logically, if his family is absent from where it once was, it is also absent from around him; he is alone and defenseless. Like the Chukes knocking each other out of the game played in a restricted area of a pool table, Louie faces another Pachuco, La Chiva, and fights it out within the extremely reduced circumference of his home center.

La Chiva actually existed, according to Montoya,[11] who while writing the poem did not think of the name's symbolic significance, nor that with it he was revealing a cause of death he purposely hid in the stanza where the death is finally treated. *La chiva* is slang for heroin. Moreover, it can also refer to death itself, as an occasional euphemism for La Chingada [The Fucked One]. Thus Montoya fortuitously combined a real rival with the sign of death by heroin overdose. In addition, note how the imagery of the last three lines mirrors grotesquely the pool-parlor games, revealing their sublimated violence. The cue sticks become knives, and the knives transform into a hypodermic syringe for shooting drugs. The game, in both cases, is won by elimination carried out by the violent action of a white agent (cue ball, heroin). One could read racial connotations into the imagery, but it is not necessary to explicate them.

The failure to reopen Louie's circle is punctuated by yet another reprise of line 1 and the eruption, finally, of the word *death* into the text. Unable to avoid it any longer, the poet calls death an insult, because Louie did not die heroically, but "alone in a rented / room." He was outside his geographic and familial space. Montoya could not have related the death scene at the beginning, but only after accumulating enough life imagery to counteract the facts of isolation. And even now, when the poet seems forced to deal with those facts, he utilizes Louie's lesson of disguise and transformation. Instead of how he died, he states that he did not die in war, nor in a gang fight—and these images become masks for the reality that slips into the reader's mind. Then, when the facts of solitude and the location, cited above, end in a dash that, again, should introduce the ultimate fact of death, Montoya utilizes the pause to evade it once more. A sudden sublimation into a fantasy worthy of Louie displaces our eye from reality: "—perhaps like in a / Bogard movie.'' This is Louie's mimetic game of raising a mundane reality to celluloid brilliance and interest. The poet insists on imitating Louie to the end, on affirming the value of Louie's creative life process, even in the face of death. Instead of one scene, there is an ambiguous allusion to many possible death scenes from Bogart's vast repertoire of famous deaths. Louie's death escapes specification and acquires a multitude of heroic, or at least dramatic, variants. The most significant and revealing irony, however, is that Montoya, who sincerely sought a Louiesque evasion of the fact, inadvertently has told us about the heroin already.

Death finally having been paid its due, though reluctantly and not without certain cosmetic adjustments, the poem returns to the question of the *end*. "The end was a cruel hoax. / But his life had been / remarkable!'' At face value, death and disappearance as the end are denied. Much more is involved, however. A hoax is an act intended to trick or dupe, or something believed through trickery. This could apply to the cinematic fantasy pole of Louie's life, with its unachievable aspirations. But since Louie is dead and his life is now a literary matter depending on the readers' perception of it, another interpretation seems more relevant. The hoax refers to the *end* as seen by the spectators, the degrading end, the disappearance which the poem has challenged since the start. The reader is warned against, perhaps even chastised for, accepting a false evaluation of Louie based on the circumstances of his death. The opprobrious image is countered by the life of class, which was displayed in the poem and reaffirmed in the last verse: "Vato de atolle, el Louie Rodríguez." This verse directly contradicts the loss of Louie in stanza 2, while reuniting Louie with his family, canceling the solitude of his death. The irony, of course, is that Louie's death was faithful to the life revealed by the poem; Montoya does not deny negative factors in Louie's life, he only outweighs them with positive art. Moreover, the *end* has now been transported from life (death) to literature (death as life), becoming an ever-new beginning; Louie's life can be replayed indefinitely.

The poem rescues Louie from the double threat of disappearance and negative imagery. In art, free from time and contingency, Louie can continue giving his generation meaning. In addition, the poem can signify a center for future generations, and perhaps Louie's creative life process can once again catalyze the *we* of Chicano identity. Not to say that we should neglect the lessons from Louie's rejection of life and his pathetic death. It was in death that the familial and ethnic *we* disintegrated. Louie's failure at life destroyed group cohesion; this is not the action the poem offers for imitation, but the tragic flaw to be avoided. The heroics offered as a model are Louie's aesthetic living, his class, his gift for improvisation; and, finally, the art of writing about life. The poem is Louie's process in action, while its truthful portrayal of Louie's negative side is proof that it rejects Louie's closures and retreat from life. The poem moves into the world.

When the poem draws back around the center, it has been transformed from the invisible absence evoked only in a bodiless name into a familiar and very real, visible presence. The words are the matter, and the poem the body, of Louie. Their beauty, fluidity, and affective power, within an unobtrusive though carefully crafted structure, create the image of a smooth, classy Louie. Significantly, the hollow void at the outset, *Louie*, is a charged, dense fullness at the end. This is the power of the word's appearance in the world: to represent an absence in such a convincing manner that the representation can actually become the reality—or at least a touchstone of reality.

The paradigm charts are clear.

	LIFE	vs.	DEATH
SYMBOLIC Threat:	~~Disguises make the man.~~ ←		Death strips all disguise, leaving only a dead body.
	↓		
Rescue:	Louie's disguises.		
	↓		
Response:	Poem as Louie's new → ~~Death~~. disguise.		
SOCIAL Threat:	~~Louie as axis mundi.~~ ←		Louie's burial equals death of the group.
	↓		
Rescue:	Louie's life images.		
	↓		
Response:	Poem as Louie's new → ~~Burial~~. presence and new *axis mundi*.		

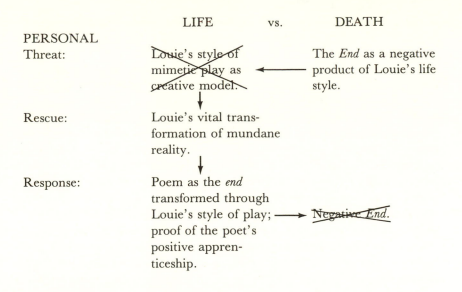

LIFE   vs.   DEATH

PERSONAL
Threat:

Louie's style of mimetic play as creative model.

The *End* as a negative product of Louie's life style.

Rescue:

Louie's vital trans-
formation of mundane
reality.

Response:

Poem as the *end*
transformed through
Louie's style of play;
proof of the poet's
positive appren-
ticeship.

Negative *End*.

J. L. Navarro's "To a Dead Lowrider"

A less well known elegy to a similar figure, "To a Dead Lowrider"[12] resembles "El Louie." It opens with a recollection of a dead Pachuco-Lowrider, displays images of him, then closes with death. The character is an anti-hero of sorts, who negates social values and dies an apparently meaningless death. Yet the poem is quite different from "El Louie."

It opens with speculation about the significance of the character's death: "It *seems* a *tragedy* that he / Died the way he did" (emphasis added). The poem's first half (lines 1–39) is toned by this speculation, although irony surfaces less than halfway through to undermine the possibility of tragedy. In the poem's second half, speculation gives way to affirmation: "It's a shame the way he died," creating a tension between two interpretations of the death. Was it a *tragedy* or a *shame*? The two words are not synonyms: the difference between them marks a drop from the heroic to the pathetic mode, from awe to pity. Yet without having seen the death, resolution is impossible. At the three-quarters point (line 60), *shame* is restated; then, after the meaningless death has been related, the poet forcefully states the judgment of shame, with which readers will probably agree. Shame is also emphasized graphically through line placement. "It's a shame the way he died" moves from almost flush left (line 40), to a twelve-space indentation (line 60); and, finally, it is divided into two lines (80–81) to leave *shame* at the end of line 80, underscored by a line stop. The poem moves from possible tragedy to shame, degrading the Pachuco's image to that of a pathetic victim.

The degradation of the Pachuco may strike us as strange in Chicano poetry, but the poem views its central figure as an outsider. The poem's first half is rhythmically punctuated with "Remember?" (lines 9, 30, 39), asked by the first-person persona, addressing a *you* introduced in line 4. The repetition implies a lack of remembrance by the *you*. The Pachuco is anonymous until line 7. The title announces a dead Lowrider, while line 3 calls him a Pachuco; the persona thus treats the character in generic terms, as a representative of a type. In the first two lines, *he* is repeated twice in a sentence deliberately structured to require the repetition of the personal, but anonymous, pronoun: "It seems a tragedy that he / Died the way he did." *Him* appears in line 4; *he* is repeated in line 5. By the time a name is attributed to the dead man, a name introduced by a possessive *his*, he has been referred to with five pronouns and two stereotypical titles. Even when known, his name is limited to the first name only. Tito's near anonymity and stereotypification reflect the threat that death may soon obliterate his identity, reducing him to a mere nameless type. At the same time, Tito's representation of those types generalizes the threat to all Pachucos and Lowriders. But here there is none of the familiar closeness between the persona and the dead man found in "El Louie," none of the latter's extended circles of relationships. Tito is an isolated individual, not remembered by the *you*, and only superficially known by the *I*.

No collective *we* forms around Tito. He is said to have "come around"; that "everyone moved for Tito" implies distance. He came from an unknown somewhere and split the subject *we*. His separation is linguistic as well; his speech is "his tongue" and "another language." The persona is so removed from Tito's human identity that he can only depict him as a thoughtless bull, with severely limited intellectual capacity and aspirations.

> Never much cared for anything, that
> Dude. He knew he lived for something,
> But he never knew what for. He only
> Reasoned to a limit. He didn't care
> For more.

The redundancies underscore Tito's closedness, as well as the persona's lack of knowledge about him. From a distance the persona can say only so much and then repeat it; he knows no more to add.

The distant perspective also manifests itself in the treatment of *Lowrider* and *Pachuco* as synonyms, an outsider's generalization. Not that one cannot be the other, but they are not interchangeable per se.

The lack of values and the obviously wasted, directionless life raise the question as to why Tito's image is rescued. Perhaps for the sake of his Chicano appearance, his self-pride, and his willingness to fight anyone who challenged him, traits linked to his image as a strident, but handsome bull. This would be a superficial reading, consonant with the judgment of his death as a shame. We can dismiss the poem at this level as a superficial, nostalgic piece, unsatisfactory or simply negative. Perhaps; however, the caution against quick misreading found in "El Louie" should make us pause and return to the text.

A reexamination of the poem fails to alter the fact that the perspective is that of an outsider, or that Tito's was a wasted life, when depicted from that perspective. Perhaps we could focus on the death scene and reconsider the term *shame*. However, Navarro's choice of words for the dialogue between Tito and the policeman who kills him—*punk, sissy*—deliberately undermines the tenor of the scene and supports the meaning of *shame*. What, then, has this elegy produced of positive nature other than the mere resurrection of an unpleasant character named Tito? Might there be another level of development? This question, and a certain amount of faith and good will, lead us back once again to the text, concentrating on its rhetorical level.

The poem is voiced by an *I* speaking to a *you* about a *he*. The three persons of speech are gathered. Yet the *I* is separated from the *you* by the fact that the latter does not readily acknowledge sharing the memory, albeit limited, that the former has of the *he*. Tito, for better or worse a Chicano prototype, is not common knowledge to the conversants. This could explain the sloppy synonymy; two distinct types, Lowrider and Pachuco, are lumped together in the category of the unfamiliar or ignored Chicano antecedents. Moreover, the obscurity of those types produces a distance not just between the *I* and *he*, which is obvious, but also between the *I* and the *you*, reducing the text to a monologue punctuated by unanswered questions. In other words, there is no unity, no community here because the historical images of the origins of the supposed community are obscure. By extension, it could be said that community depends upon a shared historical knowledge and a realistic acceptance of all facets of ourselves, even the pathetic, or "strident" ones. The threat, therefore, is redefined as the dissolution of the Chicano community due to forgetting a strident historical figure.

The identification of the real threat sends us in search of the response. The salvaged images of Tito are not enough, for reasons stated above, but there is a change in the poem attributable to him. At the end of the poem (line 80), the *I* addresses the *you* as *carnal*, the Chicano equivalent of "brother." Community has been established. Nothing has changed in society during the reading of the poem, but the poem itself has provided the experience of sharing knowledge, of accepting—in spite of not fully comprehending—but not idealizing a historical antecedent. The poem is the space of reconciliation, and Tito's life and death are the catalysts.

As readers, the silent *you* addressed by the persona, we witness a struggle and a killing; but instead of a pointless slaughter of a dumb, albeit handsome animal, it is a ritual sacrifice for the benefit of the community—in the poem's own imagery, we could call it a bullfight. The protagonist is not truly heroic, because somehow he is the dupe, the victim, of his killer. Yet he is glorious in his own fashion; beautiful within his circumscribed arena of possibilities; admirable in his raw instinct for life; pathetic, perhaps, in his falling short of human potential, but not to be blamed, as one would not blame a bull for fighting the bullfighter. Society determines his fate. This interpretation also hispanicizes the image, rendering aesthetic the life-and-death struggle within a cultural code which Chicanos can legitimately claim. As in "El Louie," the *end* is transformed through a shift to an alternate value system more attuned to the character's reality and that of the Chicano community. The poem's two alternatives exist simultaneously, with the negative one controlling the ironic surface. This reflects the Chicano reality, that of a coexistence of perspectives, one rational, practical, based on material goals; another more spiritual, aesthetic, based on how things are done.

The alternative perspectives allow the reader to appreciate Tito to some degree. This should not be misinterpreted; the poem does not condone Tito's wasted life. No amount of analysis will achieve that. The poem simply offers another level of interpretation in which Tito is absolved of blame, and another on which he catalyzes positive results. The fact that the *I* and the *you* learn from Tito, even internalize him to a degree, is demonstrable in the poem's language.

Navarro's language is much less interlingual than Montoya's. Relatively few Spanish or Chicano words are used; yet this limited use is entirely logical, even necessary within the poem's terms. When Tito speaks, Chicanismos appear in quotes (*órale*, *ese*, *aguite*, *wacho*, *rucas*, *carnal*, etc.), but the persona calls this "another language." Navarro knows this language; it is his creation. However, his persona uses only English. Language is another sign of distance. Thus, when the persona uses the key word *carnal* (line 80), it signals a break in his pattern of speech, a qualitative change. In this *carnal* rings the echo of Tito's voice from line 37, where he spoke the word. The usage of it unites the *I* and the *you*. Thus the language of the poem reflects the change achieved through Tito's resurrection; and in truth, the poem is the only space of both the resurrection and the new communal affirmation.

The essential system of heroics offered here is that of communal self-awareness and the preservation of oral history. Tito is not a hero worth imitating; he is not a hero at all. But the poem's pattern of cultural sharing and critical self-analysis is a worthy code of action to follow.[13]

Paradigm Charts

	LIFE	vs.	DEATH
SYMBOLIC Threat:	~~Tito as a meaningful being~~ ←		Death of a meaningless, thoughtless animal.
Rescue:	Imagery of a proud bull. ↓		
Response:	Death as a ritual bullfight. →		~~Meaningless death.~~
SOCIAL and PERSONAL Threat:	~~Chicano community.~~ ← ↓		Tito's strident image disunites community.
Rescue:	Tito as a shared experience. ↓		
Response:	Communal affirmation through Tito's example and language, poem as an act of *carnalismo*. →		~~Tito as disunity.~~

Abelardo Delgado's "Stupid America"

Abelardo Delgado attacks the elitist Anglo American society for not opening itself to the possible aesthetic contributions of Chicano artists in one of the early classics of Chicano literature, and still his best-known poem.[14]

> stupid america, see that chicano
> with the big knife
> in his steady hand
> he doesn't want to knife you
> he wants to sit on a bench
> and carve christfigures
> but you won't let him.
> stupid america, hear that chicano
> shouting curses on the street
> he is a poet
> without paper or pencil
> and since he cannot write
> he will explode.
> stupid america, remember that chicanito
> flunking math and english
> he is the picasso
> of your western states
> but he will die
> with one thousand masterpieces
> hanging only from his mind.[15]

The poem does many of the same things as the others. Forces oppose each other in the body of the central figure; the enemy is "america" in its stupid exclusion of Chicanos, which forces the latter into violent reaction. Abelardo alludes to the dilemma of the poet caught between two worlds and he offers a plan to resolve it. Abelardo also plays with the perception of *ends*, as Montoya does, by focusing on images of Chicano youths and then juxtaposing two interpretations of the end or purpose of the image. One interpretation, the "american" one, is to see the youth as a threat to society; the other, the poet's, is of an aesthetic desire, albeit frustrated. The Chicano is suspended in an impasse between the two possibilities; his fate awaits the outcome of the encounter, which on the aesthetic level is the reader's judgment. Like Montoya and Navarro, Abelardo concerns himself with teaching Chicanos a process of life fulfillment that will allow them to transcend the impasse in their own terms, a process involving the rescuing of traditional cultural elements—incarnated in two historical figures whom Abelardo presents as models for imitation—through a future-directed synthesis. And as we might expect, the poem is the proof of the successful application of the process it offers as a response to the conflicts depicted.

Abelardo structures the poem in three segments representing three art forms: sculpture, literature, and painting. For each there is a Chicano who would practice it if allowed to; not given access to the means of fulfilling his aesthetic aspiration, the youth's repressed desires may be channeled into destructive action. Through references to historical figures, Abelardo distinguishes the first and third segments, leaving the central one as the focus of future possibilities, where lessons gleaned from the other two must be applied. Significantly, and logically, the central segment is the literary one, specifically, that of poetry; thus, the poem is, again, the proof of the lesson.

The first segment, through the mention of carving christfigures, alludes to the *santeros*, the carvers of religious statues in the Spanish colonial area which included what is now the U.S. Southwest. This folk art form is still practiced in New Mexico according to aesthetic principles centuries old. Most Americans, including Chicanos, are unfamiliar with it. Abelardo places it before the readers to teach them about a Hispanic aesthetic presence that all U.S. residents, including Chicanos, can be proud of and learn from. Moreover, *santero* art is a synecdoche for the Hispanic society of the Southwest, unified through religious beliefs and cultural traditions, and already established before the Anglo American presence on the Atlantic coast. Abelardo challenges, by implication, the erroneous concept of the United States as a product of an east-to-west conquest. This exclusionary conception of history is based on the ignorance of the historical presence of the Indo-Hispanic culture. This justifies calling America stupid. Of course, this is the same exclusionary ignorance that Abelardo says still denies the Chicano artist's existence.

The third segment names Picasso—the epitome of the modern, cosmopolitan artist, a Spaniard of universal vision and influence. Although he is evoked as a painter, he actually practiced many art forms, including sculpture; thus, the *santero*'s cultural tradition passes into a futuristic time reference. Picasso's presence challenges the United States' claim to leadership in modernity, there being no U.S. artist to rival Picasso. Again, Abelardo places in front of the reader a model of Hispanic achievement unfamiliar to many Chicanos and not thought of as a Spaniard by Anglo Americans. And as a representative of the modern Hispanic culture, he proves this culture's reserve of genius that could flower if given opportunity.

The *santeros* and Picasso personify what is the essence of Chicanismo and its possible contributions to a society being torn apart by apparently mutually exclusionary groups—the art of synthesis. The *santeros*, finding themselves isolated from the centers of academic art and without the materials and facilities taken for granted in those centers, adapted European aesthetic principles of religious art to their environment. Theirs was, by necessity, a practical synthesis that excluded nothing that might be used to advantage; nor did it disdain indigenous influences. Picasso, finding himself in the center of academic art, with all the materials and facilities available to him, revolutionized Occidental aesthetics through his personal genius. After revamping art through Cubism, he began a series of parodies of traditional art forms, renewing and, at the same time, preserving them.[16] From traditional and modern forms, he synthesized a forward-moving art at a time of cultural impasse. His synthesis disdained no object or raw material, nor any ethnic or racial group. Both artists applied their talents and produced to the fullest of their possibilities and opportunities.

Abelardo offers these artists as models for a response to the conflict depicted in the poem. They represent the Hispanic genius for progress through regeneration, which excludes nothing of value and creates order and tradition for a spiritually sound society. They also represent role models drawn from Hispanic culture that can teach Chicanos not to cut themselves off from other groups but to adapt to their environment and synthesize any raw material at hand. The ultimate ideal would be the synthesis of the sides in conflict in the poem, to produce a redefined, wise America.

The central segment, without any historical reference, is open for synthesis to take place. Abelardo implies that the next historical achievement will take place in the realm of poetry. The youth of this segment would synthesize his oral expression and written media, if America would give him the raw materials. Without them, synthesis is impossible; but the oral expression will seek some avenue to make itself felt, just as the would-be sculptor will use his knife on something or someone. These violent alternatives would destroy not only society, but Chicanos themselves. This is the significance of the death of the frustrated painter in segment three; pointless violence destroys itself. But so do ignorant, fragmented societies.

Abelardo relates the three segments through the image of the hand as the focal point of conflict. It can be a creative or destructive instrument. Will it be allowed to construct contributions to America, or forced to destroy the society, and itself in the process? In addition, the hand represents the written tradition of oral expression.

The poet can be split by these traditions, or can synthesize them, making his hand the transcriber of the spoken word. This sounds trite, but not when one considers the newness of Chicano writing and that the Chicano word signifies Chicano experience heretofore absent in written form. The poet is to inscribe Chicano experience into the written tradition where, it is hoped, it can educate stupid America; if not, Abelardo tells us, Chicano culture may die without achieving its full potential, thus betraying the past and the future.

As the poem establishes these points, it is resolving them. It is the response to cultural exclusion and personal impasse. While stating the Chicanos' frustration over not being permitted expression in U.S. society, the poem is the expression of Chicano experience, now fixed in the written medium, from which the poet-character of segment 2 was excluded. At the same time, the poem synthesizes the Chicano experience to achieve unity. It maintains the oral curse by shouting "stupid america" and protesting injustice; but it gives the shout permanence and visibility in writing. It also synthesizes Hispanic history and the present situation in the United States, as well as a Hispanic content in the English language, forming a new product known as Chicano literature. The poem is Abelardo's masterpiece, but far from "hanging only from his mind," it appears almost everywhere Chicano literature is anthologized. The poet has transcended the exclusion and oppression he lamented, becoming himself the third model for action proffered by the poem.

Paradigm Charts

	LIFE vs.	DEATH
SYMBOLIC		
Threat:	~~Hand as productive agent.~~ ←	Hand denied tools or materials for expression.
Rescue:	Hispanic artists with productive hands. ↓	
Response:	Poem as proof of the productive, writing hand of the poet. →	~~Denial.~~

	LIFE	vs.	DEATH
SOCIAL Threat:	W~~ise~~, healthy America, ~~drawing~~ on ~~all its~~ potential. ⟵		Stupid, destructive America, denying a source of valuable expression.
Rescue:	Hispanic contributions to the arts through synthesis.		
Response:	Poem as Hispanic ⟶ contribution to American art.		~~Stupid America~~.
PERSONAL Threat:	~~Acknowledgment of Poet~~. ⟵		Poet's existence denied.
Rescue:	Poet's heritage.		
Response:	Poem as poet's proof ⟶ of accomplishment through the process of synthesis used by the role models evoked.		~~Denial~~.

In addition, I could have charted the social threat as imminent death of the Chicano through frustration and the loss of the oral culture, and the poem as the accomplished synthesis of oral and written expression.

Raúl Salinas' "A Trip through the Mind Jail"

When his barrio of La Loma, in Austin, Texas, was "demolished, erased forever from / the universe," Raúl Salinas responded by writing the epitome of Chicano barrio poems, "A Trip through the Mind Jail."[17] The home space represents the *imago mundi*, the sacred cosmogonic space without which the universe reverts to the profane chaos that menaces outside the home space's protective walls.[18] Note that Salinas locates La Loma not in Austin, which is not mentioned until the end of the poem, but in the universe. This puts the poem in the context of myth, in which the hero's role is to protect or liberate the society's cosmogonic center. The poem's persona is the hero, and the threat to the *imago mundi* strikes at his life. The hero must rescue the sacred space according to the cultural code of heroics. To do so he must find the paradigmatic hierophany and repeat it.[19] The poem will identify that hierophany and put it into action.

Salinas' immediate response affirms the barrio's persistence as a memory. "You live on, captive, in the lonely / cellblocks of my mind." Memory, that unreliable medium so susceptible to corrosive time, is invisible; the barrio is now like the masterpieces hanging in Abelardo's dead artist's mind. Like Louie, Salinas' barrio requires a new material surface on which to manifest itself. We are in the presence of the poet-persona about to liberate his home space from mere memory, to which material destruction has relegated it. This act transforms the persona into the hero; it is his rite of passage, his trial of courage. And in this case, hero equals poet.

The first stanza is two words, "LA LOMA," an emphatic thrusting of the barrio's name into the world; the next fourteen stanzas begin with the word *Neighborhood*, in which echoes that first naming. The barrio is recharted in the poem according to two internal orders: (1) place names, signposts on the barrio map; (2) the history of the persona's peer group, with specific types of experience repeatedly recalled, primarily playing and eating or drinking. The two form a spatial-temporal cross-reference, with the latter played out on the swelling circle of the former, whose expansion, in turn, is propelled by the activities of the latter. The series of outward thrusts moves toward eventual opposition, rejection, and fear, which produce an intermittent series of retreats to the center. Once again, as in "El Louie," centrifugal expansion is followed by centripetal withdrawal, until some of the same forces that destroyed Louie— drugs, alcohol, violence, and death—tear the protagonist away and leave him isolated, facing the ultimate chaos of death. "Trip" also can be divided into two halves, the first corresponding to childhood within the barrio, the second encompassing adolescence to adulthood and movement out of the home space. But always, the poem centers back around the barrio; it is the barrio.

The first view of the barrio, after we have been informed of its disappearance, comes in a kind of cinematographic zooming effect which focuses down from hills, to streets, to chuckholes, to one particular chuckhole around which there are:

Kids barefoot / snotty-nosed
playing marbles / munching on bean tacos
(the kind you'll never find in a cafe)

They play and eat, two activities of innocence and primordial definition.[20] We must consider carefully this initial image, the central
sygnifying act in the recuperated home space; its apparent simplicity
can deceive.

The children eat homecooked, obviously Mexican food, which
in the poem's terms is authentic and original. Food, and more
precisely the ingestion of anything into the body, immediately is
established as a touchstone of authenticity. In addition, the tacos
harmonize perfectly with the play activity, freeing one hand for
marbles. The game is universal, played by children everywhere,
although the way it is played varies.[21] Salinas does not specify the
form of marbles played, so we can only extrapolate from the information given, both at this point and in the rest of the poem. The
chuckhole seems to create a natural delimitation for the game-space,
evoking a version of the circle game of knocking an opponent's
marbles either from or into the circle, most likely the former. This
concentration inward to eliminate opponents is supported in the
later permutations of the game-playing motif, culminating in the
killing of one Chicano by another in game-like circumstances. The
chuckholed streets lend environmental connotations. That the streets
are never paved indicates the inequality of treatment within the
larger society. These games will be played in a setting constantly
limited and delimited by a lack of material goods determined by outside forces. The Chicanos' area resembles a war zone; they play in
the ruins created and left by society's unjust indifference. At the
same time, the chuckhole-marble circle image reveals a group
dynamics founded on aggressivity turned upon itself, instead of
against the exterior causes of the situation, like the pool-playing and
its violent transformation into death in "El Louie." This prelimi-
nary manifestation of macho competition, infantile at any age, with
its self-destructiveness, is, nevertheless, a game that harmonizes skill
and power, while it radiates significance. The founding hierophanic
act Salinas chooses for his barrio is a kratophany.[22] Unfortunately,
its dynamics of inward-directed violence remain constant in the text.
The two facets of this first image will return in permuted reprise, remaining essentially the same in spite of superficial changes, until the
persona, still trapped but in a larger ruin, spiritually feeds himself
while playing with words. The qualitative break in that final exercise
of the ritual activity marks the poem's response to the negative factors in the barrio's hierophanies.

The plurality of participants in the first image is maintained
almost without exception, thus generalizing experience; at the
end the group breaks down into individuals, coinciding with

self-destruction, though, ironically, the persona appears fully con-
ceived. The first-person singular pronoun occurs in only three of the
first twelve stanzas: in stanza 2, which actually corresponds to the
same time reference as the last stanzas, when the persona has been
isolated from his group; in stanza 8, when fear momentarily
fragments the group; and in stanza 10, when the group members
emerge from jail. Salinas clearly intended the poem to speak for his
peer group, first, and then, in ever-growing circles, for the Chicano
community at large.

In stanza 4 there is an expansion to the barrio as a social unit,
gathering at the community hall named in commemoration of May
5, a Mexican holiday, to celebrate September 16.[23] Barrio social life
revolved around the Mexican political traditions, but the heroic
names meant little to the young boys: "No one listened / no one
seemed to really care." The irony is sharp. Both dates com-
memorate struggles for independence from foreign domination,
while references to the Mexican Revolution also evoke a liberation
rebellion. Yet the retrospective focus allowed no talk about the present, much less the future. Barrio time was paced by the history of
another country, which, in the barrio's political context, had
nothing to do with its welfare. The evoked struggles, however, could
have been relevant if their significance had been related to contemporary reality. But the celebrants said nothing to the young; the
rituals were dead.

The vital ritual, authenticated by the game structure from stanza 3, was the dance. Marbles have given way to young girls dancing
together, never with the boys, who watch from the periphery.
Though only eight or nine years old, the boys are already "sex-
perts," marking the first of a series of sexual allusions in the poem,
all of which are tied to frustration. The marbles image informs the
dance with macho connotations: the girls are only objects in the
game played among boys. Significantly, one of the girls is figurative-
ly knocked out of the game by imputing sexual experience to her. At
this age the insult has no repercussions, but the boys are practicing
the macho game of honor slurring, later to be used playfully with
each other and seriously with enemies. Moreover, the incident
reveals the imprint of a sexually fixated society; the boys will retain
the pattern of sexual bias throughout life, or at least throughout the
poem. Male-female relations will be aggressive and clandestine.

Stanza 5 moves from civil to religious festivals. Food has begun
to change, "eating snowcones—raspas—& tamales." The bilingual
reference signifies the bicultural state in which the boys find
themselves; significantly, the Spanish term is placed between

dashes, graphically telling us that the language is being separated from the surrounding context. Tamales can be English or Spanish, an interlingual word accepted in either context. The circular games continue with walks " 'round and 'round the promenade,'' traditional parading of women past stationary men, or the sexes may walk in different directions, until the men decide to follow certain women. Sex is again the vital ritual, and frustration is implied in that the girls, although obviously Mexican (or why would they be at a Mexican church?), are "from cleaner neighborhoods / the unobtainables." Sex leads the group out of their closed circle by creating a desire for goals outside the circumference; the movement produces a sense of "we" and "they," of class distinctions previously implied by chuckholes and bare feet in stanza 3.

In stanza 6, the circle expands with "forays down to Buena Vista" and "cops n' robbers" games whose real goal was to spy into bedrooms. The violent aggressivity of *forays* underscores the image of the world as hostile and of the group as warrior-like; *cops and robbers* evokes the social order to which they can and will be subjected. Yet this is still play, with sex as its motivation; but the girls in the Projects reject the boys. Their only chance for sexual titillation is to watch from outside a window while others indulge; significantly, these opportunities arise while they play at crime, and actually make them petty criminals, peeping Toms. But they have no outlet for their desires within the accepted norms of their social group and must go outside of it for relief.

The first attempt involves using Juicy Fruit gum to bribe girls into sexual contact. The name itself is a euphemism for sex; the boys try to exchange the representation for the real thing, but the "good girls"—synonymous here with traditionally Mexican girls—refuse it. (Salinas infuses trivial objects with meaning, a skill sadly lacking in his imitators who think it is enough to recall the past.) The gum is a permutation of the food motif, marking a step toward Americanized prepackaged culture. Thus, the bribe actually does signify cultural betrayal, if we take the first food image as absolute. The boys unconsciously offer a reward that signifies a movement outside their culture; besides, what is sought, sex, is also culturally out of bounds. Sex aside, the act of chewing gum itself was a cliché of the American teenager in Hollywood films, tantamount to smoking in the adult woman. Mexican parents were not tolerant of it. Of course, the underlying irony is that chewing gum was supposedly a Mexican invention. The boys are moving out of their culture in search of glamorized versions of what their culture could provide, if they were willing to follow the traditional paths. But they are not willing.

Rebuffed by good girls, they turn to those who have already moved outside the culture, "stay-out-late chicks" who read *Modern Romance*. The connotations are obvious. The conflict pits traditional Mexican familial mores against modern romantic mores.[24] Frustration, nevertheless, remains. The sex is explicitly aggressive, "imposed" on the girls. Salinas locates the encounters under the shadow of the Catholic Church, toning them with the guilt that religion associates with sex outside of marriage.

The barrio's socio-religious organization, tainted with repressive sexual customs, defined the limited codes of acceptable behavior. Customs equal games; and food is the reward for playing according to the rules. Metaphorically, women become the reward sought—juicy fruit—and the macho games revolve around them. The attraction is natural; the games are the source of the frustration.[25] Life is patterned into sexually separate dancing, or the promenades, or "the games— bingo   cake walk   spin-the-wheel." The prize of the cake walk marks another step away from the original tacos. The three games are permutations of the chuck-hole game of exclusion, but different in that luck replaces skill and strength. Perhaps for this reason, the frustration and anger increase as well.

When members of the group first venture completely out of the Mexican space in stanza 7, "cross-town" to school, they are rebuffed on ethnic grounds—Mexicans are sent home for having head lice. The reason may be plausible, but that only Mexicans are sent home leads one to suspect discrimination. Ironically, the school dictates outward movement, only to classify and reject the Mexican. Irony is compounded by the positive results: a sense of ethnic community. Whereas class and geographic divisions previously existed, the school excursion unites them all as Mexicans. It also produces the group's first reaction of protest against the exterior forces that limit its movement: "Qué gacho!" [What a bummer!] The same situation will reappear, escalated, and the inchoate protest here will take on a much more definite character in stanza 10.

Withdrawn to its own space in stanza 8, the group gathers to tell scary stories that send the boys running home in fear. The circumstances of the incident are significant. The setting is Zaragoza Park, named after the hero of the May 5 battle after which the community hall of stanza 4 was named, thus situating the boys squarely within the barrio's mythical time-space. The story that scares the boys is about La Llorona, the weeping woman of Mexican folklore who haunts rivers or other dangerous areas and kidnaps naughty children. She is used by adults to scare children into obedience. The context seems entirely Mexican, but in both the park's name and the legend retold there are hidden connotations of importance. Both allude to threats of invaders aided by Mexican traitors. Zaragoza fought against the French who had been invited by Mexican conservatives; while La Llorona is associated with, at times even confused with, La Malinche, Cortés' translator and lover who helped him conquer Mexico. Thus, an imminent menace from the outside lies within the setting and the story, both of which derive from Mexican tradition. This explains how the danger of Boggy Creek—a name which rings with rural English connotations, not to mention the thoroughly English sound and its closeness to the Bogie Man—is transformed into La Llorona. The sacred center defines life within its boundaries and the chaos outside; Mexican codes define the barrio's socio-religious system as well as the exterior threats. The codes proscribe crosscultural contacts, as this stanza implies, and the boys already know that they are unwelcome in the outside society; the folklore supports the view of the world as hostile. But the boys have strayed from authenticity and are prime targets for La Llorona's vengeance. (Note in passing that the death menace takes the form of a vengeful, traitorous woman.) The boys run home, back to the very center of their original space, frightened by their own traditional explanation of the world; and in that center they find that Mexican folklore also can supply the remedy for those who stray, but have the sense to come home—a pinch of salt and the sign of the cross, "sure cure for frightened Mexican boys."

Stanza 8 is, therefore, another permutation of the original barrio image—the boys are at play, no longer with marbles, but the game essentially is still a matter of who can knock whom out of the circle. Like marbles being scattered, the group is fragmented by fear, provoking one of the rare appearances of the singular pronoun: "i think i heard" La Llorona. The space, now a park instead of a chuckhole, is their playground; but its limits, Boggy Creek, pertain to the outsider. Finally, the game results in the ingestion of food. However, the game and the food no longer harmonize, but rather are antagonistic, the latter being the cure for the former. The original image has expanded, only to return to its point of departure, the center.

The poem's first half closes on a note of fearful retreat and the finding of protection in the home. The culture provides traditional admonitions against venturing past its limits. Despite this, the boys had slowly drifted away from home; even when they were playing marbles they were already in the street. The section ends with a fearful retreat to the home itself, completing a series of partial withdrawals that alternated with the outward thrusts. It closes in upon itself in an image of a culture still able to control and protect its members through its religious folklore. Yet we should not forget that the same culture perpetuated political ideals irrelevant to the young, repressed natural instincts, and shared in ordering experience into separate ethnic groups. However, the futility of these efforts evidences itself in the inroads made by American culture (snowcones, Juicy Fruit, bingo, cake walks, *Modern Romance* magazine) and the insistent outward drive of the younger generation, chafed by anachronistic customs. In addition, the school system draws them out, albeit to reject them, reflecting the same paradoxical pressures that operate within the group. Fear and traditional mores allow the culture to maintain control, but not forever.

The second half opens with a burst of transformed imagery that conveys dramatic changes in the peer group. Whereas in stanza 3 no cafe could serve authentic barrio food, the group initiates its activities in the second half in the "Spanish Town Cafe," an obvious distancing from the home center. As the first of several "grown-up" centers, it is a permutation of their parents' May 5 Hall; and in the light of the Mexican jingoistic imagery (stanza 4), the cafe's name sounds treasonous. The cops-and-robbers games now become real stealing, and the pilfered objects confirm the cafe's betrayal image—"Fritos n' Pepsi Colas," imitation fried tortillas and the drink of the future "in" Anglo American teenager. From a contemporary perspective, this food is actually Chicano in its intercultural synthesis, but Salinas has established a Mexican pole of authenticity from which all activities must be judged.

The cafe scene also introduces a series of drugs to appear. Marijuana blends with adulthood when the cafe is called the "first grown-up (13) hangout." Thirteen could stand for the age of the boys, but it is also the numerical sign for marijuana. The association of drugs and manhood is undermined by the age itself, giving the whole scene an ironic, almost humorous tone, echoed in the pettiness of the theft. We can, however, expect the insignificant "games" to develop into more serious manifestations of the same basic action, just as in the first half marbles transmuted into sex.

The group's central activity no longer seems to be inwardly-directed aggressivity, nor is it explicitly sexual. However, the first half informs the second as the established code of imagery in relation to which any new images must be read. Thus, marijuana is an ingested element, but of no nutritional value and self-destructive, as is also their game of petty thievery. The almost total disappearance of women in the second half only intensifies the atmosphere of frustration; and when they do appear, they are linked to frustration and failure. It is as if any hope of a normal development of harmonious human relationships has been forsaken. The group has moved into the world of the adult macho, in which women are insignificant when compared to the relationship of men to men. Yet we know that this attitude is actually the result of the rigid sexual mores and of a series of frustrated attempts to break with them. So in reality the absence of obviously sexual activity effectively turns all their actions into veiled introverted aggressivity. The surface imagery has changed, but the essence remains.

The group becomes a gang in stanza 10, a development linked to gas-sniffing and muscatel-drinking escalations in their "grown-up" activities. They call themselves "NOMAS!" [NO MORE!]. It could be a cry of resistance and rebellion, though Salinas does not specify against what; this is the typical image of the directionless Pachuco seen in previous poems. The ambiguity of the name, with its connotation of limitations, underscores the gang's closedness.

As was the custom among Pachucos (a word not used yet in the poem), gang members tattooed crosses on their hands. The boys alter a traditional symbol, which saved them from fear at the end of the first half, by transposing it into a new code of pride related to street life in the U.S. urban environment. Ironically, the sign has already been defined by the context of its first usage in the poem, which continues to inform it, in spite of the boys' intentions. Thus it still connotes protection for frightened Mexican boys running from an outside threat. Consciously or not, Salinas created the perfect image of what Samuel Ramos described in *El perfil del hombre y la cultura en México*: the compensation for inferiority or fear by exaggerated aggressivity.[26] The irony extends when the tattoo, a synecdoche for Pachuquismo, gets them into trouble instead of protecting them. La Llorona, effectively forestalled by the cross in stanza 8, transforms into the police and reappears—*llorona* is slang for the police car siren, so the image transmutes through an interlingual metonymy. The cross, therefore, faces another outside threat, but now fails to ward it off. Actually, it signifies everything that causes them to be taken out of the barrio to be confined in correctional school for nine months, a gestation period from which they are born anew as fully formed "Pachuco Yo" [Pachuco I], now sporting the complete Pachuco costume. The cross has effectively converted them into what they claimed to be when they adopted it; the synecdoche blooms into the full zoot suit.

Several ironies must not be overlooked. First, the dominant, outside society once again draws the boys out of the barrio. The school (stanza 7) follows an evolution which mirrors the boys' and reappears as the correctional school; but whereas the first sent them home immediately, this one keeps them the full school year. But the reform school helps them re-form themselves into what they wanted to be, Pachucos. In this, the correctional school functions as the first school did, producing both a heightened sense of group identity and an expression of resistance. However, because the singular pronoun appears so infrequently in the poem, its usage here demands attention. That it is voiced in Spanish expresses resistance to the Anglo American society, for which the correctional school is a synecdoche. Linked to the Pachuco, the *yo* expresses the intense personal pride in a new life style, which, though it maintains a Mexican base—again the cross informs it—is not traditionally Mexican, but already a synthesis of Mexican and U.S. cultures. However, in terms of the poem's rhetoric, the *yo* indicates a fragmentation in group cohesiveness. The prison experience imposes a sense of loneliness, of individuality, of being cut off from the group; this is consistent with the other uses of the *I* in the text. But just as a pinch of salt and the sign of the cross brought the frightened *I* back into the group, the young man emerging from reform school pronounces the word *Pachuco*, which through a series of metonymies hides the cross; and the word reintegrates him into the community. Thus, ironically, the Anglo American attempts to reform the Chicano become part of a rite of passage toward a raised ethnic consciousness that defeats the purpose of the schools.

In stanza 11 Salinas focuses on the Pachucos' stifled talent, utilizing art as a metaphor for all aspirations. The "could-be artists" can only cover public buildings with graffiti. In spite of the clear sympathy for the Pachuco and the effort to lend prestige to the graffiti by equating them with Egyptian hieroglyphics, the resulting image bespeaks frustration. "Could-be" implies latent talent, while underscoring its unrealized state; hence, frustration. The Egyptian hieroglyphics' esoteric character is at once significant and restrictive. Once again, the Pachucos limit themselves.

The game-playing involved in the stanza is destructive. The graffiti are signs of aggressive claims to gang territory. They transform into signs the warrior-like world view revealed in inchoate form with *forays* (stanza 5). The graffiti included in the poem center the image of the cross, flanked by the number thirteen; marijuana and the protective-aggressive symbol are joined and placed at the heart of what the poem reveals as the sign of frustrated aspirations.

Stanzas 12 and 13 develop the negative expansion of drugs and liquor. "Chalie's 7th St. Club," with its Black music and barbecue, is the final distancing permutation of the community-hall and food motifs. The Christo Rey Church (stanza 6) transforms into Reyes' Bar (stanza 13). Logically, the paradigmatic game evolves as well. One Pachuco stabs another, while yet another murders a man. The playful, absurd nature of the violence is conveyed through the motives—the stabbing punctuates a discussion about who will drive home; the murder is the price a "square" pays for staring at a Pachuco. Note that the marbles-shooting image involves the same hand gesture as holding a gun or a knife, and its purpose is essentially the same. The game becomes a deadly crime. Similarly, drugs claim victims, with Pachucos receiving long jail sentences for marijuana possession.

The school motif receives a last permutation into the penitentiary. La Llorona looms grotesquely, carrying off wayward boys who no longer can run home. Nor can tradition forestall her. In fact, when women reappear for the first time in the second half it is to pronounce a traditional response of resignation, "Sea por Dios" [It's God's will]. These women are the mothers, who sit in court listening to their sons be sentenced; folding their arms "across their bosoms," they stamp the sentence with God's approval. At one level the image is entirely objective, realistic in its description of the women's gesture and its transcription of the response. However, in the poem the image resounds with the echoes of frustration suffered at the hands of traditional women who obey Mexican socio-religious mores. The poet imputes the same ironic guilt to the mothers as to the Pachucos; groups share ignorance, frustration, and the status of victims—victims of their own culture as well as of the larger society. With this final expulsion from the barrio, the poem shifts back to the persona's present, in which the barrio lies destroyed and the gang members are dead, incarcerated, or lost, only reappearing in the persona's memory. Now, he reveals that he too is in prison, recalling the past from his jail cell. The barrio provided him with "identity . . . a sense of belonging" in his youth and, more important, in prison: "So essential to adult days of imprisonment / you keep me away from INSANITY's hungry jaws." Lost in the chaos of the Other's space, the persona has survived because he could draw significance from the *axis mundi* which the barrio was. Its importance is so great that Salinas even forgives its negative influences, obvious in the analysis and now implied when the persona states, "i bear you no grudge." Such things are said only when one realizes that harm has been inflicted by another. However, the barrio has been destroyed in the real order of things, stripping the persona of the *axis mundi* and leaving him lost within the ordered chaos of prison. His response to the threat has been to reconstruct his journey through the barrio, bringing it from a past to a present temporal space, that of the writing itself. Thus, he states that "only the NOW of THIS journey is REAL," the *now* and *this* being the poem in which the barrio has a new material existence in written language.

The poem, then, is not the simple recuperation of the barrio, but a type of jailbreak and reintegration into community life. The poet-persona, unable to escape his cell, creates out of his barrio a metaphor of himself, "captive, in the lonely / cell blocks of my mind." The trip moves through the mind jail. He and the barrio are symbiotically joined; it gave him form and meaning, and now he repays the favor by reversing the causal relationship. But once the poem exists, once the barrio as poem has escaped the mind jail onto paper and into literature, it again serves its old function of centering the world, offering a constant exterior space of significance and identity. Through this symbiosis—or mutual synecdoche—the poet escapes his isolated cell by locating himself outside the prison's limits. In addition, the poem defines him as its author, a legitimate artist in contrast to the could-be artists of stanza 11; his potential has been realized in the work, and, therefore, he has escaped the barrio's limitations as well.

The positive result of his escape is that the game he is playing now is no longer one of exclusion and destruction, nor even of macho dominance, but of creative inclusion, reconstruction, and very unmacho self-revelation. In a gesture of tribute and reintegration, he has brought the barrio art out with him, utilizing graffiti in the poem. He attempts to make himself a synecdoche for all those could-be artists and liberate them from the cell of frustration, which ironically he himself must reconstruct in the poem if the barrio is to reappear in its true dynamics. This paradoxical positive-negative content is but another proof that the poem is the reincarnated barrio. And the action the poet performs is again that of turning inward toward a closed circle and playing with the elements caught inside it; he also nourishes himself at the same time, albeit with a spiritual food.

A final irony is that, in escaping, Salinas becomes again a captive. To renew the *axis mundi*, he must cosmicize the menacing chaos according to the primordial *imago mundi* of the barrio. He does this through an equivalent of the paradigmatic game: writing. Yet it should be remembered that, from the outset, the barrio is defined by the oppressive limits placed on it from the outside. Moreover, we should recall that an essential pole of influence in the *imago mundi* is the school, with its various permutations.[27] The school served to inform, if not transform, the Pachuco; the encounter with the menacing Other produces the Chicano synthesis. The divided Mexican community—divided along Mexican lines—becomes united in a way it could never be in Mexico itself. The youths emerge from Reform School as Pachucos, a United States, Chicano phenomenon. The encounter with the Other produces the newness, the synthesis which is neither Mexican nor U.S. American. Consciously or not, Salinas has included the encounter with the U.S. Other as an essential part of the primordial *imago mundi*. We could say that Salinas recognizes that the essential Chicano situation is to be constantly menaced by the threat of being sucked into the chaos of the U.S. order. Without that encounter, neither he nor his barrio would be the same. Chicano identity depends on all the elements in play. The poem itself repeats this situation by moving into U.S. written literature, a space that more than once has proved itself hostile to Chicano writing. (We could say that Chicano literature is an annoying chuckhole in the orderly, exclusive street of the country's English Departments.) Yet the poem is the product of the encounter; written in English, it ventures out beyond the restricted area of the poet's mind and his oral tradition. It bespeaks his experience in that Other space. Like the youths in prison, the poet has done his time within the school of English-language literature, and the experience informs the poem. However, like those youths, the poet seeks reintegration with his origins, and the poem becomes his shout of "Pachuco Yo" sent back to the community, as well as his dose of salt and the sign of the cross to ward off the ever-present Llorona. It is proof of survival and synthesis.

Once again, the heroic code of action is not the Pachuco's life style per se, but the positive channeling of his talents and spirit into creative, liberating activity. The hero is the poet; his achievement is the poem.

Paradigm Charts

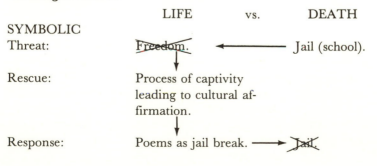

	LIFE	vs.	DEATH
SYMBOLIC			
Threat:	~~Freedom.~~	◄——	Jail (school).
Rescue:	Process of captivity leading to cultural affirmation.		
Response:	Poems as jail break. ——►		~~Jail~~

	LIFE	vs.	DEATH

SOCIAL
Threat: ~~Barrio and peer group as Chicano *axis mundi.*~~ ⟵ Disappearance of barrio.
                            ↓
Rescue: Barrio and peer group images.
                            ↓
Response: Poem as new space ⟶ ~~Disappearance.~~ for barrio and peer group.

PERSONAL
Threat: ~~Persona as sane, free; persona as artist.~~ ⟵ Captive persona; frustrated artist.
                            ↓
Rescue: Persona's communal images.
                            ↓
Response: Poem as proof of free- ⟶ ~~Captivity and frustra- tion.~~ dom and sanity within captivity; proof of artistry.

Conclusion

Four different surface structures arise from the same deep structure. It should be clear by now that the presence of the threat is essential to the dynamics of the Chicano self-image. All the poems are affirmations of a Chicano space, but none of them ignore the presence of the Other. The demand to change by the menacing U.S. Other translates itself into the stimulus to write. Tomás Rivera has said that Chicano writers are preoccupied with saving a Chicano reality before it disappears. What will bring about that disappearance is the presence of the Other, U.S. society. Yet there is also a distancing from the strictly Mexican identity. Pachucos and the barrio are intercultural phenomena; so, too, are the Chicano writers and their literature. The heroics posited are those of synthesis, with a strong appeal to the aesthetic creation of existence. In the final analysis, these poems seek a new order in the world, one that would function, perhaps, as a poem. And the poems are serious efforts to give order to that new world outside literature. They imply faith in the word's power to effect change.

3. THE HEROICS OF SACRIFICE
I Am Joaquín

If a "construction" is to endure . . . it must receive life and soul. The transfer of the soul is possible only through a blood sacrifice.
—Mircea Eliade, *The Sacred and the Profane*, p. 51.

I Am Joaquín[1] (first published in 1967) is considered the first major literary work of the Chicano Movement, and for many it still expresses best what the Movement entails. Its wide and continued popularity and the many imitations the poem spawned make it, for many, the epitome of early Chicano poetry. Whether it set a pattern for Chicano literature or simply reflected concepts and emotion inherent in Chicano culture is debatable; but since works by authors of widely divergent political persuasions contain the same paradigm, it seems reasonable to assume that *I Am Joaquín* was an accurate reading of the Chicano spirit at the Movement's outset. Much of its success can be attributed to that fact.

Style also contributes to its success. The writing is simple, free of complicated poetic tropes; the language easily accessible, communicating a readily memorable impression. Hence, repetition is a key technique. As in oral tradition, reiteration insures listeners' retention. Repeated material forms permutating motifs that, nevertheless, remain essentially constant. Thus, readers learn a process of repetition and development from which nothing in the style distracts.

Content is also simple. Mexican popular lore—including its commonest clichés—is utilized. Images, like Cuauhtémoc, Nezahualcoyotl, Cortés, the materialistic and cruel Spaniard, the long-suffering Indian, Madero, Díaz, Huerta, Zapata, Juárez, Villa, the Virgin of Guadalupe appear, with their standard signification within Mexican nationalism and popular tradition. No analysis is made, and, in effect, the poetry is not actually narrative in that these names function most often as signs, symbols, with the sparsest of characterization.[2] The poet assumes that his audience should know them; but he also realizes that a breakdown of oral tradition is a reason for writing the poem, so for those who do not know these images—especially the young—the poem serves as a teacher. (And in the Bantam edition, an outline of Mexican and Mexican-American history enlightens anyone for whom the poem is too esoteric.)

Structurally, the poem is uncomplicated. Two opposing symbolic giants frame several historical summaries. Sections treating the contemporary period posit political questions arising from residency in the United States. Thus, history informs the present, providing explanations and responses for the current situation. The second giant, which arises to save the Chicano nation—and actually is the Chicano nation—is a product of the central segment, born of the strength and unity it provides. The design is well planned and carefully executed, with a coherence that may strike the critic as simple, and which is meant to be exactly that. The poem's purpose is propaganda, consciousness-raising, not intellectual analysis or "high culture." The audience's tradition is judged to be oral and popular and the material is pared to that level. Within those boundaries it functions quite well.

The poem's main thrust is to rescue Chicanos from an enveloping chaos due to the loss of their land. The poem begins from the situation of contemporary Chicanos living in the Other's space, in Eliade's terms;[3] within that chaotic space, Chicanos must define—cosmicize—their own area. To do so they must recall the paradigmatic process that defined the culture and renew it; they must rediscover the primordial hierophany. For this reason, the Chicano Everyman, Joaquín, retreats first into his people, and then into history to seek the essential knowledge. When it is found, the people can move forward in orderly fashion toward a common goal.

Before beginning close textual analysis, it may be helpful to anticipate the major points to be found. The historical reviews will show that the paradigmatic process of definition is *mestizaje*, or miscegenation, achieved through the spilling of blood. One must be willing to shed and spill blood—a ritual hierophany according to the poem—for the good of the people. The goal of freedom and equality can be realized only through property ownership, so the revolution calls for a willingness to die, or kill, for the recuperation of land lost to the United States after the Mexican American War.

An outline of the poem's divisions and major subdivisions follows, with each marked to indicate its predominant temporal sitting.

I. Present. Lines 1–37. Lament and retreat into the Raza.

II. 1. Past. Lines 38–252. Development of Mexican mestizo culture, from pre-Columbian to twentieth century (subdivided into historical epochs).

2. Present. Lines 253–287. Community split and branded inferior by Anglo Americans.
3. Past. Lines 288–334. Chicano history as blood sacrifice.
4. Present. Lines 335–359. Chicanos united to protest injustice.
5. Past. Lines 360–406. Flashback to Anglo American invasion.
6. Present. Lines 407–441. Joaquín's determination to resist assimilation.
7. Past. Lines 442–462. Nine hundred years of *mestizaje* and survival.

III. Present. Lines 463–502. Rise of people's revolution and future projection.

Analysis will proceed section by section.

I. Lament and Retreat into the Raza (lines 1–37, pp. 6–13)

The first 37 lines mirror the entire poem in their temporal movement: present (1–8), past (9–12), present (13–23), past (24–30), present (31–37); also, in the character's movement: from passivity (1–12), to conscious analysis (13–23), to achieving historical perspective and the revealing of the enemy's essence (24–30), to an active choice of movement (31–37). The author has a plan and a method. The elements introduced here are expounded upon in the body of the poem, and at the end the direction of the chosen movement will be reversed: the withdrawal to safety (line 35) becomes an outward thrust when Movement begins (line 480). The poem's existence allows the reversal, but the essential elements are present from the start.

> I am Joaquín,
> lost in a world of confusion,
> caught up in the whirl of a
> > gringo society,
> confused by the rules,
> scorned by attitudes,
> suppressed by manipulation,
> and destroyed by modern society. (lines 1–8, p. 6)

The title line appears only five times in the poem (lines 1 [p. 6], 157 [p. 34], 288 [p. 54], 436 [p. 82], and 495 [p. 100]), marking significant points of affirmation. Here it opens the poem, establishing that its space coincides with Joaquín himself. Immediately, however, the affirmation of existence and identity is engulfed by two apparently contradictory elements, confusion and society. These two words are repeated twice in sequence, which supports the sense of whirling from one side to another. The trapped sensation is created by the passive structure of lines 3 and 5–8, and by the words *lost* and *caught up*. Joaquín is sucked in, lifted up, and spun. Even *world* and *whirl* are phonetically similar—the latter is the loosening of the former from its anchoring *d*. Actually, the world is a confused whirl; and the society, an implied order that whirls in confusion, is categorized as Gringo and modern. By contrast, Joaquín is neither; he is out of his space and in that of the Other. And as Eliade warns, the Other's world is chaos.

The first flashback into history (lines 9–12) paraphrases the saying "to lose the battle but win the war." Joaquín's ancestors lost the economic battle, but won cultural survival. Switching back to the present (lines 13–23), Joaquín faces a more complicated world than his forefathers, although essentially the same—spiritual or cultural survival and economic deprivation. Added is the possibility of economic success (freedom from hunger), albeit at the price of surrendering to a neurotic American society, with the loss of spirit. The poem offers a choice: separatism or assimilation. Yet the section should not be dismissed so simply; more is involved. The insistence on the need to *choose* (line 14) raises the poem to an existential level. Choice, the conscious willing of one's life, demands knowledge and active determination. The poem challenges the reader, presumably Chicano, to take a stand. But what seems a simple complication of traditional alternatives results in an opposition of modern versus traditional, and both involve Joaquín. Lines 17–18 restate lines 9–12: spiritual victory and economic defeat; lines 20–23 restate the modern-society imagery of lines 2–8, evoking the "lost in" and "caught up in" of the earlier lines; and American socio-psychological ills (line 21) were defined in lines 2–8. But since Joaquín is already in that whirl, the choice is between fidelity to the fathers' ways or remaining in Gringo modern society. The poem demands a withdrawal from the latter. As the poem develops, this motif will unfold as a conflict between the older people, who remember the fathers' ways, and the young, who are ignorant of them. The poem's voice sides with the former, but proposes to save the latter.

The conflict is symbolized in terms of a giant, U.S. progress and success (lines 28–30), that drags Joaquín along to nowhere. The image transforms that of the whirlwind into a monstrous force, perhaps a tornado, whose characteristics are technology and in-

dustry—modern society as the enemy. The alternative of a traditional agricultural society is implied. But if the monster is overwhelming and the space chaotic, how can one resist? The poem has
answered already—retreat—and the opening section culminates
with a withdrawal into the circle of Joaquín's people (lines 35-37).
Joaquín returns to his origins, to a centering of *our world* of order and
security, to the source of power from which he can cosmicize space.

The drawing of the circle also implies that breaking it is
dangerous. This concept is central to the poem; further miscegenation is taboo. The circle is the people and the space they occupy.
Within the circumference the space is theirs. Eventually the poem
will call for expansion to claim—reclaim—space, or land. But first,
internal cohesion must be assured; no breaking away can be
tolerated. To cement the culture, a review of the history will be
made. This is possible within the circle of the people, which counters
the whirling, chaotic circle of modern society. Joaquín has moved
back into his world, after looking back into his past and using that
vision to analyze the present. The same process will be repeated in
the poem as a whole.

II. 1. Development of Mexican Mestizo Culture
(lines 38-252, pp. 16-48)

The longest section, 215 lines, traces Mexican history from pre-
Columbian times to the twentieth century. The dialectical conflict
which produces a synthetic *I* is emphasized. This is achieved by having the *I* claim to be both sides of the conflicts, i.e., Spaniard and Indian, slave and master, revolutionary and reactionary. The poem
becomes an enumeration of heroes and, to a much lesser extent,
villains,[4] not to mention references to anonymous figures such as
masters and priests. Joaquín's synthesis is violent—he constantly
kills himself to strengthen himself. Thus, the images of blood being
shed (lines 44, 57, 101, 131, 198), killing (102, 201, 225, 231), being
killed (202, 227), and dying (116, 135, 191, 210) become facets of a
struggle-to-the-death motif. The death motif fuses with that of
historical figures in the symbol of the execution wall (106, 240).
Mexican history is portrayed as a bloody life-and-death struggle,
with death emphasized, producing a tradition of resistance to injustice and a forward thrust toward a goal, freedom (84-86), never
fully achieved in the poem. Yet the bloody tradition is the Chicano's
heritage—and future, as we will see.

This section will be analyzed according to its subdivisions.

II.1.A. CONQUEST AND COLONY (lines 38–86, pp. 16–20)

The first sixteen lines set the foundation for Mexican miscegenation in the Spanish conquest, with the indigenous elements predominating over the Spanish, being allotted ten and one-half lines of the sixteen. While the narrator says that he *is* both Cuauhtémoc and Nezahualcóyotl, as well as an unnamed Mayan prince, Cortés is introduced as the object of the preposition *of* in two possessive phrases—Indians are defined by their being, the Spaniard by his possessions. Cortés is a despot, one who possesses men; the Indians are *leader, king, prince*, and (in Spanish) a *guide*. The Spanish figure is singular, even in his national name, *gachupín*, a disparaging term; the Indians are plural, representing three different tribes—Aztecs, Mayas, and Chichimecs—and by extension the variety of Mexican culture. This, however, also explains Cortés' victory—pluralism equaled disunity in a numerically superior Indian force. Finally, the Spanish image centers on the instruments of violence, swords and fire, symbols of crusades against foreign unbelievers, while the indigenous side focuses in the image of animals in ecological balance, the traditional Mexican eagle and serpent, the center of the Mexican cosmos. However, both images share significant elements, such as a tradition of religious purpose and pilgrimage—the eagle and serpent marking the end of the Aztec search for a homeland. They also share a sense of killing for survival, as well as for conquest and domination of land—both were imperialist. These motifs continue throughout the poem.

It would be absurd, then, to propose that equal value is given to the elements in the mestizo. Neither in quantity nor in quality are they equal, though they do mix in the *I* as the point of confluence. But the poet also indicates the mixing process: Cortés, in spite of his negativity, is also Joaquín's blood and image. Blood, to be shed constantly to forge the Raza, and the image are put on equal standing. That is, the representational factor, the sign, enters into play as essential to the poem's process. Synthesis must take it into account. *Mestizaje* rests on a dual axis: blood and self-image.

Following the conquest, colonial life is represented in two aspects, civil (lines 54–63) and religious (lines 64–86). In civil life the Spaniards are masters and the Indians slaves. The latter work, sweat, and bleed for the masters. Yet masters and slaves unite in ownership of the land, an item repeated in synonyms (*land, earth, ground*) to underscore it as the basis of the society. The opposition of owner and slave is resolved in *mestizaje*, and blood is essential to the process. Though land is shared, the Spaniard holds it through political tyranny, while the Indian claims it through labor and blood. Both sides are Joaquín, but later (lines 244–252) the heroes will be those who oppose tyranny, signifying Joaquín's working-class sympathies. At this point paradox arises from the poet's need to embrace Spanish tradition in a self-image, while criticizing the conquest. At the same time land ownership is established here as a key to survival.

Religious life is depicted positively, the Catholic Church being shown as an equalizer of men under God and the propagator of the ideal of human worth and freedom, for which men fight. Christianity opposes, then, the dehumanizing modern society, though it is not absolved of guilt in the conquest. Priests were both good and bad, but this balance is undermined by the repetition of the verb *take* three times in seven lines. The saving grace is that the priests gave in return. (Later, when the give-and-take exchange reappears between Mexicans and Anglo Americans, the process fails, marking a radically different type of conquest and explaining the impossibility of further miscegenation.) The Church's positive image is underscored by the appearance of the first enumeration of mestizo elements—Spaniards, Indians, and mestizos (lines 73–75), unified under the Christian ideal. This enumeration will evolve into various forms in the poem (lines 192–197, 273–276, 481–486), signaling moments of unity—except in the case of lines 273–276, where the unifying factor is absent.

Lines 77–86 introduce the freedom struggle. From the religious ideal of *equality under God*, there arises the revolutionary formula: the *words* produce men who both *pray* and *fight* for their human rights (lines 78–80) and for the promised day of freedom (lines 83–86). An ideal catalyzes men of faith into action, producing eventual liberation. Specifically, the ideal is expressed in *words*; action is the product of verbalization, which explains the role of the poem itself—to catalyze the Chicano liberation struggle for equality under God. In addition, these revolutionaries pray; they confide in a transcendent order. The poem seeks to create that faith through and in itself, becoming the revelation of the transcendent order, becoming the prayer. Thus, the Chicano Movement is linked to Christianity, giving it the air of a religious crusade.[5] This establishes a higher law to counter oppressive human laws. Such appeals to superior values, especially aesthetic ones, are common in Chicano literature, but *I Am Joaquín* set a moral tone that became part and parcel of the Movement: a moral superiority of Chicanos over Anglo Americans that can be traced back to Catholicism.[6]

Finally, the goal of freedom establishes the expectation of a future to be achieved in the poem's terms and through its process. This sets the goal and determines the direction of the Movement beyond the poem's limits, since that time is not reached within them.

II.1.B. MEXICAN INDEPENDENCE (lines 87–134, pp. 25–30)

The next subsection's major portion treats the struggle for independence between 1810 and 1821 (lines 87–122), which, in turn, is dominated by the figure of Hidalgo. He begins as a unified image, and is split by the cry of independence that attacks the Spaniards in the name of the Virgin of Guadalupe. A paradoxical *I kill myself* section (lines 97–107) repeats the motif of internal conflict; Hidalgo is condemned by both civil and religious authorities, both of whom are Joaquín, also, who then kills Hidalgo (himself). Lines 103–107 introduce the motif of the wall of dead heroes, on which Hidalgo's head is placed to await the realization of his dreams, soon to be joined by those of others executed by Joaquín in front of other infamous walls (lines 112–113). Standing in front of anything will later trigger this motif of sacrifice for freedom. In this case, a dubious independence is won; Mexico's freedom can only be stated as a question with double punctuation (line 122).

The question marks introduce the next twelve lines, in which independence is betrayed. Motifs reveal the reasons. Oppressive forces use guns, fire, and mystic forces, symbolizing the union of Spanish Church and state. Cortés' despotic weapons are modernized, but the spirit remains: the flame, which acts through the weapons to dominate the Mexicans. The oppressed are signified by work, sweat, blood, prayer, and waiting, all characteristics previously attributed to the enslaved but resistant Indians and Mestizos. The new element added here is silence, a sign of biding time, of waiting for the promised life, that day of freedom foretold earlier.

II.1.C. BENITO JUAREZ: REFORM AND FOREIGN INVASION (lines 135–156, pp. 30–33)

The lines dedicated to Juárez are extraordinary for the sudden shift to internal unity, markedly different from the technique of dialectical oppositions. Clearly, when the threat comes from outside the nation, a leader arises to unify and save the people. Through the comparison of Juárez to Moses, Mexicans are equated with the oppressed and wandering Jews, in search of a homeland to which they have a sacred right, led by a divinely inspired leader. The image renews that of the Christian and Aztec pilgrimage to a lost homeland. Moreover, it utilizes another popular concept—Chicanos are to the United States what the Jews were to Nazi Germany. This sets up the demand for the establishment of a Chicano national state similar to Israel. It also implies that Chicanos can rightfully use the same tactics of terrorism and violence if necessary.[7] This will take place under a leader like Juárez, who will unite the nation against foreign invaders and their reactionary Mexican allies. Juárez is referred to as a little giant (lines 150–151), the first giant to oppose the oppressive giant from the opening segment; thus he prefigures the eventual birth of the Movement giant, who also will arise from the little, that is, common indigenous people. Juárez' enemies are kings, monarchs, and presidents, prefigurations of the Anglo American–West European technological society. Most important, when the threat is external, the Raza unites under a god-sent leader and fratricidal fighting is suspended.

It should be noted that this image of Juárez is that of Mexican propaganda and popular tradition and is not factual. Juárez' attempts to link Mexico and the United States, which he admired, are ignored, as well as the failure of his reforms. This is an excellent example of the poem's uncritical utilization of standard Mexican nationalistic imagery, its appeal to the clichés of Mexican populism, perpetuating stereotypical imagery, while using it to establish a Chicano heritage. This is perfectly consonant with the simplification process of oral tradition[8] and with the cosmicization process of a home space. One repeats what is already known and accepted in order to prove one's authenticity and invoke the paradigmatic patterns.

II.1.D. MEXICAN REVOLUTION (lines 157–206, pp. 34–41)

The title line opens the next subsection, signaling a moment of affirmation and revelation, in this case the close emotional and ideological tie the poet seeks to establish with the Mexican Revolution. Emotionally, the link is with the popular leaders Villa and Zapata; but, ideologically, a difference is made between them. The two heroes are juxtaposed (lines 158–168), and, though Villa occupies more space, Zapata is closer to Joaquín's essence. The persona "rode with" Villa, but says "I am" Zapata. Both seem positive images: Villa signifies emotion, power, and violent action, the work pole of work-and-prayer; Zapata's ideology of land ownership by the people is the prayer. Villa is another giant—a "tornado"—rising from the people to face the oppressive giant. But tornadoes lack direction and are chaotic. The poet prefers a hero with ideological direction. Zapata's motto renews the land-ownership motif from the colonial section (line 62); and, when passion and fire produce a failed revolution, the ideology continues. This is the significance of the use of past tense for Villa and present for Zapata.

Any doubt about the poem's ideology is dispelled with a specific espousal of Zapatismo in the next fourteen lines. Land is worth dying for. And since Zapata's goals have not been realized, those who claim to be Zapatistas must be willing to die to continue the struggle.

As in the independence section, the revolution splits into fratricidal camps (lines 183–197), which eventually synthesize into the second enumeration of mestizo elements. Comparison shows a change of emphasis and order. While lines 73–75 grouped Spaniards, Indians, and mestizos, lines 192–197 first list four Indian tribes—Yaqui, Tarahumara, Chamula, and Zapotec—then the mestizo, and, last, the Spaniard. In the first enumeration, equal participation produces the mestizo, while Indians far outweigh the Spanish in the second. In addition, the mestizo, the end product, separates the Spaniard from the process in the latter. It should be noted that the expanded Indian representation is achieved with tribes not considered "highly cultured," compared to Aztecs and Mayans, thus emphasizing its popular base.

The last lines (198–206) produce a synthesis of victors and vanquished, the dead and their killers, reactionaries and revolutionaries. The *I* is the revolution's bloodshed, the synthesizer of positive and negative poles into life and progress.

II.1.E. WOMEN (lines 207–218, p. 42)

A marked change of tone signals the emergence of women into the poem. The historical flow is interrupted by projecting their presence abstractly, free of specific references. Women die and live anywhere, any time; thus, woman becomes a mythical (timeless) presence, a constant value in a world of historical flow, a synchronic touchstone at any point in a diachronic process. This is underscored by giving her an image of religious *mestizaje*. She is both the Virgin of Guadalupe and the Axtec goddess Tonantzin—she endures, no matter what system rules. Under any name the goddess remains essentially the same.

This section is a temporal and religious pause, a momentary rest in the poem's persistent movement. The woman's role is to maintain traditions (symbolized in her black shawl) through her faithful presence, but not to determine history, which is here the man's sphere. Even the male named, Juan Diego, is feminized in his attributes of faith and humility. The whole section is markedly feminine. The passive, stereotypical role to which the woman is relegated is lamentable, but, once again, the poem traffics in Mexican clichés. It calls for a withdrawal into that culture, and women represent its traditions. The poet ignores the active role women took in history, preferring to limit them to the passive mother image.

In the poem's terms, however, the women's segment is structurally and thematically important. It separates Mexican history from the Chicano portion to follow. The change of tone and ahistoricity force readers to adjust their mood, break stride, before meeting Chicano heroes. At the same time, the motherly image constitutes a link between the two sections. Chicanos are tied to the Mexicans by parentage and tradition, yet separated by location —geographic location in reality and structural location in the poem. The woman's image creates the effect. The poet uses her, though he denies her a specific historical role.

CHICANO HEROES (lines 219-243, pp. 44-45)

Three Chicano heroes, Joaquín Murrieta, Elfego Baca, and the Espinoza brothers, represent the states of California, New Mexico, and Colorado respectively. At the time of the writing, these states had produced Chicano leaders of national significance: César Chávez, Reies López Tijerina, and Rodolfo Gonzales. The poem's heroes prefigure these Chicano Movement leaders.

Of those named, Murrieta receives the most attention. He represents armed, violent resistance against an enemy who commits two unforgivable crimes: stealing land and raping and killing a man's wife, thus attacking two elements which represent life and tradition. Murrieta's violence, like that of the others, was in self-defense; they all are willing to kill to protect their land and women.

When killed, all become severed heads atop the wall of independence. The motif joins the Chicanos and Mexican heroes from the independence section, uniting them in a common struggle.

II.1.G. CHICANO / MEXICAN UNITY, RÉSUMÉ
(lines 244-252, p. 48)

The Chicanos—Murrieta and the Espinozas—are raised from the status of outlaws to that of freedom fighters through association with

Hidalgo and Zapata, acknowledged heroes. Contiguity attributes to the Chicanos the Mexicans' ideals, while lending coherence and progression to history from pre-Columbian Mexico to the Chicano Movement. The heroes share death at the hands of reactionary enemies; their heads stand on the wall together. They had the courage to face deceptive and hypocritical tyrants (lines 247–252). To *face* equals to *stand up to*, the motif of resisting an enemy capable of violent retribution. The reference to tyranny recalls line 59, thus framing segment II.1 in resistance to oppression and making that resistance a constant of Mexican-Chicano history. This serves to divide history dialectically into a progression of warring camps, of *us* and *them*. Since the heroes died without realizing the moment of freedom, the struggle must continue into the present where the tyrannical force persists.

Up to this point, however, the opposing forces have blended dialectically, through fatal bloodshed, forming Joaquín. Only when an exterior force threatened did the dialectic cease. The poem embraces all Mexicans, because the real enemy is the present manifestation of that tyrannical force, which happens to be, in the Chicano situation, again exterior. Yet we can expect the poem to begin imposing the choice, though it has already defined which side the true Chicano will take—that of the common people and against tyrants.

This historical vision is a gross simplification. Ideologically and poetically, the poem offers clichés, without analysis. History seems logical, simple, understandable; complications are ruled out in a melodrama of good and evil. Even paradox, which might connote confusion, is so systematically utilized that it becomes a predictable rule. To the chaos of modern society is opposed a reversion to traditional views. Supposedly, if one withdraws from modern society, history becomes clear. Thus, at midpoint, the poem ties off history into a compact, graspable whole just before returning to the present. The present is still unresolved, but now it can be appraised with a historical perspective, which shows that the forces at play are the same.

II. 2. Community Split and Branded Inferior
by Anglo Americans (lines 253–287, pp. 51–52)

The poem's second half opens with Joaquín standing, looking back, and simultaneously seeing the present; he has assumed the heroic standing position and, though still inactive, he has changed. To the look-and-watch motif (lines 31–32) has been added the historical perspective. The poem has educated the *I* to see differently. Also, placing the present moment at midpoint causes a pendulum effect of swinging from past to future through Joaquín, the center of the historical process. Of course, we should recall that the poem's first half ended with the image of tyranny, creating a center disputed by opposing images. The confrontation has Joaquín standing and facing tyranny, emphasizing his heroic disposition.

In the present the *I* remains split, graphically represented in the mutilation of the title line:

I,

of the same name,

Joaquín (lines 259–261)

The *I* is separated from its name, and its verb of existence, *am*, is missing. This chaotic lack of identity is attributed to living in a country that has obliterated Joaquín's history and stifled his pride, imposing inferiority on him.

After 215 lines of history, to attribute inferiority to a lack of history must mean that something was overlooked. The above lines graphically represent it with the empty space between *I* and *Joaquín*. Though they share the name, one is not the other. What they lack, what was not given in the first historical overview, was Chicano history between those early Chicano heroes—who were actually Mexicans cut off from Mexico—and the present. This seems to demand another retrospective journey.

What remains of this segment leads to the same conclusion. The third mestizo enumeration actually splits the *I*. The setting is now the United States, so the binding process is different—the melting pot (line 280), which demands a rejection of ancestry. This explains the perplexing statement that Indians have endured and can be called winners; they have refused to assimilate, choosing to remain separate, despite the hardships. The mestizo has yet to overcome the temptation, accepted by some, to sell out (line 283) for token rewards. The poet restates the choice between following the old ways and accepting American neurosis (line 21). The melting-pot metaphor structurally mirrors the whirling chaos of the opening lines—the present is still menacing.

The poet's categorical denunciation of assimilation / miscegenation in the United States raises the question of why it is valid in Mexico and not here. Is this racial prejudice? Or does history support the poet's stand? Again, the period between the first confrontation and now, which might supply the answer, could enlighten us. The poet must revert once again to history for the missing answer.

II.3. CHICANO HISTORY AS BLOOD SACRIFICE
(lines 288–334, pp. 54–62)

That something essential is about to appear is announced when the next segment of the poem opens with the title line; the specific aspect of life to be reviewed is conveyed in the second line—the multiple ways Joaquín has bled. This shorter historical overview concentrates on the catalyst of miscegenation: bleeding death. The poet seeks two things: something overlooked previously, and Chicano history since the early confrontation with Anglo Americans and since the Mexican Revolution, where the first overview left off.

Mexican history is first encapsulated in a mural-like image (lines 290–298), in which shapes reflect each other structurally, creating a flow of forms relating all the objects in mutual signification. Moctezuma's bloody altars become the bent backs of Indian slaves, whose bleeding lash marks turn into whips held by masters, who shed their pure blood while standing at yet another wall. Blood gives purpose to history and unites social classes, in Mexico, creating the expectation of eventual justice for the oppressed through the same bloody process. Note that the image originates with altars, evoking the motif of sacred purpose.

From that compact image, the poem expands into a vast historical panning shot of every battlefield in Mexican history on which the dialectical forces bled in synthesis, closing with the word *revolution* (line 307), which was also the ending point of the first overview. Mexican history has been scanned in search of some overlooked event; and it is found.

Perhaps because Joaquín was not prepared for the confrontation until his Mexican identity was recovered, the definitive historical event in Chicano history was, incredibly, passed over in lines 38–252: the Mexican American War of 1846–1848. The poet now targets an incident which combines a battle with the symbolic altar (walls, heroes facing the enemy, sacrificial victims, resistance to tyranny): the fall of Chapultepec Castle in 1847. The *children* (adolescent military cadets, known as Los Niños Héroes) defending the castle jumped from the walls instead of surrendering. The poet offers a morality play: when threatened by invasion, real heroes—even children—die for their country. Heroic death is rewarded by the eternal life of fame. This message appeared earlier, but now the enemy is the United States, and when the threat is external, we were taught, synthesis is voided. Although all the factors for *mestizaje* were present on the Mexican side, what was lacking was the bloodshed on the U.S. side. The children die in hermetic resistance.

The violent apparition of the Anglo American divides the segment, as it divided Mexico, separating Mexicans and Chicanos. The second part, set in the present, introduces a review of three bloody routes Chicanos historically have followed in attempting to continue the *mestizaje* process in the United States. Prison and the boxing ring structurally represent the closed isolation in which Chicanos are trapped (lines 318–328). The latter combines hunger and boxing in referring to the tradition of ethnic minorities using sports as a means to social mobility. Crime is another. These back doors to American society are evoked to show that Chicanos have tried to follow established paths to acceptance. Another traditional door, military service, is introduced next, with references to World War II, Korea, and Vietnam. The poet claims that Chicanos have paid the blood price in established assimilative rituals. Having shed blood willingly in U.S. wars, they cannot be blamed for lack of participation. Yet they are still excluded. The sacrifice has been futile. Why?

As is his tendency, the poet frames the segment with one image, in this case that of pure blood (lines 295 and 329). Nothing in this poem is unintentional, especially not a mention of blood, the central image of its paradigmatic process. In addition, in the poem's final and climactic section, there is an affirmation of pure blood (line 499) made by the transfigured Joaquín; its usage here prefigures that last affirmation. So we must analyze it carefully. Purity of blood is attributed to two different groups, to the cruel masters (line 295) and to the Chicano soldiers (line 329). Though separated by centuries of history and miles of geography, they become one through the metonymy of blood, representing the synthesis motif. In the Mexican section, blood flowed equally from everyone, workers, slaves, and owners (lines 304–305). As we know from lines 54–63, these groups formed an *I* through mutual land ownership. Also, the master's pure blood mixed with the others' blood, and it happened against the setting of sacred altars. Mexican battlefields become extensions of those altars, spaces where the ritual of the ideal of equality under God can be realized. In the Chicano part, Chicanos bleed in restricted areas—boxing rings and prisons (like the pool tables, chuckholes, barrios, and cells of Chapter 2)—or in wars fought on foreign soil, where Chicanos have no role as owners. As in the Chapultepec incident, U.S. troops are imperialistic invaders, and the blood shed—according to the poet—is only the Chicanos'. (Worse, Chicanos shed blood fighting as imperialistic mercenaries.) It is nonsynthesizing bloodshed, because Anglo America has refused to accept the sacrifice as proof of equality. History teaches Chicanos that their exclusion is unwarranted and that to keep trying is useless.

II.4. Chicanos United to Protest Injustice
(lines 335-359, pp. 64-66)

When the present moment reappears solidly, Joaquín is standing, facing a legal court, a permutation of the force of tyranny he faced before. It finds him guilty, not of an actual crime, but for his Raza's glory. This glory of unity comes from the poem, whose existence has imparted to the *I* the knowledge necessary to allow him to stand proud and strong in the face of injustice and not to expect acceptance. He is sentenced to his familiar role of laborer, slave, but with the difference that the land is not his. Land, culture, and women have been equated in the poem, so it is said now that Joaquín's culture has been raped. Ironically, this leaves an opening for response. The woman has been violated, but not killed nor abducted. She must be avenged, according to the macho code which the poet explicitly claims (line 343). This demands a willingness, like Murrieta's, to fight and kill to protect one's home. The poet appeals to the unwritten law; blood will be shed, but it is the Other who has brought it on his own head.

II.5. Flashback to Anglo American Invasion
(lines 360-406, pp. 69-74)

This segment divides into two subsections, one summarizing the history of confrontation in which the invaders reject miscegenation (lines 360-388), and another in which the rejected arts are explained as a life source (lines 389-406). The Chicanos' poverty and oppressed state are *rewards* for the descendants of chiefs, kings, and revolutionaries. Chicanos helped the gold-seeking foreigners, but were robbed in exchange. The process of miscegenation was opened to the Anglo American, who turned it down, ignoring Joaquín's purifying *fountain*, that of natural harmony and fraternal love (lines 386-388). Since the only fountain that has flowed here is blood, this means that the invaders refused to mix theirs, missing the chance to enter into the vital process of *mestizaje*.

Another motif underscores this rejection. When *mestizaje* began, the Spanish priests *gave* the religious principle of equality in exchange for what they *took* (lines 70–72). Now, in a similar situation of conquest, there is only a one-way flow of goods. Chicanos gave; Anglo Americans took, though they left what was of real value (line 383). While the Spaniard gave the ideal of equality, it is just a word in the United States (line 351). The lack of interchange is the failure of miscegenation, and thus of life in the poem's terms. Anglo Americans chose to remain outside, and outsiders must be fought.

The rejected values were, specifically art, music, and literature, defined according to the poem's ideology. Art is that of the Mexican muralists, Rivera, Siqueiros, and Orozco, the *illustrators* of the Mexican Revolution.[9] Art is defined as a revolutionary act for mankind's salvation. Aesthetics do not enter into consideration. Music includes both *mariachi* music and the *corridos* (a type of popular ballad), with the *corridos* also representing literature. Music is joy, happiness, and love. *Corridos* are history—traditions, legends, and actual events —turned into song, the storehouse of the dialectical process of life and death, of joy and sorrow; they are the life of the people, and the people are Joaquín (lines 400–406). The poem, which also is Joaquín, defines itself as the *corrido*, thus inscribing itself within its self-established code of values. This explains its use of cliché, of repetition, of simple language, of few but key images. Also, it opposes the Chicano oral culture to U.S. written culture, attempting to locate itself in the former, while actually being part of the latter—an ironic *mestizaje* with the rejected and hated Other.

That *corridos* are storehouses of tradition and culture associates them, and the poem, with women, who have been depicted in the same way. This implicit metonymy introduces the next segment on the family.

II.6. Joaquín's Determination to Resist Assimilation (lines 407–441, pp. 77–82)

The woman's passivity continues, as does her role as a bridge to Chicano heroism. As the storehouse of tradition, she is a cultural mirror in which Joaquín studies his reflection. Simultaneously, she watches him, activating the mirror into a judgmental instrument armed with the totality of history. Significantly, Joaquín's declaration of purpose springs from seeing himself reflected in another's eyes, which at the same time place him in historical perspective, lovingly. The woman equals the *corridos*, and both equal the poem. They are all passive, faithful sources of culture, and commentators who call the man to action. If action is not forthcoming, they also will reflect his failure. Joaquín joins the woman to face life; that is, he accepts the poem's challenge.

Through the poem's "eyes" he sees and comprehends his situation. Joaquín cries in anguish for his children who move into the social death of U.S. society, from which they cannot remember Joaquín. At this point, the title line reappears—the threat of disappearance is forestalled, first, by sheer affirmation of existence. Then there follows a declaration of purpose: to fight, to win, to teach his sons who he is (lines 432–441). These lines form an interior duplication of the poem. Joaquín, assuming the poem's historical perspective, sees his children being swallowed by the monster from the first segment; he affirms his being and the need to will the historical perspective to his sons, to save them. If they are to die, let it be as heroes. The poem itself is that struggle, that perspective; it is Joaquín. The *sons*—and daughters?—who read it will know him, receiving from him their own significance and purpose.

II.7. Nine Hundred Years of *Mestizaje* and Survival (lines 442–462, pp. 82–86)

Once more the poet resorts to the past for strength before moving forward, this time beginning with the reconquest of Spain from the Moors. Blood again is the central image in historical process. He states that he has *endured*, *survived*, and *existed*, preparing us for the climactic shift into the future tense in the final lines. And the past has been lived amid the worst of U.S. society's social neurosis enumerated here in seven lines (456–462). What at the start was a chaotic monster, impossible to grasp, is now dissected and inventoried. This is possible only because Joaquín now has a historical perspective and a positive self-image, with which he can put his environment into rational order.

III. Rise of People's Revolution and Future Projection (lines 463–502, pp. 93–100)

For the last time, the poem shifts back to the present with the motif of "and now." Elements unite to form the revolution, a dormant giant rising to face the first menacing giant. The goal is a better life, that golden moment of freedom foretold ages—and many lines—ago. From all directions a unified *we* starts to move; the standing and waiting motifs are superseded by action. The defensive circle now expands outward to reclaim its rightful space, producing the last enumeration of mestizo elements, but now they are names of U.S. Hispanic ethnics, all under the term Raza, and all the same. Identity is achieved through race (looking the same), experience (they *cry* and *sing* alike; that is, they share a history of struggle), and reaction to experience (feeling the same). This is surely simplistic, but entirely consonant with the poem's vision.

The last ten lines state the refusal to be devoured by the modern giant. The title line is repeated, followed by the last summary of Joaquín's essence: resistance against a strong enemy through spirit, faith, and pure blood. (Note that the self-image always includes the threat from the Other.) Joaquín's last affirmation of identity flows from that essence: he claims to be both the prince of the Aztecs and the Christ of Christianity, a historical and religious *mestizaje* of heroes willing to die for their people in a bloody, sacred sacrifice. Although the entire poem has prefigured this discovery, the paradigmatic creative act here finally is named explicitly. The poem has shown that history is a continuous progression of mestizos performing the paradigmatic action of their primal heroes, killing them and dying as them. Joaquín has come to understand that process and the need to continue it, with all its connotations of violence and bloody sacrifice. It is the necessary paradigmatic heroic code. And now that the history of the nation has been infused with a clear mythical, sacred significance, Joaquín projects himself and that process into the future, toward that as yet unrealized moment of freedom, stating that he shall and will endure. The shift from *shall* to *will* signals a change from a simple statement of futurity to a declaration of determination to form a future through willful action. (In the Spanish version, the last two lines simply repeat a determined *perduraré*, losing the forceful change of the English version.) This ending reflects the entire poem, a movement from passive to active life, with the goal left in the future.

Paradigm Charts

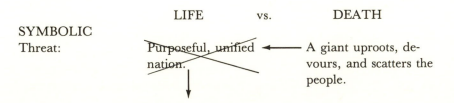

	LIFE	vs.	DEATH
SYMBOLIC Threat:	Purposeful, unified nation.	←	A giant uproots, devours, and scatters the people.

LIFE   vs.   DEATH

Rescue: A signifying ritual of
                     blood sacrifice.
                         ↓
Response: Poem as protective
                     giant evoked by
                     knowledge of history; ——→ ~~Menacing giant.~~
                     reading of poem as
                     the repetition of the
                     ritual prayer calling
                     for the ritual act.

SOCIAL
Threat: ~~Purposeful, unified~~ ←—— Modern society repre-
                     ~~nation.~~   sents chaos for tradi-
                         | tional Chicano
                         | culture, demands
                         ↓   assimilation.
Rescue: Historical images of
                     the Chicano nation.
                         ↓
Response: Poem as ordered his- ——→ ~~Chaotic modern~~
                     torical identity and   ~~society.~~
                     basis for future.

The personal chart should be prefaced by calling attention to the fact
that Rodolfo Gonzales, the author, is one of the national leaders of
the Chicano Movement. Therefore, the definition of the leader's
role is of personal significance to him.

PERSONAL
Threat: ~~Leader accepted by~~ ←—— A traditional distrust
                     ~~common people.~~   of leaders as dic-
                         ↓   tatorial.
Rescue: Images of leaders aris-
                     ing from the common
                     people and incar-
                     nating their totality.
                         ↓

Response: Poem as proof of the
                     poet-leader's belief in
                     the supremacy of the
                     common man in the ⟶ D̶i̶s̶t̶r̶u̶s̶t.
                     Chicano Movement.
                     Poem makes him an
                     educator, prophet,
                     heir to title of mestizo
                     leader.

Conclusion

The poem produces change and is the vehicle for it. Like the women it portrays, it confronts readers through its mirroring presence, challenging them to evaluate themselves and make a choice. Chicanos are directly challenged to assume Joaquín's role. The poem is so simple, so well designed, so easily grasped that it appeals to the reader. Many may not comprehend its justification of blood sacrifice or the call to violence, but they are attracted to the readily identifiable clichés, the familiar content. The poem functions as *corridos* or popular songs or folktales do, moving one emotionally, but not stirring analysis. Yet, as in them, there is an underlying moral, based on a Manichaean simplification of the world into good and evil. When one is lost in the chaos of modern living, such simplifications offer a refuge.[10] The poem's power derives, first, from its simplistic ideology and form; second, ironically, from its pretentiousness. The poem dares to invoke a cosmic, religious, and transcendent principle upon which the Chicano Movement can be founded; it unabashedly claims a divinely revealed purpose for itself. The fact that it does so in popular terms, in the most demagogic rhetoric, in no way lessens its pretentions, though it does raise questions regarding the implied estimation of the people it addresses.

4. THE TEACHINGS OF ALURISTA
A Chicano Way of Knowledge

Quetzalcóatl-Nanauatzin is the sun-god of the priests [Tlamatinime], who consider voluntary self-sacrifice the highest expression of their doctrine of the world and of life.
—Jacques Soustelle, *La Pensée Cosmologique des Anciens Mexicains*[1]

Alberto Urista, known as Alurista, has published three collections of poetry, *Floricanto en Aztlán* (1971), *Nationchild Plumaroja* (1972), and *Timespace Huracán* (1976). They are didactic books that attempt to teach Chicanos to understand themselves and their situation, and to overcome the threats to their existence. Alurista shares the anti-industrialist, anti-technological, anti-capitalist attitude of *I Am Joaquín*, as well as the purpose of consciousness-raising through an appeal to self-knowledge and ethnic pride. However, his use of pre-Columbian philosophy, an emphasis on mythical time, a third-worldist view of universal harmony, and an acceptance of all races in the formation of a new culture of pluralism make his heroic system markedly different from Gonzales'. To understand Alurista we must explore two sources of his vision: Carlos Castaneda and Nahuatl poetics.

Alurista's first two books begin with epigraphs from Carlos Castaneda's *The Teachings of Don Juan: A Yaqui Way of Knowledge* (*TDJ*).[2] (The third book was to include a third citation, but the editor refused to use it.)[3] The epigraphs come from Don Juan's explanation of the "enemies of a man of knowledge"; that is, what prevents people from becoming, like Don Juan, beings in harmony with the cosmos. Men of knowledge renounce rational thought in favor of a separate spiritual reality, the truth of life, becoming free and self-fulfilled, even within the restrictions of modern society. Don Juan explains that when a man begins to learn, the unexpected newness of the experience produces fear, the first enemy.

> Fear! A terrible enemy. . . . concealed at every turn of the way, prowling, waiting. And if the man, terrified in its presence, runs away, his enemy will have put an end to his quest. (*TDJ*, p. 84; cited on the title page of *Floricanto*)

Fear can turn the man into "a bully, or a harmless, scared," defeated man; but if he accepts it fully and continues to learn, fear will give way to clarity. Yet clarity blinds him by erasing doubt.

> It [clarity] gives him the assurance he can do anything he pleases, for he sees clearly into everything. And he is courageous because he is clear and he stops at nothing because he is clear. But all that is a mistake; it is like something incomplete. If the man yields to this make-believe power, he has succumbed to his second enemy and will fumble with learning. He will rush when he should be patient, or he will be patient when he should rush. (*TDJ*, p. 85; cited in *Nationchild*, p. [12])

Trapped by clarity, a man becomes a *buoyant warrior* or a *clown*. To avoid it he must defy clarity, using it only to see, wait, and move carefully; he must think "that his clarity was a mistake" (*TDJ*, p. 85). Then he will have true power—enemy number three.

> Power is the strongest of all enemies. And naturally the easiest thing to do is to give in; after all, the man is truly invincible. He commands; he begins by taking calculated risks, and ends in making rules, because he is a master. [Power will turn] him into a cruel, capricious man. (*TDJ*, p. 86)

He must control himself carefully, realizing that power is never really his; he must "reach a point where everything is held in check" (*TDJ*, p. 87), where power is used wisely.

The last enemy, old age, one must resist by not surrendering to fatigue; constant struggle will produce one brief moment of fulfillment.

Each confrontation is a rite of passage; together they form a maturation process. Alurista offers it as an alternative to the "American way of life." In this he adopts a typical 1960's attitude: the whiteman's materialistic, rationalized society is decadent, self-destructive, and alienated from nature. Alurista pictures him as trapped by inorganic possessions which he thinks he controls. As victim of the enemy power, Anglo Americans create a cruel, capricious society, powerful but doomed. Survival requires a withdrawal from it and a return to a spiritual harmony with nature. Castaneda provides a model—an Amerindian "way of knowledge" and a guide to a "separate reality." Moreover, since Indians have survived the genocidal European conquest, in spite of being powerless, they can be a model for Chicanos. However, Castaneda provides no aesthetic theory, and his character Don Juan preaches noninvolvement in any social system, even alternative ones, which negates Alurista's social commitment.

Pre-Columbian Nahuatl culture, a highly organized society with a philosophical-aesthetic system, provides Alurista with a spiritualized poetics. The title of his first book explicitly names its source: *flor i canto*, "flower and song," a Spanish version of the Nahuatl term for poetry, connoting the entire system of Nahuatl thought, in which poetry was considered the key to knowledge.

A *tlamatini*—Nahuatl for philosopher or wise man—was a combination teacher, psychologist, moralist, cosmologist, metaphysician, humanist, historian, and genealogist. Moreover, according to Miguel León-Portilla's *Aztec Thought and Culture* (*ATC*), the *tlamatinime* were "responsible for composing, painting, knowing, and teaching the songs and poems in which they preserved their scientific knowledge" (*ATC*, p. 16). Poetry, which facilitated oral teaching, was more than a useful vehicle, however, it was "the only true thing on earth" (*ATC*, p. 75). The ephemerality of existence made the possibility of knowing any truth doubtful. Poetry was the only source, "a peculiar type of knowledge, the fruit of authentic inner experience, the result of intuition. . . . which, through symbol and metaphor, allows man to discover himself and then to talk about what he has intuitively and mysteriously perceived" (*ATC*, p. 76). This vision of divine origin makes poetry one of the few things that could escape destruction in a world of fleeting existence. Poetry was an attempt to transcend evanescent being. This quality made the *tlamatini* a sacred bard, through whom man is "able to communicate with the Divine" (*ATC*, p. 79). "Only he who comes under the divine influence which scatters flowers and songs among man is able to speak of 'truth on earth.' . . . [He possesses] 'a heart made divine (yoltéotl)' " (*ATC*, pp. 77–78).

A fundamental concept of the *tlamatinime* was that of the face and heart. Alurista explains it and its relationship to poetry when he writes about the Nahuas' sense of the ephemeral existence of things and the underlying eternal movement.

> En el mismo ser humano se postula esta dialéctica entre lo eterno y lo efímero a través de la metáfora "corazón" y nos mueve dentro, es el continuum de la vida que se transforma con la muerte para retornar a su eterno origen divino, por lo

tanto, "corazón" es lo que dura. "Rostro" es lo que perece, es la personalidad, el cuerpo y la mente, vehículos del corazón eterno del Dador de la Vida. El rostro nos abandona día a día, mas el corazón continúa su movimiento dentro y fuera de su manifestación corpórea e intelectual. La "flor" es el rostro y el "canto," el corazón. La Flor y el Canto han de humanizar, enseñar y alegrar al corazón y al rostro de los pueblos acercándoles así a la creación, al Creador y a sí mismos a través del movimiento y la medida que cause harmonía perodicidad, dialéctica relación entre los pueblos dando lugar así a la unidad de todos los seres.[4]

Through his poetry Alurista aims at forming the Chicanos' face in accordance with the transcendent values of the Nahuatl heart, the philosophy of the spiritual harmony of all creation. Poetry is a sacred act capable of revealing truth, transcending the chaos of ephemeral life. To do so the poet must be a *tlamatini*. The consciousness of the sacredness of his words—the sincere belief that these words do not simply reflect reality, but create it—leads to the messianic tone of Alurista's work. At its best, it touches reservoirs of intuitive revelation; at its worst, it sounds preachy and arrogant.

Of Alurista's books, *Floricanto en Aztlán* is still the best example of his poetics and the most widely read as well as the most influential. Also, it is the source of everything he has produced since. Therefore I have chosen to dedicate my limited space to the analysis of *Floricanto*.[5]

As its epigraph announces, *Floricanto en Aztlán* analyzes and counters fear, specifically the Chicanos' fear of the Anglo American, presented in the book as the Man or Mr. Jones. The quest referred to in it is the realization of freedom from fear. Chicanos must actively pursue it, but without knowledge it is unattainable. They must, first, know what they fear; second, know that their tradition provides responses to the threat; and, third, overcome it. Alurista analyzes the situation; attempts to debunk the oppressor; and offers an alternative drawn from Chicano roots, but consonant with their contemporary state. Analysis demonstrates how he goes about it. It would be too lengthy to study all one hundred poems, so close textual reading will be done on the first ten. With the techniques and motifs established, their further development will be discussed to show how he realizes his project.

The first two poems appear side by side, a graphic placement pertinent to the discussion after each has been analyzed separately.

when raza?

when raza?
when . . .
   yesterday's gone
and
   mañana
mañana doesn't come
  for he who waits
no morrow
  only for he who is now
to whom when equals now
he will see a morrow
mañana la Raza
  la gente que espera
no verá mañana
our tomorrow es hoy

  ahorita
que VIVA LA RAZA
  mi gente
our people to freedom
  when?
now, ahorita define tu
  mañana hoy

la canería
y el sol

la canería y el sol
  la mata seca, red fruits
the sweat
  the death
el quince la raya
  juanito will get shoes
and maría
  maría a bottle of perfume
y yo me mato
  y mi familia
también suda sangre
  our blood boils
and the wages
  cover little
  only the lining of our
    stomachs
we pang
  but mr. jones is fat
with money
with our sweat
  our blood

why?

(1) "when raza?"

Taken at its simplest, the first poem asks, *When will we achieve freedom?* It urges Chicanos to make today the awaited tomorrow by defining it so, ("ahorita define tu mañana hoy" [right now define your tomorrow today]); an act of will and interpretation imparts meaning to reality. The poet plays with signs of temporality until their meaning blurs, the signs becoming *words* defined by human action, and now the action is writing. Life defines words and life can only be lived in the present; tomorrow is possible only if now is not postponed. Inactivity makes all time disappear ("la gente que espera / no verá mañana" [the people that wait / will not see tomorrow]). *When* comes to equal a time chosen and realized through self-assertion, which, in turn, is freedom. Fulfillment is to grasp time and define it through action.

The poem's introductory status allows only brief reference to causal factors: "when . . . / yesterday's gone." When the historical perspective disappears, the future loses meaning—"and mañana / mañana doesn't come"—and the present is nullified. The two lost times bracket a nonexistent present. The motif of the loss of historical identity is linked to possible extermination. To prevent the latter, Chicanos must define the present as theirs; but since it lies invisible, they must first recover history. To retrieve the past while creating the present means to find one's living heritage, a historical now, a true mythical sense of paradigmatic time.

Cut off from spiritual roots, people find themselves in profane time, in the Other's chaotic territory. Their history will give them the ancestral knowledge of communal rituals they can repeat to cosmicize space, order chaos, and reestablish cultural health. Time becomes again sacred.[6] Alurista sets out to do it.

The title's question assumes more significance when we consider that *raza*, here and elsewhere in the book, is not set off by commas. The "oversight" does not hinder understanding it as direct address, but allows another possibility: "When will there be a race?" asked of the Raza itself. It implies that Chicanos, lacking self-determination, remain, at best, a conglomerate. The goal is to become Raza, to activate the communal ties. With the present bracketed into profane time by the loss of past and future, both *when* and *raza* are put into question; at the same time, they are interdependent—to become community is to control time, to make oneself the center of temporal order.

Alurista calls for radical revolution. Time is society's regulating agent, its organizational infrastructure. Submission to alien time is slavery within the Other's time-space. Alurista's existential reorientation would undermine society. The philosophical (spiritual) essence of the revolution is typical of him; freedom requires spiritual as well as physical harmony with nature, the cosmos. Alurista will reveal that such harmony is a Nahuatl inheritance, based on solarcentrism (the sun as the central hierophany), which he opposes to the artificial divisions of time based on unnatural labor. Hence, the sun will, at times, have negative value, as when labor is exploitative and the laborer an enemy of nature. Self-determined, natural labor harmonizes people into the environment, allying them with the sun, nature's and life's matrix. A return to natural rhythms strikes at the heart of modern society; the return to self-determination strikes at the heart of capitalist society. Alurista is both radical and revolutionary.

(2) "la canería y el sol" [the cannery and the sun]

Alurista introduces Mr. Jones, the exploiter "fat with money" produced by Chicanos' sweat and blood. Exploitation here explicates the loss of the past and future and the bracketing of the present in poem 1. Jones possesses Chicanos' labor (time plus action), thus controlling their present; however, a temporal subterfuge keeps workers from thinking about their situation. Attention is focused on the future, which never comes. Time is "el quince la raya" [the fifteenth, payday]. The colloquialism for payday, *la raya* [the line], also alludes to the company store, where pay is marked off by a line that never cancels the debt. This form of slave labor is Alurista's metaphor for capitalism. Wages, labor, exploitation, and time are bound in a system controlled by owners. The company store promises an always postponed tomorrow of freedom, the future-oriented time of poem 1. The poem—and all Alurista's poetry —must be read within this context of labor exploitation.

Wages buy necessities, covering the stomach linings, but leaving Chicanos hungry—"we pang"—in contrast to fat Mr. Jones. Hunger, with its concomitant motif of food, repeatedly appears in the book, with food becoming a sign of cultural identity and natural harmony. To *pang* comes to signify hunger for freedom. Yet the laborer here buys shoes for his son and perfume for María, which in light of the above imagery seems contradictory; neither item is absolutely necessary, perfume is a luxury, and both are consumer products of capitalism sold in the company store to keep the worker bound. Trapped within capitalism, he has accepted as needs unnecessary goods. Alurista concretizes capitalism in these specific, common objects.

At this point in the diachronic reading, shoes and perfume derive significance from the social code within which the family is trapped: children need shoes; women like perfume. But both interpretations cast the Chicano in negative light when explored, and Alurista runs the risk of the negativity being attributed to him. The desire to buy shoes, in spite of poverty, connotes wanting to move into the middle class. Perfume is worse because it seemingly betrays a concept of woman as the passive idol, adored but limited by man, beautiful but frivolous and superfluous. Together the items chauvinistically divide sex roles: men—active in the outside world, practical, down to earth, useful; women—passive, withdrawn from the world, unrealistic, capricious. And the Chicano kills himself (y yo me mato) and makes his family sweat blood (y me familia / también suda sangre) for these items.

The synchronic perspective, however, corrects this first impression. Alurista has a penchant for redefining a sign through adjustments, reversals, or inversions in the signified. This is essential to his didactic purpose of offering an alternative vision of reality. *Shoes* and *perfume* are examples; from negative beginnings they become nuclei of motifs in the imagery of liberation. Chicanos will be portrayed as walkers (poems 6, 7, 11, 20, 36, 41, 42, 57, 63, 67, 74, 76, 78, 82, 92, 96, explicitly; implicitly in others); walking assumes the connotation of the pilgrimage-to-a-promised-land tradition of the Aztec ancestors, and, thus, of following in their footsteps, a contemporary action which actualizes a historical heritage. By focusing on *shoes*, Alurista introduces the walking motif through allusion. Simultaneously, he ironically demonstrates how far Chicanos have drifted from their heritage, while staying intuitively within it. That *shoes* are deemed important shows that walking remains central to their life; to assume that the feet need protection shows their unawareness of a centuries-old tradition. As the book progresses, *huaraches* reappear, and the man will be forced into the street barefoot.

Perfume functions similarly. The error is to assume that beauty must be purchased in artificial scents; nature supplies its own aroma. Through a series of metonymies, woman is transformed into—or revealed as—the aromatic flowers (roses) of the goddess Guadalupe-Tonantzin (poems 34, 41). Her skin is aromatic, with "Ponds of azucenas / blancas de nieve en tu voz" [lilies / white as snow in your voice] (45). The aromatic woman, and the Raza, will contrast to the stench of Mr. Jones' society; they compete for the verb *to permeate*. While "the stench / of the cannery permeates / the air" (16) in an image of capitalist pollution, the Raza's self-assertion is "rosas rojas [red roses] . . . alive with scent / to perfume / and permeate amerika / with sarapes aromáticos" (7). The sarape, in turn, becomes the central image of harmonious pluralism based on Chicano humanism. Flowers and "el perfume de mi raza / permeates the free flight / of my . . . solara tradition" (37), a flight that eventually transforms the Chicano poet into the sun itself (98). In "la carne de tus labios" [the flesh of your lips] (41), dedicated to the woman, she is given clearly liberated images: "el plumaje guerrero [the warrior plumage] / in her arrogant walk / to pace / and have / to run behind no more," which could be said to be male-related virtues in Alurista's code. She is then said to have "flores / con aroma / las de tonantzin" [flowers / with aroma / those of Tonantzin] (roses again). And the woman gives birth to the Raza (53), the "Chicano infante" (54), the "brown eyed *sun*" himself.

Thus the woman's natural aroma is an essence permeating Alurista's entire imagery and ideological complex. But to know the true significance of *perfume* and *shoes* requires the synchronic perspective. At the risk of appearing chauvinistic at first glance, Alurista teaches us not to accept "reality" at face value, especially when still determined by Mr. Jones, Inc.

The sweat-blood-heat image, central to the poem and the book, traditionally evokes hard work: to sweat blood under the relentless sun. Here it is exploitative; sweat and blood equal money to fatten Mr. Jones. The key image of the sun—which appears in the book explicitly thirty-four times, making it the most used image—is introduced as a power in league with exploitative forces. It dries the *mata* [plant], metaphor for the Chicano laborer who produces "red fruits" of bloody sweat—death. The fruit of labor will later evolve into the *tuna* [prickly pear], symbol of the desert cactus' productivity: a sweet, red food, analogous to the sun itself, which feeds hungry Chicanos. But in the first instance, the sun and fruit are negative. Alurista often begins with negative connotations or stereotypes, only to reverse them through the poem; here, however, there is no reversal in the poem itself. The sun is oppressive here because it is locked into the system of exploitative labor, which structures time so as to rob workers of life; it only marks the passage toward another *quince de raya*. The sun makes Chicanos' blood boil, a negative image here, but one which eventually signifies a positive disposition to resistance.

The sun will be rescued from exploitative forces through the recuperation of the Nahuatl tradition of solarcentrism. Also, in terms of imagery, the book will establish the intricate network of Chicano-sun ties, mentioned above. Thus, at play in the book is the movement of an image from one code to another; in terms of spiritual quest, this means learning how to see reality differently. Alurista utilizes the techniques of interpretation as he teaches them. By poem 10, when the sun next appears explicitly, it has shifted into the Chicanos' column, free from the cannery image. It reappears with negative connotations only when labor resumes an exploitative significance.

Structurally, the poem again brackets the present within images of loss. Whereas absent past and future bracket an implicit today in poem 1, *el quince la raya* and *mr. jones* bracket the Chicanos' daily existence in poem 2. But while poem 1 locates most of the poem outside the brackets, poem 2 surrounds the poem in apparently negative imagery. Nevertheless, the two poems treat the same reality and together represent more than either alone. Their juxtaposition is another lesson in seeing beyond the obvious, in how the knowledgeable eye perceives the harmony of cosmic space. We must study how they interact. Please reread the poems and *look* at them as a single visual unit, as if contemplating a painting.

Framed by *when?* and *why?*, the poems pose essential questions concerning Chicano survival. To achieve *when* would eliminate *why*; by understanding why they are oppressed and then eliminating the causes, Chicanos will activate their present, creating their *when* and the Raza. This diagonal pattern of oppositions is found in other elements. The ideal *now* of poem 1—*VIVA LA RAZA*—opposes *death* in line 4 of poem 2. These oppositions contrast the *now* of living in the present to the *now* of waiting for an elusive future. The crossing pattern is clear.

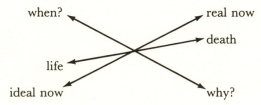

By tracing these force lines, we also finally discover the reason for the loss of the past in poem 1. Its placement corresponds diagonally to the presence of Mr. Jones in poem 2; this is corroborated by matching the oppressive brackets of both poems.

Yet whereas the elements in the first chart form canceling oppositions, the Jones brackets are causal factors of time loss in poem 1. The future-centered slavery allows Jones to control the present and cancel the past. His function in poem 2 is not opposed in poem 1, simply transferred. The bracketed, absent present in poem 1 is explained by the bracketed present of absent life in poem 2.

This discovery leads us to reevaluate the pattern of oppositions, and what at first seemed a balance of forces proves to be a canceling of the left column by the right. The space created by the two poems on the page mirrors the company-store image by forming a balance sheet for Chicano accounts. The right hand liabilities column dominates the left hand assets column. Immediately there comes to mind the traditional political division of left versus right, and there is that correlation: the left is revolutionary, the right reactionary. The

Chicano presence on the right side is the traditional family, while the sentiment on the left is revolutionary. Moreover, the left is abstract, ideological; the right is composed of concrete images, like the sun, blood, shoes, etc. Alurista advocates not only a spiritual alternative, but also a material one, with changes in either order mutually dependent on the other. The recuperation of lost *yesterdays*—which begins in poem 3—will cancel Jones' influence in the left column; in turn, this will begin a shift in the power flow, because historical knowledge will explain *how* oppression was institutionalized, an explanation which will begin to answer *why* it exists. As Chicanos realize, through the poems' lessons, that they must resist exploitation, they may begin to withdraw from the system and work for themselves. It will be a long process, but it must commence, and can start with reclamation of the barrio as a Chicano space—hence the poems on defining, controlling, and celebrating the barrio (7, 36, 42, 71, 78, 87, among others). Jones will not surrender without a struggle; his agents, the police, will continually hassle Chicanos as they walk barrio streets; but Chicanos finally will force him into the sun to reveal his lies and run him down the streets naked and ashamed. In the end the streets will be alive in celebration. It is Jones and his capitalist system that must be canceled completely from both columns. Chicanos must control their own space.

Note that the majority of the lines in poem 2 are Chicano-content verses. It is only Jones' presence that perverts labor, as it does the sun itself. Labor becomes money, which through pairing and inverting with the repeated image cluster in the same poem, equals death.

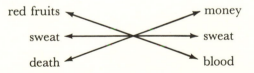

red fruits   money

sweat   sweat

death   blood

To cancel the monetary-reward system would allow Chicanos to control their work. They would still sweat, but their blood would flow in the sweet fruit of the *tuna*. Money and death would disappear from the equation. Alurista advocates a coup against Jones to liberate the Chicano family from capitalistic bracketing. Ironically, the poems show that Jones' presence depends on the Chicanos' labor and passivity; by taking control of themselves—they are the means of production—they will make the fruits of labor theirs. The energy unleashed from the canceling of the *yesterday's gone* bracket in poem 1 should void Jones, Inc., in poem 2, which would cancel the illusory-

mañana bracket remaining in poem 1. Free of the brackets, *now* would become a Chicano reality.

Viewed together the poems form a characteristically Chicano space: the sytems interface, tensions interplay—to say nothing of the interlingualism of the language. The actual encounter of forces and the formation of a Chicano reality occur between the columns, where a line separates and joins them. Chicanos must draw from both sides, while abandoning neither; must claim the center and expand outward by synthesizing the poles—a constant expansion stoked by the material consumed by, and incorporated into, the swelling nucleus. The book itself functions in this manner: the two poems offer a complex of images, a nucleus that will expand through evolving images, motifs, and structural patterns, constantly transforming, but never losing a traceable line, an umbilical cord to the propagating matrix.

The expanding movement is not, however, merely horizontal. The bracketing is vertical, with the ultimate restraining lines drawn by *when?* and *why?* Jones' immediate menace veils the fact that only Chicanos can answer the ultimate questions of their lives. Abolishing the *when* and *why* brackets in their worldly form would reveal the eternal philosophical questions of time and existence. To the sterile modern (non)response of Occidental culture, Alurista opposes the vital Nahuatl philosophy of solarcentrism, the *flor i canto*.

With the Chicano world located in the center, in an apparently empty, new space defined by Chicano life, expansion projects horizontally and vertically at once. But the poems' force field is diagonal, so what is produced is a radiating circle. From the outset, Alurista weaves the ideal content and the visual displacement of the poetry to create the central image of his entire work: the sun, the cosmicizing hierophany.

And Chicanos, like their Nahua ancestors, are children of the Sun . . . within the space of Alurista's literature. Alurista repeats, from the start, the ritual of adoring the sun and, through it, orders the chaos in which he, and his people, find themselves.

This may seem a critic's game, but it is serious. Alurista knows the role of spatial movement, of visual and physical relationships in the pre-Columbian philosophy. Time was inextricably tied to space.

He visually creates the materialization of the ideas—areas in conflict, which, if seen and understood through the philosophy of total harmony, can be transformed into a cosmically harmonious space. The poems open that space, not just on the ideal plane of the signified, but on that of the sign as a visual art object. He asks the reader to actively transform the world, now; and since the immediate now is that of reading, his literature teaches the reader to act and it is the space of that action. He becomes a *tlamatini*; readers become believers. The poetry, in the encounter, becomes what it was for the Nahuatl wise men, a hierophany, ''lo único verdadero en la tierra'' [the only true thing in the world].

From this nucleus Alurista develops his literature. The next eight poems demonstrate how the motifs begin to function.

(3) ''i can't''

Recuperation of the past begins. The Man attempts to annihilate Chicanos by interning them in a maze (a labyrinthine bracketing) comprised of ''detention camps / the heat / and troops.'' But the poet claims the land through his fathers and grandfathers, ''our caballeros tigres / y caballeros águilas'' [jaguar knights / and eagle knights], pre-Columbian warrior clans. Indigenous affiliation is emphasized by stating that independence came only when the Spaniards left, a concept from a standard Mexican Hispanophobia. Freedom should not be lost *now*, a reference encompassing the period since the mid-1800's, when the United States invaded the Southwest. *Now* assumes mythic dimensions, expanding according to the poet's will; this allows the war for the territory to be treated as a still unresolved struggle. In poem 11 one learns that the betrayal of the Guadalupe-Hidalgo Treaty left the matter pending.

Chicanos are exhorted to *will freedom*, an act of self-determination, a definition of meaning. Yet, though freedom springs from spirit, the total being is not ignored. Alurista defines freedom as being ''amos [masters] of our bodies / masters of our hearts / y nuestras almas libres [and our free souls].'' Body and heart correspond to the Nahuatl face and heart, humanity in its ephemeral / eternal being, according to Alurista. The soul, however, seems to introduce a Christian concept, perhaps necessary because the Nahuatl afterlife was, for the majority, not eternal—and the poet calls for eternal life in the last line. The Christian soul allows for the eternal life of the person as an individual.

Most interesting here is the poet-community relationship. The poetic *I* is both separate from and part of the communal *we*. The poem begins: "*i* can't / keep from crying / *my* gente sufre [people suffer] / the man, he hassles / and *our* pride is stomped / upon *my* death!" (emphasis added). The *I*'s reaction to his people's suffering is emphasized; and the loss of communal pride is linked to the poet's death, as if he were the source. This is reinforced later in, "i will my freedom / and it wills my people's," which clearly establishes a causal relationship dependent on the *I*. Perhaps Alurista's *I* is a communal pronoun, but the poem begins with the image of personal reaction, fixing the particularity of the *I*. This is consonant with Alurista's desire to be a *tlamatini* and a Don Juan à la Castaneda; guides are special, an elite group. Despite Alurista's protests (see his article "La estética indígena"), neither the *tlamatinime* nor their poems were the patrimony of the common people. In the book Alurista guides, educates, opens living space, all from the perspective of an "I-who-know-and-am," a *tlamatini* with *yoltéotl* (a divine heart), the personal link between the divine and the human. This authoritative tone permeates Alurista's writing.

The *tlamatini* aura lends the poem's last lines a specific meaning. The poet again calls for willing "manhood into eternity / to perpetuate / and live for ever / in our LIBERTAD." Eternal life was a nagging concern for the *tlamatinime*, because they were unsure what it consisted of. However, they believed that poetry would escape destruction due to its divine origin. To live forever was to become poetry, to have a poetic tradition, keeping in mind the total sense of poetry as history, philosophy, religion, science, etc. Alurista avers poetry's sacred power to create life.

(4) "the man has lost his shadow"

Picking up the blood-and-sweat labor image, Alurista declares a strike against the Man, whose turn it is to sweat blood for his guilt and ignorance. (Ignorance / blindness is the Man's main characteristic.) He must bleed to a death of "his own making." An inhuman devourer, he kills and lusts for power and possessions. By extension, humans do not kill, nor do they crave power or possessions; and it is assumed that Chicanos are human.

The *shadow* also distinguishes Chicanos as a metaphor for tradition and heritage. The Man has lost his through his inhumanity. Chicanos recuperated their past by claiming it in poem 3, in which they also excluded the Man from their space. Thus, in poem 4, the Chicanos' past—shadow—is again present. Recovered *yesterdays* initiate the denial of Jones, leaving hm to die in his own system.

The shadow image is understood fully only in the light of other poems. The images clustered around *shadow* here refer to others in the first three poems. Poem 4 develops from and with them as a unit. The shadow image is particularly interdependent, because it implies an image absent in poem 4—the sun as part and parcel of a destructive power, as it functioned explicitly in poem 2, and implicitly, as "heat," in poem 3. The Man dies in poem 4 from exposure to his destructive system of poem 3, from which Chicanos have withdrawn ("ya basta" [enough!]). However, even if they remain in the system, Chicanos now have their ancestors' shadow to protect them from direct exposure. This is a coded allusion to pre-Columbian solarcentrism, which Alurista later calls "solar heritage." Chicanos' heritage allows survival, while the Man's egocentrism alienates him from nature, which equals suicide.

(5) "libertad sin lágrimas" [liberty without tears]

A restatement of poem 1, this poem differs in its recuperation of *yesterday* in the form of "caballeros [knights] / clanes tigres [jaguar clans] / proud guerrero plumaje [warrior plumage] / free like the eagle / y la serpiente [and the serpent]." This past, however, becomes a future, being introduced by a series of future, direct willings of freedom: "we won't let it / freedom shall not escape us . . . / we shall / now / are . . ." Projected by will, *now* opens to encompass future and past.

(6) "hombre ciego" [blind man]

Power blinds the Man to his human possibilities, enslaving him to "cepter [*sic*] holders." The freedom-asserting Raza, on the other hand, will create a "cepter of justice / and equality / humane / and proud." Opposing scepters frame the poem, restating the conflict between the Man's dehumanizing system and the Chicanos' humane one. Between them, the freeing, opening process occurs.

One of the goals of the Raza must be to free all victims of false power systems. The power system is linked to labor: "la última gota" [the last drop] evokes the sweat-and-blood motif. However, Chicano wounds have closed—by rejecting exploitation in poem 4—and a scab of will has formed that heals in freedom, reinforced by ancestral heritage, walking with them in the form of a shadow. Their freedom is the assertion of love and the casting of their shadow, projecting the past into the future. Chicanos also can cast their shadow into the Man's shadowless void, ironically opening his eyes, freeing him from his inhumanity. This fulfills the purpose of the *flor i canto*: the unity of all beings. Before the man can rejoin the human race, however, he must stop acting like a crazed animal, stop killing others and himself. Chicanos must "bind his paws / and file his fangs" by depriving him of power and possessions. Like a victim of the enemy of Power, the man is out of control. He must be freed by being taught to keep everything in check.

Obviously, Alurista's thematics and the dynamics of his message develop with each addition, swelling the original space opened in poems 1 and 2. New here is Chicanos' self-assertion of their humanity humanizing all people, an idea repeated in poems 7, 9, 10, 58, and 61. The Chicano Movement assumes the cosmic purpose of saving the human race.

(7) "la cucaracha" [the cockroach]

From a crippled cockroach, an image from a popular song of the Mexican Revolution, the poem moves to the breeding of walking cockroaches in free barrios. The crippled roach is caught in capitalistic inequality. The walking roaches will arise from ethnic assertion —"assert our bronze"—and the creation of a sword, a permutation of the scepter (poem 6) into a weapon of justice. Again Alurista converts negative to positive within a single object to frame the poem, with self-determination the catalyst.

America again is called suicidal, a deadly though ephemeral façade. Suicide takes an image related to labor motifs, "the stench of fog," linking it to the cannery smell and pollution, preparing readers for the clash of organic and inorganic forces. The Man is the destroyer of the environment.

Alurista repeats the transformation of Raza from poem 1, making it a verb here: "we have to Raza / nuestra voluntad [our will]." To *Raza* equals *to realize*, but with the obvious ethnic connotations. In his redundant fashion, Alurista explicates this with the "assert-our-bronze" line quoted above.

Introduced here are the red roses of passion, asserted, of course. In later poems the roses will be the miraculous ones left by the Virgin of Guadalupe (12, 34), while passion becomes characteristic of struggling Chicanos. Here, the flower image quickly switches from visual to olfactory, its scent permeating America in an expression of Chicano redemptive power. Amerika (the *k* spelling is a cliché of Chicano poetry) is to be beautified by Chicanos; that is, it will be given a spiritual purpose. Note that the Virgin is also the Nahuatl goddess Tonantzin, and, thus, Alurista posits the re-Indianization of America.

Another image appears for the first time: the sarape, here representing the multiplicity of fragrances of the passion. The sarape image reappears at significant points, blending into others; but since its usage here only anticipates its explicit codification in poem 10, analysis will be reserved for that section. When the sarape is revealed as a full image, it radiates significance into other images it has been a part of. This is Alurista's manner of cross-pollinating his flowers with related connotations.[7]

The poem also marks the first use of *tenoch*: "with the pride of tenoch." *Tenoch* is Nahuatl for a grove of cactus with prickly pears, or *tunas*. According to legend, the Aztecs saw an eagle screaming the call of holy warfare from the top of a *tenoch*, marking their homeland. The symbol has become the Eagle and the Serpent and signifies Mexico. The pride is, then, that of Aztec culture in its pilgrimage to a promised land where the Aztecs would rise to dominance, and, surely, a reference to the Mexican nation in its independence from Spain. Alurista places it at the end of the poem as a goal, blending it with the walking motif of searching for the land of freedom. The poem moves from lameness to walking and to the goal of Chicano motion and Movement, a heritage from the past. Future and past mold in an expanding now.

Tenoch is also significant in its primary meaning. *Tunas* are to become the symbol of the Chicano spirit flowering amid adversity (poem 18) and the Chicanization of the red-fruits-of-labor image from poem 1. The *tuna* is a fruit of Chicanos' own, grown among thorns in the desert, where the Man cannot go because he lacks a protective shadow. In addition, it is juicy and refreshing, an appropriate food for hungry and thirsty Chicanos who walk through the wilderness. It transforms bloody death into sweet life. And the source of this transforming miracle is the pre-Columbian center, Tenochtitlan, Mexico and all it symbolizes.

(8) "las canicas y mis callos" [marbles and my calluses]

A repeated action (playing marbles) frames the poem; but this time instead of an inversion of values, there is a revelation of significance. One suspects a transcendent significance in the game when at the start it is called communion with the land; but the poem rapidly changes subject to Chicano food versus the typical U.S. hot dog. Eating dons sacred connotations—tortillas equal the Eucharist of the Catholic mass. Hot dogs, then, become a sacrilege forced upon the poet. Besides obvious ethnic reasons, the explanation is that the tortilla is a product of the people's sweat-and-blood labor in communion with nature. Hot dogs, by extension, are a synecdoche of the exploitative system, an archetype of consumerism. Alurista is not averse to using the most trite clichés.

When the poem suddenly shifts back to marbles, with "it is ours to play / marbles," the game assumes the connotations of the intercalated food imagery. Playing marbles is metaphoric for self-determined life. Alurista makes it explicit: "i was free in the dust / of my marble land." The threat to that freedom is symbolized in the forced eating of hot dogs, which is further toned through references to school bells; the hot dogs are probably a school lunch, and thus a sign of the school's acculturation role being protested. While marble land is the school playground, it is also equated to an integrity of maturity which must not be lost. The marble land becomes a territory that encompasses the players, but the action itself defines the space.

The ambiguous image alludes to a famous Nahuatl image of human existence: "In the palm of His hand He has us; at His will He shifts us around. We shift around, like marbles we roll; He rolls us around endlessly" (*ATC*, p. 122). León-Portilla explains the image:

> Ometeotl [the supreme god of duality] holds man in the palm of his hand and sustains him within in it. He introduces activity into the world. . . . We are born never to rest, but to live, to work, to suffer, to fight, and to seek a "face and a heart." Man yearns for what is true on earth, for only by finding truth will he put an end to his restlessness and find within himself the foundation he seeks; that is why we . . . roll like marbles. But the most tragic thing about our existence is that, in spite of our feeling of freedom, we do not know our final destiny. (*ATC*, pp. 122–123)

Alurista links the simple children's game to his chosen philosophy, superimposing past, present, and future. Chicanos receive a divine reference: both they and God play. Finally, by using an image from the culture he is trying to revitalize, he binds Chicano and Nahuatl cultures. The poem becomes a metaphor for the cultural movement he advocates.

(9) "chicano heart"

As the eternal element of being, the Chicano heart is the living tradition of solarcentrism; and, as in poems 6 and 7, its spirit will save America. Boiling blood (2) and will (1) now join passion (7). Among the conjoining motifs, confrontation arises. A cerebral America, incapable of human action, opposes living, singing Chicanos. Thinkers versus livers; inorganic versus organic; artificial versus natural; the motifs are all evoked. America brackets itself in its rationalism, which Chicanos have escaped. Boiling blood is now a positive force for human existence, instead of a sign of exploitation; this results from the sun's reappearance as part of the Chicanos' heritage. Whereas the sun participates in the Man's system framing poem 2, the Chicanos' solar heritage, their eternal heart, frames poem 9; and within this frame, the Man can only limit himself. The tables have been turned. Spatially speaking, Chicano space has expanded enormously since poem 2, transcending the Man's brackets.

An important motif is introduced here, that of music: "our heart sings in passional symphony." There had been one earlier music allusion (poem 7), but now the music is much more complicated, a symphony, with its highly developed form and a tradition of centuries of sophistication. Alurista will use music of all kinds, from Rock to Classical, to symbolize the universality of the Chicano spirit, deliberately expanding it beyond Mexican nationalism.

(10) "el sarape de mi personalidad" [the sarape of my personality]

In poem 7 the sarape represented the multifarious Chicano spirit as it would "permeate amerika." Here it becomes the central image, while retaining its connotation of miscegenation.

The framing image is the sarape, functioning like the marbles in poem 8—a simple, personal statement assumes universal significance at the end with the shift of elements within the image cluster of which the sarape is the center. The poem begins, "el sarape de mi personalidad / comes in fantastic colors / basic / essentially fundamentales." The colors are the basic ones that produce all others.

Perhaps the redundancy of the last three words should warn us that Alurista is planning some play with them. At the poem's end the three words are repeated, *essentially* becoming the Raza's *essence*, which is *fundamental* and *basic* "to the chromatic wheel of humanity." Alurista creates expansive movement within the image, while maintaining the central object, thus demonstrating the spiritual movement he calls for—a redefining of the world from a sense of self-knowledge. And this redefinition should alter humanity's pattern.

The Man's presence is implied by the refutation of the opinion that Chicanos are lazy: "lazy you say! / how blind." By now we know that to be blind and to not know or understand are signs of the Man; his presence is the unvoiced misreading of the sarape as the clichéd image of lazy Mexicans. Alurista attacks a stereotype by redefining a sign in Chicano terms: "the spectrum of my wool is life itself," a verse prefiguring the final revelation of Chicano essence as basic to humanity.

Once Chicano identity is firmly established and the world redefined from it, we can entertain the idea of the unity and equality of all people. For there to be unity, all factions must have a secure self-image, an assurance of cosmic worth and purpose. The poem does this with the image of the sarape. True to form, Alurista projects the image in time—"the radiance of our quilted heritage"—to reclaim a historical tradition. He forecasts the unity of all, but eschews the melting pot, with its connotation of identity loss, in favor of the sarape, focusing first on the object and then on its colors to convey his image of a pluralistic society. "La essencia de mi Raza es fundamental [the essence of my Race is fundamental] / basic / to the chromatic wheel of humanity / free to compound in secondary colors / retaining the basic texture / our woolen skin of color bronze." The colors can blend in any combination once the elemental colors achieve equality. The blatant Gringophobia in Alurista's poetry is countervailed by a current of idealism based on ethnic and racial equality.

Motif Development

The first ten poems demonstrate how Alurista opens a space with an expanding code of imagery. The development of that imagery can now be traced through its central motifs.

The Man continues blind and ignorant (14, 19, 20, 29, 37, 40, 41, 66, 69, 72, 76, 86, 90, 91, 93, 96, 98), inorganic, plastic, murderous, unecological, and traditionless. Though he has the potential to be saved (6, 58, 61), he probably will continue to be suicidal (58). In the end (99) he still tries to limit Chicanos: "the man say we making noise / when we quiet all the time."

Chicanos constantly seek freedom, at first through willing self-determination (1, 3, 5, 6, 7, 9, 10, 11, 12, 13, 15, 18, 20, 24, 27, 31, 49, 61); then, as if the space for self-willed action had been established, the focus shifts to more active images, such as walking and flying. The walking motif, beginning with shoes in poem 2, continues throughout (6, 7, 11, 15, 20, 36, 41, 42, 57, 63, 64, 67, 74, 76, 82, 88, 92, 96). In truth, it is another image of self-assertion of heritage. In poem 20 the Chicanos walk the barrio streets and are stopped by a policeman who does not know that their walking signifies the holy tradition of pilgrimage to freedom, and specifically the Aztecs' journey to Mexico. This projection into the past is followed by another into the future as the Raza asserts its freedom: "to design our streets / and pave our paths / self-willed eternamente [eternally] / so that we may resume our walk / without a hassling badge" (20). Walking is a metaphor for a rescued tradition of freedom.

Flying, traditionally signifying freedom, appears early on in perhaps its most common mythological reference, Icarus (12). Flight signifies the necessary return to the sacred solar source. Icarus' flight ended in disaster, of course, but Alurista purposely uses the risk aspect to create the tension of fear, which the book seeks to overcome. "i was rotting / in fear / —no more / i fly and risk a fall" (77). Flight transcends fear, not death: "fly! / die in laughter of your wound" (84). Fear is the accepted element of risk involved in self-determination.

Walking and flying are linked through another motif, the cockroach. Poem 7's transformation is repeated in poem 15. From crawling after crumbs and being crushed, the cockroach goes to walking "like poets walk on dreams / and philosophers on ideas . . . like campesinos walk on toil / and operadores [operators] on buttons / on machines / y fábricas [factories]." The cockroach is equated to all Chicanos, with an emphasis on laborers. By including poets and philosophers, Alurista reduces them, and himself, to a common level of laborer. Then, in poem 34, the cockroach will never crawl again; having found its wings, it will fly to heaven in the feathers of Teotihuacan. Like the poet-*tlamatini*, the flying roach prays for food for the people. Later, the poet's singing is equated to flying in an image of obvious mythological references: "Chicano, here / i am bright spotted in the sky / ulysses Chicano / ciclope gringo i'll see you / to hear me sing / to fly / a volar and terminar [to fly and finish] / lo ya comenzado [what has already been started]'' (98). Flight concludes the pilgrimage home, after years of warfare (Ulysses) and the overcoming of the unseeing monster who would intern Chicanos to feed upon them (Cyclops), a permutation of the Man's image from poems 2 and 3 that raises the struggle to mythological status. The Chicano has become the sun itself, assuming the image that from the start dominated the central space of the poetry. Alurista frames his book in sun imagery.

The sun appears explicitly in thirty-four poems and implicitly in many others. We have seen how, in the first ten poems, the poet rescues the sun's image from the Man's system by linking it to pre-Columbian imagery. It becomes the goal of the expansive flight, the center of the egalitarian cosmic world. When ''cultural assassination'' threatens to devour the poet, he runs to the sun of his fathers, ''the one that printed / on my sarape / fantastic colors / through the prism'' (30). As the source of the metaphor of ideal social pluralism, the sun is the hierophany of sacred harmony. In last line of poem 30, the sun becomes the sacrificial pyramid where life was infused into the Raza. Life and death unite in a solar ritual, discussed more fully below. Here, the sun is a value worth dying for. Metaphorically, Alurista posits equality based on individual differences and makes it an ideal worthy of Chicano sacrifice; if Chicanos must die, it should be for this ideal, not for the Man's profit.

The Man is an anti-solar, nocturnal creature in his duplicity. He has perverted the sun (1) and attacks by night (30, 44). But if exposed to the sun, he cannot survive (4), because the sun is truth and justice. If stood ''naked before the sun / the man can't see'' (44), so the poet advises Chicanos to force him out into the sun to reveal his lies (95). In poem 99 Alurista calls for revolution to run the Man down the streets, naked and ashamed under the burning sun. It should be remembered, however, that Alurista advocates pluralism, and Chicanos are urged to use their natural warmth to burn the Man in a redeeming ritual (80), allowing him to ''reinstate himself as a warm human being'' (68). In the sun's light—that is, when the poet's philosophy triumphs—equality and brotherhood will rule, because ''bajo el sol / cualquier barro sale bronce'' [under the sun / any clay comes out bronze] (46).

The sun exemplifies Alurista's technique of expanding an image to metaphorically demonstrate the expansion he desires for the Raza.[8] It begins as a captive element in poem 2, though the interaction of the first two poems liberates it, prefiguring what will take place in the book, where it is freed to become the source of energy, as well as the goal, of Chicano flight. The poet eventually becomes the sun (98). The expansion is temporal as well, with the recuperation of pre-Columbian solarcentrism. The sun becomes the new generation of Chicanos. The new race is born a bronze fruit (53), the color produced by the sun—the sarape's essential *texture* is bronze (10) and all clay turns bronze under the sun. The Raza is the sun's child. In "chicano infante" (54), Alurista cannot resist the obvious pun of *sun* and *son*: "brown eyed sun / on the pyramid of joy." In "sacred robe" (57), "i saw the crimson / blown by the wind to see / —rimmed with gold / to see me like a son / flowing forth to sea."[9] The birth of the new Raza is directly related to the recuperation of solarcentrism as the primary hierophany, as the past and future meld in the now of the ritual which is the poem.

The sun and time are inextricably bound. In poem 2 time is labor measured in the sun-marked days of the company-store calendar. To escape from labor-time would actualize the *when* of poem 1. In poem 4 the poet refuses to work for the Man, while his own time expands into the past and future, though always centered in the *now*. After the new child is born, the poet asks that he be taught the lesson of time: "let their times be doing / (time *is* all the time)" (56). Time is for activity, not for waiting; *now* is the only time there is. The Man does not know this essential truth, nor does he learn it. In poem 93 he is still ignorant: "he not know tomorrow's hoy [today]."

As we might expect, Alurista closes the collection by reversing the initial time image. The poet strolls through the barrio; "mañana el jale / pero 'orita' el tiempo es mío [tomorrow work / but 'right now' time is mine]" (96). The system persists, but the Chicano has learned to concentrate on *now*, making time a personal expression of community life. This directly attacks the labor-oriented, future time of capitalist society. The last poem is a festival, a celebration of free time, as if to say that Chicanos have learned to seek life in their own time-space. And that time-space will be one of rejoicing and communal togetherness in freedom.

What comes, then, of the question of fear? Obviously, the poet surmounts it, stating that he no longer fears the Man because he has devoured his fear and digested his own blood (88). We must analyze his liberation process.

The eating and drinking images used to express liberation offer a clue. The same poem states that he now drinks, but his thirst was quenched "many minds ago." We should recall that the persona once fled from cultural assassination (30) to take refuge in the sun, which turned into a sacrificial pyramid—again the self-devouring image. Death as a vital, life-giving ritual is evoked. The key to unlocking the chains of fear is Death.

This fits clearly into Alurista's orientation. While explaining factors involved in the struggle to become a man of knowledge, Castaneda says that dramatic exaggeration is useful. (This might explain Alurista's histrionics and sense of drama.)

> He [Don Juan] imparted through dramatic exertion the peculiar quality of finality to all the acts he performed. As a consequence, then, his acts were set on a stage in which death was one of the main protagonists. It was implicit that death was a real possibility in the course of learning because of the inherently dangerous nature of the items with which a man of knowledge dealt; then, it was logical that the dramatic exertion created by the conviction that death was an ubiquitous player was more than histrionics. . . . The idea of impending death created not only the drama needed for overall emphasis, but also the conviction that every action involved a struggle for survival, the conviction that annihilation would result if one's exertion did not meet the requirement of being efficacious. (*TDJ*, p. 196)

This explains death's role in Alurista's thought. He must convince Chicanos of its imminence so that they will face and overcome it.

In poem 2, death formed part of the brackets entrapping Chicanos. Even the sun was negatively involved. But amid oppression, Chicanos had their cultural heritage, though unaware of it in poem 2. Later, *shoes, perfume, food, panging* all reveal themselves treasures of both past strength and future direction; the sun shifts to a positive element, and even time becomes Chicano time. Space expands, transcending the brackets, although the Man keeps trying to reimpose them. The Man himself will be spiritually debunked; stripping him of his actual power is impossible, so Alurista portrays him as soulless, traditionless, suicidal, and dead, and thus not worthy of our fear. Yet death itself is impossible to defeat; and, truly, if it were eliminated, the urgency in the poetry would disappear. The threat is necessary for dramatic effect. So death is at the heart of fear, and Alurista attacks it by drawing on Castaneda's teachings: despite everything, people are impermanent; but "one still had to proceed and had to be capable of finding satisfaction and personal fulfillment in the act of choosing the most amenable alternative and identifying oneself completely with it" (*TDJ*, p. 199).

To persuade Chicanos to break out of their limited existence, Alurista shows that remaining inside means death (2, 3). Life is outside (83), and Chicanos choose to go forth, in spite of the danger: "i know what awaits me / . . . the stench / . . . but i still walk / out to live" (42); and "swallow pain / and live / in flight free rugged hawk, fly! / die in the laughter of your wound" (84). The ability to take the risk comes from a sense of life's impermanence and of cosmic transcendence in which death is natural. One does not court death (13), but one cannot let it bracket life. Death is faced and put into perspective; fear of it is accepted as natural, but not as an over-riding obsession.

Fear of death assumes meaning within a transcendent code of life. Death is made into a ritual through the evocation of pre-Columbian ceremonies. Chicano ancestors are pictured at the sacrificial pyramid giving life to the Raza (30). Death must be a sacrifice for the people, not for the exploiter. If one commits oneself to the cause of expanding Chicano life-space, to making *when? now*, then death becomes part of life. Alurista again expands one image, life, to encompass another, death, which had it bracketed.

Floricanto is highly complex, thematically and structurally. It suffers from redundancy, trite poetical usages (both in imagery and in technique), and preachiness, though they can be explained as efforts to communicate through oral, folk, and popular codes. Its virtues are the cohesiveness of its imagery, the clear development of its message through the organic growth of those images, and the sense of totality in the collection. One might wish that Alurista had cut some poems; but his sense of well-roundedness, of the wholeness of the number 100, are justified by his philosophical / aesthetic base. He seeks a stable, full, cyclical space.

The space of *Floricanto*—the book's material presence in all its lengthiness, as well as the intellectual / spiritual space of its image clusters—is a metaphor for the Chicano space Alurista calls for. It opens from the question of existence, analyzes the restrictions, and expands beyond them to create that existence, the time-space of it. The forces contained are the Chicanos', or at least those which we have come to associate with Chicanos.

It is here where Alurista's true power and achievement lie: his poetry has provided a system for interpreting Chicano reality which is still with us today. Some might call it irrelevant, or decry its nationalism, or oppose its idealism, but from the perspective of Alurista's poetics it is difficult to deny its efficacy as a book. And if we recall Castaneda's words, to survive, every act must be efficacious. Whether Alurista has achieved the goal of his other mentors, the *tlamatinime*, of speaking truth on earth, is another thing altogether. We can only say that the book is a faithful beginning.

Paradigm Charts

	LIFE vs.	DEATH

SYMBOLIC
Threat: ~~Freedom of men under the Sun.~~ ←——— Fear of a man / beast who entraps and devours humankind.

Rescue: Of a solar tradition of harmonious nature in which the Man is a negative animal, unworthy of fear.

Response: The book as a fearless celebration of free life in harmony with nature. ——→ ~~Fear of man / beast.~~

SOCIAL
Threat: ~~Self-determined community with historical consciousness.~~ ←——— Capitalist society enslaves people with never-realized material promises; fear of moving out of the system.

Rescue: A heritage of self-determined culture based on self-sacrifice for the harmony of community in nature.

Response: The book as a survival for self-determined living within a capitalist society. ——→ ~~Fear and enslavement to materialism.~~

	LIFE	vs.	DEATH

PERSONAL
Threat: ~~Alurista as~~ *~~tlamatini.~~* ◄——— Lack of contemporary
                                                          Chicano community
                                                          with its own spiritual
                                                          beliefs.

                          │
                          ▼

Rescue: Of a Chicano heritage
                 of belief and ritual
                 updated to contem-
                 porary needs.
                          │
                          ▼

Response: Book as com- ————————► ~~Lack of commu~~nity.
                 munity teacher and
                 proof of Alurista as
                 tlamatini.

5. THE HEROICS OF SELF-LOVE
Sergio Elizondo

The kind of world one wants depends on the kind of world one is trained to want, and equipped by training to get.
—Ernest Becker, *The Structure of Evil*, p. 187

In *Perros y antiperros*,[1] as the title implies, Sergio Elizondo establishes a dualistic world of confrontation between the Anglo American and the Chicano. Though his Chicano is much more Mexican and less a cultural synthesis than those of Montoya, Alurista, and others we have seen, he carefully distinguishes Chicanos and Mexicans and emphasizes U.S. residency. Like Gonzales and Alurista, he sees the struggle as one between a technological, over-rationalized, materialistic, and capitalistic society, short on moral fiber, dehumanized by its divorce from nature, exploitative and racist; and a traditional, still humane culture which has preserved its healthy ties to the land and family through love, hard work, and the shared experience of having been exploited. Elizondo also expresses the conflict in terms of written versus oral culture; and since he, like others previously seen, feels that the young are losing the oral tradition, he sets out to become its anonymous voice, repeating his people's history. The book has the aspect of a journey through time and space, with the poet wandering the Chicano Southwest like a Medieval romancer, repeating news he has heard from the inhabitants, giving his poetry the texture of oral literature. Though both the author's statements[2] and the highly lyrical style belie the subtitle of *epic* added by the publisher, there is a definite development which makes the book more than a collection of poems—a development that follows our paradigm.

Like other writers, Elizondo starts with the image of Chicanos under the defining influence of the other culture. The title announces the threat. The Dogs are the Gringos (in the sense of non-Hispanic Europeans), while Chicanos are defined as *anti*, a reaction which makes the Other central to their identity. Through hatred, Chicanos have lost their own self-image as the center of life. The poet is determined to shift the concentration back to themselves. He begins by reversing the title, starting the book with "Antiperros." The Chicano is still fixated, but at least the focus is on one's own culture.

"Antiperros"; "Perros"; "España" [Antidogs; Dogs; Spain] (poems 1-3)

The first three poems announce the book's structure: from hatred and fixation, to historical analysis focusing on Chicano resistance and survival, to open ridicule of the Gringo.

The first two lines state the factors in the conflict.

"Land lost, flame of love
Land destroyed, I am full of love" (poem 1, p. 5)

The Gringo's presence has ruined the Southwest, but the response Elizondo offers is love, a word that assumes multiple significance. *Flame* is the first allusion to the sun, the key to a motif of harmony with nature, which also comes to mean political revolution and human affection. The motifs will eventually unite, in later poems, in the imagery of the woman, who is synonymous with land and tradition. The revolution must free woman, land, and tradition so that they can thrive in the form of the family. Love becomes the driving force of cultural reaffirmation, distinguishing Chicanos from Anglos, the latter stereotypically pictured as unloving, even among themselves. The book aims to teach Chicanos that self-love, instead of hatred, should be their central defining activity.

"Antiperros" reveals a sense of sour grapes. Young Chicanos discuss life across the tracks as sterile—but the United States has taken it even to the moon. Though siding with the young, Elizondo recognizes that they lack historical perspective to understand their situation. Such factors as the tracks, the exploration and conquest of space, and the flag, will be revealed by the poet as signs of negative life not worthy of jealousy.

Debunking begins immediately, while the poet establishes his symbolism. Essentially, through conquest the Gringo has established an over-rationalized society. *Tracks* initiate a conflict of geometric imagery, in which Gringos are associated with straight lines, while Chicanos are characterized by the roundness of nature. Anglos measure in square miles what the Spanish estimated with the eyes, round orbs that measure in circles ("Perros," p. 8); Anglos retreat from nature, opposing straight lines to the curves of the heart

(p. 8). As will be seen in later poems, the Chicana has rounded veins (p. 36) and a curved walk (p. 16); the roundness of the poet's eyes watches the curves of the flower (p. 48); Chicanos develop under the eyes of the Virgin of Guadalupe (p. 20); and God is a curve (p. 60). While Anglos fragment the world, Chicanos harmonize with it.

Anglo conquest, treated historically in "Perros," is characterized in "Antiperros" through the imagery of the moon landing. The U.S. flag, a "fake rag stiff as death," makes death the Gringos' sign from the start; the flag represents sterility ("white enamel clinics"), decadent affluence ("retch of fat sweat"), dehumanization ("the steel of their lost souls"), and the decay of capitalism ("filth" of money). Through technology—trains / rockets—Gringos take their "insolence" everywhere, the moon being only the latest place, though significant in that it is cold, pale, dead. In response, Chicanos will develop their own flag, the United Farm Workers', made of natural cotton and planted firmly in the earth and under the sun and the Virgin's eyes. This flag, prefigured in several poems, appears fully in "Padres, hijos; ayer, hoy" (pp. 30–34); it signifies the union of land, sun, labor, and love in the Chicanos' effort to recover their own nation, Aztlán. To achieve it, the Anglo must be further debunked along the lines of the motifs established in "Antiperros."

"Perros" summarizes the history of Gringo-Mexican confrontation from the mid-1800's to the 1940's. The first line "They reached our ranchos," declares land the heart of the conflict, while asserting that Chicanos possessed it before Gringos arrived. The latter came in sorry condition, "dying of hunger" and "pursued by / the dust of death," words that frame their first image—though "begging friendship," they bring death. They are then characterized through synecdochical possessions. Their felt hats, in the context of "Pennsylvania" and "bibles," become black Quaker hats, inappropriate for the sunny climate. Their "prickless" spurs imply an unfamiliarity with Western range culture. There arises the greenhorn image, with Puritan overtones. The spurs image is also typical of the oral-culture technique of veiled obscenity. The Anglos are supposedly sexless, mechanical people; of course, we are to believe, at the same time, that they are animals that reproduce like dogs. Elizondo would have us see them as anything but human.

The Bibles raise the difference in religious orientation, as well as the conflict of written versus oral traditions. Protestants adhere to the written word, while Catholic Mexicans supposedly obey a law based on social interaction and love. Puritan elitism is also implicit, with the concept of the chosen people; by extension, Mexicans are the unchosen. This is the same insolence taken to the moon in "Antiperros." The frontier motif appears in the wagons. The Conestoga's design caused it to be compared to a ship with canvas sails; the plains became another ocean. Elizondo evokes the interpretation of U.S. history as east-to-west movement begun in Europe and extended to the moon. However, "our ranchos" converts that movement into an invasion of settled areas; hence, theft.

Humanity is denied the immigrants in their lack of an open glance and friendly handshake. Their mirrorless eyes refuse to reflect the Mexican image. Eyes become a sign of Mexican / Chicano humanity, as well as an act of judgment and affirmation.

Stanza 2 introduces the Mexican in images of human and natural harmony: "My grandparents beards of tortilla smell." A culturally specific food permeates the symbol of generations of presence, while Mexican life centers around the family eating ritual. With "skin of sun on earth," Mexicans become the synthesizing epicenter of a nature that Gringos fragment, conquer, and resist. Ironically, Mexicans' humanity led them to help the immigrants, who later proved traitorous. The latter's families thrived, "became falsely round," until like a pack of dogs they took over. They hid their *straight* nature, pretending to be human; but the offspring spoke an inhuman language that betrayed the deception.

Stanza 3 introduces the loss of land through the use of that strange language; the "bibles on their asses" of Stanza 2 transmute into a "shitpile of books in court." The Outsiders, having devoured enough, relieve themselves on the natives in the form of written culture. Simultaneously, the land is ruined; crops die under salt water, an image of tearful sorrow. Water plus land plus sun plus work plus love produced Chicano culture; when the water is ruined and the land taken, laborers become migrant farm workers slaving in the sun. What allows them to survive is familial love.

The Anglos were welcomed into the Mexicans' homes, then took them. *Home* signifies the Southwest, the Mexicans' homeland; it also comes to signify life style. The Chicanos' home will be the source of strength and transcendence, while the Anglos' home is the stereotypical inhuman, plastic environment described in the final poem. The book explains the loss of *home* (land), the retention of *home* (love), and the development of a *home* (Aztlán) ideology to retrieve the first. Elizondo also discredits the Anglo home to prevent Chicanos from coveting it.

In stanza 4 Mexicans retreat into barrios, where they wait, maintaining oral culture, and opposing Anglo technology with love, exalted as stronger than a century of motors. The twentieth century brings labor unrest on both sides of the border (stanza 9). Elizondo refers to a strike in the Arizona copper mines, but the image encompasses the Cananea Strike in Northern Mexico in 1906. Led by Anarchist sympathizers, workers wanted international unions. U.S. troops suppressed both strikes, having been called to Cananea by the Mexican governor. Elizondo shows the Mexican Revolution betrayed by Mexicans themselves in favor of common industrial interests. Also, he links the Chicano Movement's ideals to those of the common people of the Mexican Revolution, while divorcing them from the Mexican government's manipulation and betrayal.

In strictly poetic terms, stanza 9 functions without external references. "Dirt miners" can only mean workers of the land, now cut off from their spiritual life source, the sun. Workers make "suns," an image of the revolution's flame, the goal of social and economic equality based on land ownership. Significantly, the struggle for "suns" is tied to shouts of love, which, in turn, are like lanterns illuminating the miners' dark world. Love renews the sun on earth, while sun-love guides the revolution.

Stanza 10 affirms survival through love, with the home and family growing. The glow of cigarettes fills the night, denoting preparedness that reflects the miners' underground suns; revolutionary spirit passes from generation to generation. Wrapped in their culture ("blankets") and withdrawn from the dominant society, Mexicans survive into the present, biding their time.

The last two stanzas burst with joy and cultural affirmation, the first shouts since the Mexican Revolution. The house is renewed (love), animated by polkas (music as tradition), and the man dances when the spirit illuminates his eyes. The poet uses *faroles* [lanterns] for "eyes,"—a word that previously linked love, sun, hope, and revolution (stanza 9); the spirit is alive. The driving force is "a strong and liquid friend / tickling on my balls," an image explicated in "Padres, hijos; ayer, hoy" (p. 30), in which the young, rebellious Chicano speaks of "an honest friend / that by clear waters I await." The friend turns out to be the United Farm Workers Union. There will also be a link between the union and the woman (in "Nota Mexicana," through the metonymy of cotton skirts and cotton flag). Thus the Chicano is happy with the friend who will bring back his land and culture. Here, however, we can only take the image as alcohol and sexual arousal. This explains the intoxicated tone, the dancing on one foot, the shining eyes, and the tickling testicles. Yet love has already been tied to revolution and land, so in truth it is the same. Also, we are given three of the necessary images: sun, water, love. Only land and work are missing. The former awaits the determination to win it back. Until then, the revolution is like a strong sexual urge. Work reappears at the end, linked to sex.

The poem ends with "the dark young girls of Texas / going to pick cotton!" The image is not frivolous; it centers the focus on the woman, who incarnates all the other values. She is seen going to work for the exploiter. She must be freed. Moreover, the poet is projecting to the book's future—cotton, the Other's crop, will become the UFW flag (in "Padres, hijos; ayer, hoy"), a sign of reclamation of Chicano labor. The woman's skirt will be like the flag ("Nota mexicana"), because she is the culture's center; this she proves by eventually speaking the word *Aztlán*, the Chicanos' unifying ideal. These images direct the reader forward, prefiguring essential responses to the stated problems.

"España" presents an innovative image of the mestizo to oppose to the Gringo. Spain and Mexico form the silver and bronze strings on a guitar that plays sounds "clearer than all the suns." Two national traditions flow in Chicano music, a living heritage. With this strength, Chicanos can now strike back, marking a change from the lack of power in "Perros." The exercise of this strength takes a typical Elizondo vent; the Anglo is ridiculed as a dog, in contrast to the Chicanos' nobler animal image, the horse.

"Mi cuento" [My story] through "Marcha" [March] (poems 7–16)

Poems 7–16 (pp. 14–43) form a unit in which Chicano Movement ideology arises from the search for love. The unit is framed by poems about the Chicano experience in contemporary wars, World War II ("Mi cuento," Poem 7, p. 14) and Vietnam ("Marcha," poem 16, p. 42), and historical reviews of the loss of the Alamo ("Pastourelle," poem 8, p. 20) and the exploration and loss of California ("Aquí entras Califas," poem 15, p. 40). The historical poems utilize the image of the land as a young woman captured by the enemy. In the central poems, young Chicanos speak to their parents about their loved ones, whom they wish to marry. Out of this situation, framed in past and historical references, arise the UFW flag and the word *Aztlán*. However, there is also a touch of warning about inherent danger: two poems on machismo ("Buenos hijos de la Malinche," poem 10, p. 26, and "Machismo chismo, chismo," poem 14, p. 38) frame the center of love and political birth.

"Mi cuento" treats Chicano participation in World War II, the disillusionment which followed, and the redirecting of nationalistic spirit into resistance to oppression. The war is pictured as the Chicanos' rite of passage to freedom. Chicanos fought for American democracy, from which they were later excluded. Elizondo praises the bravery, but explains that it was a mistake. Yet it did produce a shout, which after the silence of previous poems signals a step forward. When rebuffed by postwar America, the soldier takes refuge in a traditional manner, trying to make something out of his experience by expressing it in music. He has returned to his own tradition (*lira*, an archaism for "guitar") after singing the big-band songs of the Anglo.

Two stanzas follow, one each for the man and the woman. The first restates the war–coming-of-age motif, then flowers into a prefiguration of the UFW flag image: "Dark through my parents' wings of passion / darker through the sun of my labors, / white through the eyes of the Virgin, / hot like the red chile." The darkening of the skin tone as a sign of pride and of militancy will be repeated explicitly in "Padres, hijos" (p. 32), where Chicano consciousness is linked to the UFW flag. However, Elizondo is careful not to condemn the older generation, while calling attention to the younger generation's positive change. Here, the eagle's wings originate in the parents' passion—love is survival power. The young must give love direction, hence the need for the Movement and the flag's importance. At this point the flag's elements remained disembodied, the unit only prefigured. Its seeds are the wings, the colors, the sun's darkening of the skin, and the tie to a unifying faith. The Virgin of Guadalupe recalls the indigenous tradition, while her eyes evoke the motif of natural curves. The reference to *chile* is not simply for the color red, but to emphasize, first, sexual connotations; second, fiery militancy; and third, food's all-important role in cultural and familial preservation.

The female stanza balances and compliments the male image, not only in the softness and sweetness—swaying, curves, honey, warmth, roses—but in the song of her speech, to match his song, and her sun-melted, dark skin. In addition, the heat in her eyes links her to the sun and the Virgin, making her, simultaneously, both the Movement's spiritual source of energy and its goal. This is not machismo, however, because Elizondo does not relegate the woman to passivity. She is active in the image of a bee, a tireless worker who fertilizes nature while tending the home of a highly organized society, and a fierce fighter who dies in battle. The image matches the male eagle in its animal qualities. Her clearly sexual image is positive within the connotations that Elizondo has established for sex and love. (I am tempted to carry the image out to call the male a drone, which might be valid considering the poems to come which satirize machismo, but I will leave it as a suggested item for thought.) These stanzas prefigure the eventual union of male and female, but for the moment, they stand separated in the fields of exploitive labor.

The poem closes with fifteen lines framed in writing images drawn from graffiti. The Chicano quits work and retreats to his barrio, where he writes on walls so his eyes can read his own expression. Five lines of life images follow, culminating in flight, the fulfillment of the eagle-bee-sun heritage. Even the policeman's menacing guns cannot hold him down; he challenges them. The poem ends with "con safos," the graffiti signature of pride, challenge, and possession.[3] These verses form a *placa*, or barrio-gang graffito, emphasizing the role of written expression in the birth of the Chicano spirit, while tying literature to the popular word.

"Pastourelle" is an allegorical version of the fall of the Alamo. A rural maiden is raped by an arrogant stranger; she is the Hispanic Southwest, he the U.S.A. The Alamo, a home of devotion and humility built by strong hands, is the image of a country people dwelling in peace and love, a pastoral scene, with young virginal girls safe under the eyes of the Virgin of Guadalupe. Both Mexican and U.S. eagles threaten the peaceful scene, preparing the way for the UFW eagle that will arise later to protect the people. Instead of describing the war, the poet stresses that Mexicans fought on both sides; by attacking written history for ignoring Mexicans, the poet links the loss of land to the exclusion from written media. The poet promises to remedy the exclusion; the Mexican heroes can rest, because the poet lives to tell the story in his poetry.

At this point, with the conflict defined and the flowering of Chicano ideology about to appear in the text, the poet ends two poems, set in different historical periods, with writing images. The poet avers the need to write the oral tradition into the dominant media of print. Perhaps young Chicanos are fixated by the Anglo image (poem 1) because they are already a reading generation, out of touch with the oral tradition; the poems have sought to remedy that. Elizondo enters the enemy's domain to stake a claim for a Chicano presence and provide the young with an alternative within the written media. Yet his material is carefully *unwritten*; that is, its tone is deliberately oral, with emphasis on the voice, on the humor and word play of the oral tradition, and the rhythm and even the rhyme of the corrido. At this point the poetry assumes the voice of the young brothers, who, now armed with the historical perspective of the preceding poems, state their mature stand in "Chicanos" (poem 9, p. 25): "I'm Chicano, / because that's the word I named me. / None has given me that name, / I heard it, and I have it, / A child no more: I am a man."

Immediately following this poem, Elizondo places an ironic piece meant to characterize Chicanos. The title, "Buenos hijos de la Malinche" [Good sons of Malinche], is a Mexican phrase that Octavio Paz has explained in *The Labyrinth of Solitude (LS)*. Malinche, Cortes' translator, "becomes a figure representing the Indian women who were fascinated, violated or seduced by the Spaniards. . . . the Mexican people have not forgiven La Malinche for her betrayal" (*LS*, p. 86). She represents the open, the violated, as well as the sell-out to the invader. Macho is the opposite—the violator, the hermetically sealed aggressor, "pure incommunication" (*LS*, p. 82). The sons of *la chingada*—La Malinche—are the "strangers, bad Mexicans, our enemies, our rivals" (*LS*, p. 75). Yet Malinche is the Mexican Mother, and for Mexicans to reject her is to reject their origins and deny their hybridism. "The Mexican does not affirm himself as a mixture, but rather as an abstraction: he is a man. He becomes the son of Nothingness. His beginnings are in his own self" (*LS*, pp. 86–87).

Elizondo uses this concept both to satirize Mexican machismo, symbolized in the title, and to contrast it with a new attitude which we could call Chicano or third world. Machismo not only makes it impossible for women and men to relate to one another as equals, but also prevents communication between men. With the title Elizondo evokes the machista dynamic of isolation, and goes on to say that Chicanos even accept that they live according to it. Yet this assertion requires that a secret be silenced ("secreto callamos").

The poem, however, goes on to reveal the secret: Chicanos have no Oedipal complex, do not lust for their mothers, and do not feel that they violate their wives, as the Paz characterization of the macho says. Thus Elizondo denies that Chicanos are machos. He also denies that Chicanos reject the miscegenation symbolized by Malinche; rather Elizondo exalts it: "Jews, Blacks, Indians, and Chicanos / as I said, brother, / through our mothers are we brothers." Irony functions here not only in the contrast between Elizondo's assertions and the invoked Paz intertextual context, but in the fact that Chicanos themselves silence their reality in order to wear a false, foreign mask of machismo. Following the first clear declaration of Chicanismo in the previous poem, this poem warns of the danger of traits inherent in Mexican culture, traits that are no longer Chicano but which could be readopted and ruin the new-found identity. Chicanismo, as we have seen, depends on the acceptance of one's total history, on love and family, and on the open process of miscegenation. Elizondo gave us such an open image in "España," a direct contradiction of the Mexican rejection of the Spanish heritage. Machismo—the egotistical denial of history, love, and openness—seems to impose itself on Chicanos, as a fascination with the Anglo reality imposed itself on them in "Antiperros," though this time the false vision comes from Mexico. And once again Elizondo refocuses the Chicanos' vision on themselves.

In the poem "Machismo, chismo, chismo" (poem 14, p. 38), the macho dies in the isolation of his *I*. The structure of stanzas in inverted triangles represents the dissipation of the macho process; and as inverted pyramids, they are anti-sun signs. Yet, more than mere satires, they signal dangers to be avoided. Elizondo places the two warnings about machismo between poems of historical reference and poems of revelation, as if machismo were the single most significant deterrent to Chicano unity. This is logical when one considers his emphasis on love, women, and family.

"Mi casa" [my house] and "Padres, hijos; ayer, hoy" [Fathers, sons; yesterday, today] (poems 11 and 12, pp. 26–34) form a unit, encompassing the lost territory of the Southwest. The two poems claim the area as the Chicanos' home—land, water, and humanity in harmony. In addition, after the cautionary note of the macho poem, it is significant that "Mi casa" is addressed to the mother and "Padres, hijos" to the father. The young Chicano speaks to his parents, and in the second poem he speaks of the young girl who was given to him in marriage by the king of Spain, but who is now lost. The image is of the land grants lost after 1848. To regain the bride is to regain the land. The same young man speaks of his friend by the water, the UFW with its flag—fulfilling the image begun in the first two poems—that will lead the way to the recovery of the land / bride. The son explains to the father that servility is no longer acceptable; he will now *see* and *speak* clearly, and light fires if he must. However, the poem closes with a melancholy note, which in context can only be a nostalgia for the maiden's hand—the land —lost still to the Anglos.

In "Nota mexicana" [Mexican note] (poem 13, p. 34), the maiden appears. "Give girls of your love. / Undulating skirts of cotton." The skirts are synecdoches of the UFW flag and all it signifies. The girl is asked to give her hand, to recover the loss in the previous poem. She answers with her eyes—like the Virgin of Guadalupe —and words like jewels; the preciousness of her words prepare the way for the signficance of what she says at the end. Her image is traditionally Mexican: she works in the kitchen as a dutiful daughter, helping her mother make tortillas for the father; she wears braids and sings songs compared to the Virgin's rosary. She is the epitome—stereotype—of Mexican womanliness. And when she speaks to her father about her young Chicano, she says that he is from Aztlán. Thus, out of love is born the name of the Chicano nation, as binding as the UFW flag, and here synonymous. We might object to the stereotype and to the *Mexicanness* of the girl so divorced from the intercultural Chicanas. However, it should be noted that this traditional oasis does not produce results. The young people speak to their parents, but receive no answer; and after the three poems, they are still apart. Perhaps the traditional family procedure no longer functions. The meaning is ambiguous, but Elizondo's image of the traditional, virginal, Mexican ideal is (too) clear.

"Aquí entras Califas" [Here you enter Califas] and "Marcha" [March] (poems 15 and 16, pp. 40–42) close the historical frame of this section. Together they form a conquest, loss, and the start of reconquest of California. Both poems function through motifs established earlier.

Elizondo uses Chicano slang to contrast two visions of California. *Califas* is the beloved unforgettable girl; but the girl / lost-land motif bodes ill. Originally settled by Spaniards, Indians, and Mexicans in search of El Dorado, this land of promise was named after a fantastic island in a Spanish novel[4]—a utopian adventure still unrealized. Modern *California*, though not depicted, is evoked by the word itself—the girl has matured into a woman. California remembers her mestizo origins, but in the light of present times, which the reader brings to the text, references to Indians gathering roots and fruit mask images of Chicanos who still wander the land picking crops; however, such images no longer signify freedom, but rather serflike labor for those who usurped the dream. Califas remains the loved image, while California lies under another's roof, awaiting rescue.

Key words here reappear as titles of other poems. *Sueño*, the dream of lost land, becomes a poem about the betrayal of the Mexican Revolution (poem 22, p. 54), while *descanso*, rest in one's own land, titles a poem which culminates the Chicano development in the book (poem 32, p. 68).

In "Marcha" the first and last stanzas are veterans' marches. First come the dead who fought for the U.S.A.; then, walking joyfully, come Chicano Movement *veteranos*, slang for gang members and ex-convicts. Between the two lies a stanza of *ubi sunt*, lamenting

Chicanos killed in war. The poem closes with a reprise of "Mi cuento"—a veteran, who thought he would move up in society, finds himself marching in a UFW protest, which means that nothing has changed in Anglo society from World War II to Vietnam, but the Movement gives the Chicano veteran an organized alternative his father lacked.

"Del Nueces al Bravo" [From the Nueces to the Bravo] through "Deliro" [Delirium] (poems 17–27)

In "Del Nueces al Bravo," Elizondo sets a summary of the love-land-girl motif in South Texas. A barrio is described, with activity centering on the bakery, where young girls gather to socialize. Soft Spanish words evoke the virginal girl from previous poems; again they are repositories of the family traditions centered around eating. The persona then reveals his unspoken love for one of them, the lovely María.

From the center, María, the poem swirls back out to the barrio, then to the fields—where María, through comparisons, personifies nature. Within María's diffused presence, the persona could live as if "in a story." *Story*, however, has been tinged with negative connotations and should alert us to possible ironies. In the last stanza the persona sleeps under the sun, dreaming of copper, like his skin, and of galloping on Chicano mares, ending on a note of joy.

Something, however, is amiss. The closing image is a notorious stereotype of the lazy Mexican, and, in Elizondo's imagery, it rings negative. It clashes with the images of nature's awakening in the first stanza: vigilant palms are linked to women, assuming a character of Mexican traditions being preserved; a cock crows to the rising sun, an image of the revolution. The images draw on Elizondo's code, within which daydreaming is opposed to striving for liberation. Tracing the image of deceiving daydreams under sunny Texas skies, we recall that in "Perros" the land was lost in *false blue skies* (mistranslated as "false blue eyes").

Perhaps the first danger sign is the sudden switch to night in the second stanza, and the soft mist which covers South Texas. The awakening of stanza 1 is reversed in stanza 2. Later, the young man cannot speak to María, when in "Padres, hijos," the young Chicano had spoken clearly, and in "Nota mexicana" he asked the girl for her hand. The desire to live in a *story*, with the diffused presence, instead of with the real María, is another negative sign.

Even the money image is mistaken: a copper coin with the Eagle and Serpent, a Mexican coin. The Chicano of "Mi cuento" knew that his pockets were American. Chicanos live here, not in Mexico; and a copper penny is nothing, even if it were U.S. currency. The persona is mixed up, but Elizondo's irony is keen.

Where has the persona gone astray, and what is Elizondo saying? Following the poem's movement, we arrive at the center: María; but after her appearance, the poem drifts off course. Closer inspection reveals another element: María is a maid who spends eight hours a day—sun hours—working for someone else. Like California, this source of tradition is controlled by an employer; but the persona leaves her in exploitation in favor of escapist dreams of Mexico, instead of facing reality in the United States. The woman is the land, so he cannot escape fully; but he tries to. Perhaps Elizondo—consciously or unconsciously—is saying that South Texas is an area of apathy, of escapism based on its closeness to Mexico, of dreamy delusions of not having to face Chicano reality in this country. Or perhaps he is just portraying the sleepy impression the area gives to the stranger. Ambiguity allows either interpretation.

"Del Nueces" introduces a series of poems that, as a group, warn against drifting into complacent isolation. The dreamy bubble bursts when death takes hold of the text for seven poems (21–27). Death is a woman in the first poem, "Muerte," hiding behind a palm, the initial image from "Del Nueces," in which the danger motif began to possess the text. Yet death continues to be the Anglo as well. The Chicano shows no fear, challenging death with his knife. "Sueño" recalls the death of the Mexican Revolution with the defeat of Villa. Love enables the survivers to go on. Poems 23–26 reduce death to a familiar, oral-tradition image of the "Bitch." The tone is disrespectful, playful; the humor is obscene. Elizondo is familiarizing death, taking possession of it, to ethnically neutralize it. By putting it into culturally recognizable terms, he makes it less fearful. The purpose is to integrate death into life. Not that it will disappear; but if explained, life can go on. "Delirio" treats death / life in affectionate terms, as a liquor in a bottle with the eyes of a beautiful, fair-complected woman. Death continues to pursue, even seduce the persona; but now it has been brought into life, contained within another object which allows it to be seen, but restricts its movement.

"Lullaby" and "En casa" [At home] (poems 28 and 29)

To pull out of the death cycle, Elizondo evokes two life elements central to his imagery—sexual love and the family. "Lullaby" entreats the girl, missing since the betrayal of "Del Nueces," to give her body to the *dead* persona, victim of the last seven poems. She revives him, taking him from *the hard life* to *Life like that is never short*. Her presence extends life; even if death should come, life would have been full. Moreover, the persona now speaks directly to the girl, finally communicating without intermediaries. The text is moving toward the realization of love.

"En casa" culminates the house-home motif at the personal level. The text arrives at the Chicano home after searching through history and geography for the lost home. The woman is its heart, with peaceful images surrounding her. Culture oppression is absent. Not even death can break the continuity the persona will achieve through the oral tradition which the woman passes on to the son. Father and son receive continuity, and the woman becomes what she has been throughout the book, life's matrix. Moreover, the woman, no longer working for another, is free to enjoy the fruits of her labor, which are now her family and love. The home has been regained; the woman, rescued.

"Murrieta en la loma" [Murrieta on the hill] and "Murrieta Dos" [Murrieta Two] (poems 30 and 31)

At this point the text has only to personify the concept of the Movement. The family center must project outward into the struggle, lest the home become another false utopia. The poet calls on the oral tradition to retrieve the image of Joaquín Murrieta, the Californian who resisted Anglo encroachment in the past century. He is portrayed as an incarnation of many previously seen images. He is a mule driver in 1836, linked to the Spanish colonists in "Aquí entras Califas" through the animal; this extends his presence back centuries. With "1836," the date of the Alamo ("Pastourelle"), not that of the invasion of California over a decade later, Elizondo deregionalizes Murrieta and his significance as an image. The same effect is achieved through his Texan hat. Murrieta encounters Anglos, shares his water and tobacco, then wishes them well, repeating the welcome in "Perros" and alluding to both the theft of water and the vigilant night-smokers in the same poem. Though peaceful, he protects himself with an onion knife—a farm worker's tool, like the Chicano's knife in "Mi cuento" or "Muerte"—and a horsehair robe, a link to the horsemen from "España." Stanza 4 is one, very significant word: "Veo" [I see], a verb which (like eyes) assumes the meaning of human dignity, resistance to oppression, and love, as well as the book's purpose of bringing young Chicanos to see a total self-image. In stanza 5 Murrieta recalls the image of labor + militant resistance = revolution, with the expected violent reaction from the Anglos, who put down a strike with pistols and insolence, two Anglo signs since the start. The poem takes the strike from "Perros" to summarize a history of struggle. The last stanza draws from "En casa," where the woman wove the lifegiving threads of oral history; in "Murrieta en la loma," "The threads of Chicano murmur / wove stories about me." Elizondo creates parallel images, binding metonymically the family and the social movement, making the Chicano Movement a family affair.

"Murrieta Dos" amplifies the image of the hero, transforming him into the spirit of Chicano tradition. Yet the images may seem contradictory in their negation of origins, direction, substance, and even the legend of violent militancy. At the same time, several key images are repeated, such as the son of Malinche, Spanish ancestry in a mestizo blend, and land and water. This combination of identifiable images and explicit negation depersonalizes the Mexican / Chicano heritage. The hero's voice says that, though called Murrieta, he is actually a spirit who transcends specific persons; he is all those who have died to live on in the Chicano struggle. The poem also denies Murrieta's image as a killer of Anglos; Anglos killed themselves. It is significant that Elizondo writes, "They say I am Joaquín," a specific reference to the Gonzales poem, and then denies the killer image and personalism. Against the ideology of blood sacrifice and the personality cult of the leader found in *I Am Joaquín*, Elizondo counterposes the nonviolent spirit of the UFW. This is obvious throughout the book, in which the UFW images play such a vital role.

"Descanso" [Rest] (poem 32)

Murrieta's spirit is extended back to Quetzalcóatl by having the pre-Columbian god ride through the California hills, as the Spanish colonists and Murrieta did. Elizondo combines the two leading hero figures in Chicano literature in this way. However, he appropriates the image by surrounding it with his own imagery. Like the weaving woman, Elizondo creates a tight fabric of many threads, expecting the reader to see the entire cloth in each individual part. Motifs reappear: lost land, Anglos fencing it off and stealing the water through force of arms, ruination. The spirit of resistance survives, despite the defeat of the Mexican Revolution, to be reborn in the fruits of common labor. Elizondo insists that the Movement must be labor oriented, that the real tie to the land is not a mythical pre-Columbian ancestry nor a peace treaty, but the fact that Chicanos work the land and deserve to profit from the labor. Thus he chooses the image of water that flows and makes the land fertile. But it is the "Zanjeros," the workers, who tend the irrigation systems, who guide the flowing spirit to make the land produce. From water, the spirit becomes air and sun. Four elements are present; the fifth, love, is the Chicanos' labor. The spirit lives on through them.

The last three poems have repeatedly stressed the Southwest as one area, encapsulating the text's intention of recapturing the territory lost to the United States in 1848. The text has repossessed the area. Like water passing through an irrigation system, whose lines crisscross the land, the spirit flows through the interwoven system of motifs in the text. Having achieved its purpose, the text rests in "Descanso" before returning to the original confrontation.

In "Antiperros" young Chicanos seemed fixated on Anglo society in a way dangerously close to sour grapes. The text has reoriented them with historical, mythical, and socio-political imagery, concentrating their vision on their self-worth. Now, armed with the self-confidence of its own existence, the text attacks Anglo society directly, satirizing and ridiculing the American Way of Life in the last poem.

"Camino de perfección" [The Way to Perfection] (poem 33)

The title of the final poem is ironic; the poem, viciously satirical. The Anglo is pitied as a victim of his own world of plastic sterility, cut off from nature, love, and religious transcendence. Nothing survives ridicule. The poem can be divided into six sections for analysis:

1. *Birth and tradition.* The tone of mock pity is established from the outset: "Poor Brute! / What a life he had!" The Anglo is dehumanized as well as placed in the past tense as if dead. The implication that he is dead is underscored by the name of the hospital where he was born: *Memorial*, a word connoting a monument to a dead past. From birth he is alienated from nature by his own inventions; the plastic spoon and the white clinic are the birth images.

Plastic is used ten times in the poem (*artificial*, three times); nothing the Anglo has is natural. The usage here plays on the usual "silver spoon" image for upper class or privilege. The metonymy through *spoon* preserves elitism, while *plastic* devalues it. Tradition is reduced to a line of births punctuated by fear and defecation; fertility is thus unnatural, and we are supposed to believe that this is because Anglos situate birth in white clinics with cold steel walls. The baby is immediately wrapped in and surrounded by plastic, given artificial stimulation and food, vaccinated against nature, and washed daily. Two images contrast specifically with the Chicano imagery of the text. The child wears diapers of synthetic cotton and shoes of plastic cotton; real cotton symbolizes the Chicanos. The baby bottles of plastic contrast with the hand-blown bottle of "Delirio." Even in death Chicanos are more natural.

2. *Growing up.* The child is protected from nature and life. The initial image cuts him off from the land; he was not allowed to play in dirt caves, because of a mania for cleanliness. *Tierra* [dirt; land] however, so charged with significance, evokes the connotations built up by the text. Ties to the land permit survival; thus Anglos are doomed, while Chicanos will live. In addition, Elizondo claims that Anglos never learned about fighting after school; life came too easily.

3. *Military service.* Forced to encounter other races, the Anglo refuses to interact with them. Racism is depicted as nonacceptance of different eyes and skin, both of which were linked to land in previous poems. Water is wasted by the Anglo to wash and purify everything, instead of being used to produce life, as Chicanos use it. And at the end of this part, stimulants appear as another synthetic form of living.

4. *Work and family.* Work, the sign of puritanism in "Perros," becomes obsessive, making all five of its appearances within twenty-five lines. It tones marriage, which is supposedly a simple extension of work for Anglos. These are unloving people, more interested in each having a car than in being together. Their love bed is, of course, never used, though they do produce a little Brute born in the same sterile tradition.

5. *Recreation.* The Anglos' recreation is as artifical as the rest of their lives: campers; artificial, plastic lakes; artificially hatched fish; and plastic radios to drown out the sounds of nature. Their "desperate" rush to nature ends in alienation from it.

6. *Transcendent meaning to life.* The final first-person prayer of thanks to the "God of Plastic," attributed to the President of the United States, parodies the well-known rhyme "I don't care if it rains or freezes, as long as I have my plastic white Jesus." Elizondo

adds some words, perhaps for emphasis or to break down the smooth rhythm and harmonious cadence of the original. The parody lacks the easy flow, but thus draws attention to the content for satirical purpose. It would not do for the final insult to reflect a successful sense of rhythm.

In all, the poem is, in my opinion, an example of overkill. Its placement and purpose in the book is justified as a return to the original confrontation, and perhaps the vitriol is understandable in light of the text—kindness and trust have been shown to bring nothing but betrayal. However, there is something amiss in the poem which I can only attribute to the choice of images. The sour-grapes sensation from "Antiperros" has been reinforced rather than dispelled. The language is far from the "words / pure and good as days / in truthful poverty" of the young in the first poem. Moreover, because the images center on much of what has become part and parcel of Chicano existence and aspirations, the poem sounds hypocritical. The attack is not on Anglo life, but on modern life, and it would be hard to convince people that that life is as sterile as Elizondo pictures it. There is an implied fear that material comforts, or even sanitation, would erode Chicano culture. Nor is any alternative to modern life given, except an ambiguous return to the land implied in the text. The text is trapped in the quandary of much Chicano writing, that of negating what is already a part of the self. Elizondo implicitly criticizes the rejection of Malinche by Mexicans, but then rejects one of the Chicanos' parents, the United States. He cannot, however, escape it in the text itself. Constantly we are given images of Chicano formation through contact with the United States. To try to reject it is like trying to take the Anglos' presence out of Elizondo's poems; many would not make the least sense. Finally, the poem is weak because it deals in stereotypes, appeals to the lowest instincts and prejudice, and falls into the vices supposedly used against Chicanos by Anglos. This may be repayment in kind, but it still sounds like sour grapes. (In a private conversation, Elizondo confided that "Camino de perfección" was not written as part of the book, but that the editor wanted to include it. Elizondo was right.)

Conclusion

Like other Chicano writers, Elizondo sets out to create a Chicano space within the United States by redefining history to include a Chicano presence and by redefining the values by which life is judged. He also sees the need to give the young their heritage ignored in schools; but, unlike Gonzales, he does not picture them as disappearing into mediocrity.[5] Elizondo's young despise Anglos, but lack the self-knowledge to counter them. Gonzales *saves* the young; Elizondo *helps* them understand what their instinct and experience have led them to begin already. Gonzales wants to create the Movement; Elizondo offers the Movement assistance. He sets out to change the youths' perception (hence the *eyes* motif) so they will stop seeing only the Other. He realizes the goal by tracing history from a Mexican / Chicano perspective and focusing on the new Chicano family based on traditional values and a Movement based on the family. This vision of the Movement differs markedly from Gonzales'. Whereas Gonzales holds that tradition is preserved through violence, Elizondo's agents are family and love. Hence Elizondo gives women an active role compared to Gonzales' passive women. Hence, Elizondo's emphasis on the United Farm Workers, a pacifist group whose patron saint is a woman. Both authors speak of land recuperation, but differ in the element with which land is paired—Gonzales: land and blood; Elizondo: land and love. Elizondo wants Chicanos to *see* and *love* themselves. His book is an act of seeing and loving them; thus he repeats the hierophanous act which he says defines the culture. And repetition is a re-creation.

Yet the poet returns to the anti-Other fixation in the end. He demonstrates once again that the Anglo American presence is essential to the Chicanos' self-image, one based, in part, on the threat from the Other.

Paradigm Charts

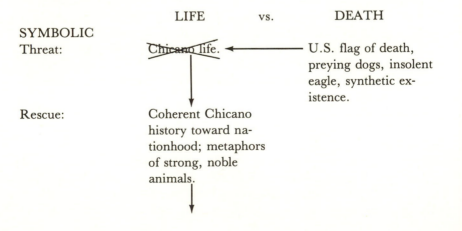

	LIFE	vs.	DEATH
SYMBOLIC Threat:	~~Chicano life.~~ ←		U.S. flag of death, preying dogs, insolent eagle, synthetic existence.
Rescue:	Coherent Chicano history toward nationhood; metaphors of strong, noble animals.		

LIFE   vs.   DEATH

Response: UFW flag of Aztlán ⟶ ~~U.S. signs of death.~~
                 as nation of natural
                 existence; Chicano as
                 horseman, UFW
                 eagle.

SOCIAL
Threat: ~~Chicano self-esteem.~~ ⟵ Anglo American
                                            technological,
                                            materialistic society;
                                            progress.

Rescue: Of Mexican tradition
                 of love, survival;
                 emergence of Chicano
                 ideology; negative im-
                 agery of Anglo
                 Americans.

Response: Poem as affirmation ⟶ ~~Anglo American~~
                 of Chicano self-   ~~society.~~
                 esteem; as debunking
                 of Anglo American
                 society.

PERSONAL
Threat: ~~Mexican-born, older~~ ⟵ Chicano youths' dis-
                 ~~participant in Chicano~~   trust of older genera-
                 ~~Movement.~~   tion; fixation on
                                            Anglos excluded Mex-
                                            ican presence.

Rescue: Mexican antecedence
                 of Chicano Move-
                 ment. Youth emphasis
                 in poem's persona.

Response: Poem as proof of ⟶ ~~Distrust.~~
                 poet's active par-
                 ticipation and cham-
                 pioning of the young.

6. THE VOICE OF SILENCE
Miguel Méndez, Poet

History is a speech act. . . . Even substantive remains such as buildings and historical sites must be read, i.e., located in a context of verbal recognition and before they assume real presence.
—George Steiner, *After Babel*, p. 29

Miguel Méndez' constant concern is that silence will engulf Chicano culture because of the breakdown of verbal interchange central to oral tradition. The speaker-listener relationship between the old and the young is disappearing; disinterested young people ignore a diminishing generation of wise old ones. Isolated from Hispanic written literature, Chicanos need their oral tradition to withstand the inroads of foreign cultures and to maintain a cohesive group identity. Older generations must not die unheard.

At the same time, Méndez distrusts written materials vis-à-vis cultural identity. Written media have been controlled by the conqueror, Anglo American and Spaniard, and exploited by the ruling classes, U.S. and Mexican, to the detriment of racially, ethnically, and economically marginal peoples. Official national histories and written literature falsify the Chicanos' role. Yet, as Chicanos move from an oral culture to a written or electronic one, the definition of their self-image passes into the hands of outsiders or assimilated Mexican Americans. One could argue the advantages or disadvantages of this image change, but Méndez brooks no argument—it is negative. Writing may be necessary for Chicano survival, but it is not to be trusted.

Méndez responds by invading the realm of the printed word with writing which he seeks to convert into the expression of the Chicanos' oral tradition—encompassing folklore, history, religion, mythology, songs, and genealogy. By preserving it in writing, he counters the imminent breakdown in the oral method. Written texts can wait for interest to rekindle. Writing itself can constitute, however, another threat; it exposes the culture to outsiders, to the oppressor who consumes the written word as a matter of course. Cultural secrets endow power to the possessor, so they must not be divulged carelessly. Méndez' revelations hide behind a mask of silence; the texts are inscrutable to the undeserving reader, becoming meaningless readings equivalent to silence in their opacity.

Méndez' concept is closely akin to Robert Graves' explanation of Celtic oral tradition in *The White Goddess*.[1] Like the Celtic bards, Méndez seems to practice the defensive techniques of the "dog, Roebuck and Lapwing"; that is *guard the secret, hide the secret, disguise the secret*, while simultaneously voicing the secret for those who deserve it. This technique is appropriate when one lives in, or invades, hostile territory. For Méndez, that territory is double: the geographic area of the United States and the space of the written word. This difficult task determines Méndez' style and structure. Without repeating what I have explained elsewhere,[2] a résumé of his prose pieces may better explicate this point.

In "Tata Casehua,"[3] an old Indian chief, Casehua, wanders the Mojave Desert in search of a Yaqui child, uncontaminated by whiteman's blood, to inherit his kingdom. A young boy, instinctively attracted to Casehua, begins an apprenticeship of sorts. He must prove himself truly interested (he repeats questions before receiving answers), brave (willing to challenge the killer river), and faithful (refusing to be distracted from his mission). Having completed his task, he hears the desert's silent voices reveal Casehua's forgotten identity—he is a Yaqui hero who resisted Mexican military invasions. His heir assured, Casehua reintegrates into the desert. In Méndez' novel, *Peregrinos de Aztlán*, the oral versions of the lives of the oppressed are contrasted with the false and deprecatory versions written in official records or the press. When the central character, in whose mind the oral versions float, dies, the reader becomes the repository, not only of truth, but of the knowledge that truth has been suppressed. The reader is challenged to utilize that knowledge. Both works also test readers with esoteric vocabulary, plot fragmentation, an ornate, baroque style, and an at times self-righteous moralizing. But if one persists to the end, reading carefully, a historical and moral revelation is offered. Méndez' texts are rituals of ethnic and class testing. Readers prove their Chicanismo, proletarianism, or, at least, their sympathy by understanding the characters, and by sheer endurance. Those who pass are privileged to witness a sacred unveiling of oral tradition.

Los criaderos humanos (épica de los desamparados) y Sahuaros [The human stockyard (epic of the forsaken) and Sahuaros] follows the same pattern as the prose. However, whereas the latter concentrates on the reader's role, and only implicitly on the writer's, the poetry

book explicitly treats the writer's function in society. The protagonist and first-person narrator is a poet, meant to resemble the author.
And since both the concepts and the techniques repeat those of the
prose, *Criaderos* can be read as Méndez' *ars poetica*.

To all appearances, the book contains two separate poems. The
first relates a poet's wanderings through the desert in search of his
origins; he meets the strange inhabitants of a horrible human stockyard, witnesses an attack by their rulers, and escapes. The poem's
tone is serious, grave, befitting its subject; and the political allegory
is obvious. The second poem, lighter and more joyous in tone, is an
ode to the desert's beauty. Whereas the first tells a story in epic-
narrative fashion, the second functions as a lyric piece, seemingly
without plot. Differences allow them to be read separately; the
capitalization of *Sahuaros* in the title, contrary to Spanish convention
that capitalizes only a title's first word, and an interior title page for
"Sahuaros" seem to underscore a division into two poems.
However, Méndez is maneuvering defensively again; the two poems
are bound through motifs, imagery, and, most significantly, the
book's purpose. They form one poem because neither can achieve
full meaning without the other. But the subterfuge is essential to
Méndez' method and goal, so analysis will start with "Criaderos"
as a single unit.

"Los criaderos humanos"

The 1310 free-verse lines, in the first person, of "Criaderos" form a
centering movement of dual discovery: one, what the *criadero* signifies; two, who is the narrator and what are his functions vis-à-vis the
criadero. The socio-political allegory is clear, perhaps too obvious.
The poem can be divided into the following sections.[4]

I. Lines 1–85. Introduction to setting and persona.

II. Lines 86–542. Responses to questions by the desert's voices.

III. Lines 543–1105. The *Criadero*.
    1. Lines 543–672. First encounter with inhabitants of *Criadero*.
    2. Lines 673–1105. Attack by oppressors; epiphany.

IV. Lines 1106–1310. Reaction, retreat, discovery of narrator's
    purpose, death.

I. INTRODUCTION TO SETTING AND PERSONA
(lines 1–85, pp. 1–4)

The introductory verses are structured by questions about identity, the persona's and the place's. Although explicit answers come only after the narrator reaches the *criadero*'s center, here the essential factors are supplied.

Line 1 asks how the persona arrived here; line 2 admits that he does not know. This void begins to fill as information accumulates. In a world of wasted routine, without past or future, the persona has walked like a pilgrim seeking his roots, place, and essence; we can expect the poem to provide them. The personal focus introduces a source both of virtue and of conflict. The individual perspective will change, as the persona accepts communal ties, but it will not disappear. Line 22 introduces the thrice-repeated (49, 80) question about the identity of the setting, posed by the persona in reaction to what he sees. The place is quickly characterized: sadness is queen, misery sovereign; a place that "oprime y lacera el alma" [oppresses and lacerates the soul] (23). The soul here is the persona's, because according to him the inhabitants are soulless (84). This introduces two major themes to be developed in the poem. First, the inhabitants' souls will be acknowledged, a qualitative change in the text's portrayal of their existence. Second, the persona's elitism—having a soul makes him superior to the inhabitants, whom he does not yet know—will be challenged and overcome in the poem.

The persona's initial reaction to the place is to exclaim, "¡Dios mio!" [My God!]—an expression that becomes his signature motif, repeated six times (21, 93, 197, 465, 942, 1282), coming to play a key role in his transformation.

The place's situation is communicated through images of infertility; and the absence of water, words, voices, past, and future. Between the first two questions about the place (22, 49), the persona describes images of death and futility, framed by litanies sung by dead cicadas and a strange burial: "La tierra / se traga a la tierra" [The earth / swallows the earth] (47–48); the image is later explicated in a reference to a farm worker "que antes de morir ya era tierra" [who before dying was already earth] (1072). The absence of water and blood nullify communal rituals—a crucifixion, Christianity's central rite; sexual love; and land cultivation. "Riveras y milpas / ansían el torrente / cual hembras olvidadas" [Rivers and cornfields / desire the torrent / like forgotten women] (28–30). Méndez evokes objects now absent to establish a lost-golden-age motif. Mother Earth would flourish, as she once did, if irrigated, a sexual image implying the need for males to resume their *macho* role; impotence will be attributed to oppression. Méndez' imagery is crass: what is needed is a good stud; the earth is an anxious *hembra* [female].

Méndez' familiar motif of the silent voices of the past appears here in the form of hidden sobs, flowing through waterless arroyos, rustling vegetation where there is no growth, and in the lack of birds or songs. Again, absence is emphasized by reference to vanished items; also, the poem begins to recuperate the past by naming those very same items.

At the heart of the frustrated family, the parents of dead children (50) stand like crying statues (42), implicitly trees—their pain (history) is *petrified*, which means that the tears do not flow. Since tears are the land's only humidity (611–618), history is equated to water—and sperm, so badly needed to restore life. Each image's connotations swell the central image of absence. Since both past and future (dead children) are lost, the land exists in a miserable present; and the persona's situation is no better. Hence, the persona and the land share a venture of fulfillment.

The final question about what this place is focuses on the *pueblo*, which means both "town" and "people," marking a step toward the personal. The persona combines the two in stating that it is an "escenario trágico / poblado de actores sin alma / sin obra ni drama literarios" [tragic stage / populated with actors without souls / without literary works or drama] (83–85), which places the community question squarely into a literary reference. Literature humanizes; like water and sperm, it fertilizes. As the land longs for water and the woman for man (27–30), so the sand longed for words (53–58). Water, sperm, and words are metonymically equated as objects desired by the desert. The poem must provide the liquids of life.

The persona begins to do so by shedding tears in reaction to his initial perception of this land. Unknowingly, he offers exactly what is desired, and this act of sympathy stimulates the voices to break silence, beginning section II.

II. RESPONSES TO QUESTIONS BY THE DESERT'S VOICES (lines 86–542, pp. 4–25)

Lines 86–534 continue to penetrate this place through the testimony of the desert's creatures. The first one, a bushlike beast rooted to the ground, announces, through lips like withered geraniums, that this place is a *criadero humano*. The horrified persona calls on God to explain this creature, but then walks away. The creature pleads with him to return adding, "Aquí / solamente la resurrección de la clorofila / es esperanza de vida. / Dolor de humanidad es reconocer la propia culpa / y aceptar la acusación de la conciencia" [Here / only the resurrection of chlorophyll / is the hope of life. / The pain of humanity / is to recognize one's own guilt / and accept the accusation of the conscience] (105-110). *Resurrection of chlorophyll* becomes a central motif signifying the return to ecological harmony and the golden age. Yet the persona's repulsion signals an aloofness from the world's woes. The creature denounces this attitude: to refuse one's responsibility for suffering is to be less than human. The irony is clear—both the inhabitants and the persona are less than human at the start; mutual humanization is needed.

Yet the persona insists that he wants to "penetrar al pueblo raro" [penetrate the strange town] (111), underscoring both his desire to understand and his position as an outsider that separates him from the goal. The desire leads to the next encounter (115-154): he catches a creature beating his dog and castigates him, boasting that he too was once a beast, but now is gentle. Once more he assumes a superior stance, ironically undermined through contrast with the dog, who forgives the creature.

The persona again walks away, avoiding mirages or luminous lagunas as if they were real, his movements controlled by illusions. Later (390-391), the eyes of the oppressors—the Hombres de Cristal [Crystal Men]—are called blue lakes, metonymically linking them to the mirages; both limit and determine the freedom of the oppressed. The persona unknowingly is a prisoner, to an extent, a circumstance which belies his arrogant aloofness.

A pair of seemingly furious beasts are encountered next (189-302). Frightened, the persona invokes God and prays for protection before asking the beasts about the place's history. The animals, actually tame ploughing oxen—impotent males over Mother Earth —relate the story of the golden age of chlorophyll and its destruction by the *Rapiña* [Rapine], conquerers whose electric saws deforested the land, causing water to vanish and the land to lose color, becoming a desert. Their bombers dropped eggs of hate onto Mother Earth, an image of sterile rape. When animals took the trees' place, the *Rapiña* bled them, turning the blood into gold.

When the persona wonders who these oxen are (347-349), yet another voice arises to explain that they are part of the starving masses, emasculated and subjugated by the Crystal Men of the blue-lake eyes, who command the *Rapiña* and the Blacks (351-412). The terms of the allegory refer to capitalism and racism; the country is specified through references to moon flights and conquest under the symbol of the eagle—the United States (399–412).

This speaker is the image of the older generation about to die with its oral tradition—an ancient tree, survivor of the electric saws, witness to history, but with no one to talk to. The persona has luckily encountered a wise tree/man; he persists in his questions until the usually silent voice speaks. When the tree's voice fades into the wind, an aged woman, La señora Enredadera [the Climbing-Vine Lady], who is the tree's granddaughter, continues the oral-history lesson (464–514), providing, finally, enough knowledge to enable him to penetrate the *criadero* itself.

III.1. FIRST ENCOUNTER WITH INHABITANTS OF *CRIADERO* (lines 543–672, pp. 25–31)

The *criadero* is a village of mole-like beasts, periodically bled dry by the *Rapiña*, and desiring only to become trees to escape. They surround the persona, eliciting from him, at last, his identity—he claims to be a teacher, a counselor to the young, a poet, and a brother. The inhabitants swarm him adoringly, but he, frightened, wants to escape again. In spite of his claims of brotherhood, he has not accepted his likeness or responsibility.

III.2. ATTACK BY OPPRESSORS: EPIPHANY (lines 673–1109, pp. 31–51)

The *Rapiña*, and their mercenaries the Aguijón [Spurs, Goads, Pricks], suddenly attack, while the persona watches from the safety of the old tree. All inhabitants are bled, even children, whose blood makes the most precious jewels. Gold for churches and consumer goods for the rich are produced as well. The raid occupies many lines, allowing Méndez to introduce some of his favorite themes of oppression.

Méndez despises war, but realizes that military service has been a traditional path for minorities to assimilate. To combat this he satirizes the professional soldier through the Aguijón, who kill for social-economic rewards. These green-clad soldier-slaves (730) are the most human of the oppressors, but they still kill for a share of the booty. Proud of their position, they glorify their bloody deeds in patriotic songs, claiming to be liberators of the poor. But Méndez cannot treat them completely negatively; after all, they come from humble origins, from ourselves. Beneath the façade he finds echoes of pain—they cannot forget their humble roots nor their original humanitarian ideals. To hide their history they distort it, but their cynical children only pretend to believe the stories (1012–1105). The satire exemplifies Méndez' willingness to criticize his own group. Yet the Aguijón are the most human simply because they are not one-sided like the others. Though this coincides with Méndez' intention to make them more appealing, it points out the poem's major flaw, the use of stereotypes. Méndez refuses to portray the oppressors' humanity. Other Chicano writers share this fault, but that makes it no less damaging here.

No Méndez work would be complete without an attack on the written word as the oppressor's tool. During the raid an old man complains to a Rapiña that his deeds cannot be condoned by the letter of human or divine law (834–835). The Rapiña responds, "las verdaderas razones son las únicas que pesan. / No te fíes de la ley escrita / la que se impone la trae la hembra desde la matriz / y se pasea en el semen del macho" [the true reasons are the only ones that count. / Don't trust in the written law / the one that counts is the one a woman carries in the womb / and it floats in the macho's semen] (837–840). Méndez has expressed similar thoughts about written history elsewhere,[5] but here it comes from the oppressor; moreover, it provokes a vision of the regeneration of the golden age. At this point, the incident remains ambiguous; the explanation must await the application of the allegory to the author himself.

In the middle of the raid, the *criadero*'s characteristics are recapitulated (862–903): hunger, shame, bitterness, rancor, hate, racism, self-destruction, slaughter, silence, atrophied intelligence, and misery. The segment's structure is significant. It opens with an exclamation: "¡Este es un criadero humano!" [This is a human stockyard!], a line repeated in 883. Between the two exclamations, the *criadero* is described abstractly, with the repetition of "Here . . . Here . . ." Following the second exclamation, the description focuses on the creatures. The movement from place to inhabitants is the same taken by the poem. However, one now expects a tripartite structure, three repetitions before response; and so it is again. From place and inhabitants, the focus goes to the persona. But when we expect him to react, to speak, he remains hidden behind the tree, watching, still the aloof observer.

The old tree, shaken by indignation, speaks instead: "Malditos los que fingen ternura / los huérfanos de humanidad malditos. / Mil veces malditos quienes instigan las guerras. / Malditos los que pronuncian en falso / el nombre del bendito / que expiró en la madera de mis brazos" [Damn those who feign tenderness / the orphans of humanity be damned. / A thousand times damned those who instigate wars. / Damn those who speak falsely / the name of the blessed / who expired in the wood of my arms] (912–917). Since by this point the persona has made the invocation of God his sign, the tree's accusation of hypocrisy is aimed at him. This denunciation completes the triptych with a revelation about the persona, structurally linking him to the *criadero*, while thematically separating him into the category of the responsible.

The three repetitions produce a response, the persona's reaction: tears inundate him, and they, in turn, bring an epiphany. The persona accepts his identity as both an oppressor and the oppressed, seeing his grandparents and grandchildren in both groups, and himself as dying while simultaneously killing his own children (934–941). The present expands into the past and future through family ties and fratricidal self-annihilation. And in the center stands the poet-persona, with the poem's power concentrated on him, as if seeking resolution. He invokes God once again and feels the sorrow of having been born. He is transfixed in the realization of his inescapable humanity. Emerging from his hiding place, he receives the brunt of the attack; painful essence is given him (964). He recognizes his guilt, as the first beast foretold he must, and is transformed: "Lloré minutos fugaces de arrepentimiento / renegué de la impotencia / de no anular dentro de mí mismo / la maligna condición que nos convierta / tal como son las bestias" [I cried fleeting moments of repentance / I cursed the impotence / of not destroying within myself / the malignant condition that converts us / into something like beasts] (970–974). He leaves the *criadero* a changed man.

IV. REACTION, RETREAT, DISCOVERY OF NARRATOR'S PURPOSE, DEATH (lines 1106–1310, pp. 51–60)

He walks in search of the future and encounters a "strange man" who had appeared twice before (333–346, 519–527), fascinating but repulsing the persona. The creature is ugly, constantly changing his animal likeness—cockroach, monkey, owl, cat, snake, monster. He appears when the persona and the poem seem about to reach an important juncture and serves to delay the discovery. The first time the persona has just come across the *criadero*; but after the creature appears, the *criadero* disappears for some 210 lines. We are told little about the creature that time, but the "electric sensation" he causes metonymically links him to the enemy. His second intervention came when the persona has been befriended by the wise old tree; at

that point he frightens the persona away, again delaying the progress. After the second time, the persona is warned that the ugly
man is a poisonous intriguer, a traitor and deceiver who sells his
own family (528–534). Yet it will be only after a third apparition
(1127–1154) that his identity is revealed: he is an *arachnid*, a spider
who weaves false, luminous webs of perfidy to entrap the credulous
(1155–1163). The persona wonders why people still fall for the
deception, believing him a redeemer. This hermetic image of the
treasonous brother has an allegorical correspondence I have explained in detail elsewhere,[6] but here any image of a redeemer in a
poem seeking redemption must be analyzed, even that of a false
prophet. Méndez supplies only metonymic and synonymic clues.
Arácnido is a pedantic synonym for *araña* in Spanish. Who in
Méndez' world could be a spider and an academic pretender at
once? Carlos Castaneda, who once claimed to be Carlos Aranha,
Portuguese for *araña*. The fibrous, luminous aura around the
creature (525) should have alerted us; Castaneda uses it to describe
how beings look when seen with trained eyes.[7] Castaneda's supposed Yaqui knowledge made him a media success, a rich man,
eventually a Ph.D. and youth-cult guru. The fact that he is Hispanic
—a Peruvian—makes him a treasonous brother. Méndez denounces
Castaneda as a false prophet, and the persona avoids him.

The persona, meditating on what he has witnessed, compares
the emaciated inhabitants to the fat Rapiña, thinking that the latter
look like freshly plucked chickens, ready to be roasted (1199–1200).
This thought provokes laughter all around him—he has been
''monologando en voz alta'' [monologuing out loud] (1203), a good
definition of Méndez' poetry. The jubilation introduces a radical
change in the environment—nature reveals her plenitude with an
enumeration of edible plants. The laughter is compared to the sound
of flowing water, and through metonymy the desert receives what it
has desired since the start of the poem. The poet declares his love for
the plants and his special tie to the cactus since childhood; he is
returning to his origins. In the morning, after sleeping in the protective shelter of a sahuaro—within the storehouse of oral history—he
awakens to witness the rain. The sky ''nacía llorando serenamente''
[was born crying serenely] (1248), in stark contrast to a sorrowful-
burial dawn at the beginning (24–50). But ironically, the peaceful
dawn apparently spells the end of the poet's search, not in rebirth
but in death. He finds himself walking on a river, like Christ on the
waters, back to the land of his birth, death. He invokes God's name
and requests that his death be not disappearance, but rebirth,
preferably as a beautiful tree to console the suffering people and to

sing about God's universal love. The poem ends, saying that this enchanted city is the route of his destiny.

The ending seems paradoxical. After such violent satire, the text's revelations, the positive transformation in the persona, why does he simply die? We expect more and are left dissatisfied. The ending seems escapist, too personal. We must reconsider some factors to understand it.

From the introductory segment the poem has insisted on the personal venture. The persona was seeking his origins, place, essence. His epiphany makes him less aloof, a responsible brother, but on a personal level. When his identity is revealed, it is as a poet, a teacher, a gentle man. As such his role cannot be escapist nor that of an objective, nonparticipating observer. The question is, how committed must the artist be; to what extent must one participate?

At this point we must return to the scene in which the Rapiña denounced written law and produced a vision of the golden age. It seems to say that to achieve regeneration, the oppressed must take up the violence of brutes, become like the Rapiña. The Rapiña, like the monster in "Tata Casehua," tests the hero's resolve. To live the law of the animal would equal the poet taking to the streets in rebellion. The vision is another mirage. This is why Méndez puts the statement in the mouth of the enemy, mixing it with what he himself considers the truth about written media; it is meant to be tempting. Méndez is testing the reader as well. The violent path would betray the persona's newly discovered human essence. His role is to fight with words, not with weapons. He can reduce the oppressor to the ridiculous—but he dies and the lesson seems to go for naught.

"Sahuaros"

He does not simply die, however, but rather is granted his dying request and resurrects as the singer of universal love, a tree to shelter the suffering. "Sahuaros" is the enchanted city of his destiny where the poet-lost-wanderer is transformed into a desert Virgil, guide to tourists and seekers of their origins, like the Chicano reader. His words will transform the trees into living monuments to the Chicanos' legitimate written tradition. Where in his arrogance he saw the beings of the *criaderos* as soulless because they lacked literary tradition, now, from his new empathetic mode, he reveals a literary tradition centuries old. Where the *criaderos* were anonymous, now there rises a troupe of famous figures. In short, "Sahuaros" responds to the needs of "Criaderos," revealing images, fertilizing the soil, liberating the land.

The poet of "Sahuaros" is the same persona as in "Criaderos," but no longer is he lost nor at the mercy of hostile forces; his transformation is now complete. "Sahuaros" begins, "Pósase el firmamento sobre el suelo. / De lejos / parece agua lo que solamente es azul" [The firmament rests on the ground. / From afar / it looks like water, but is only blue] (1311-1313). The persona begins by identifying a mirage as nothing but color, a simple façade, an exercise in acute and comprehensive vision contrasting with the control those mirages had over him in "Criaderos." Thus, "Sahuaros" begins by relegating the oppressor—for the mirages were his eyes—to a debunked, distant presence. Readers know they are in a transformed world.

The poem then recapitulates the "Criadero" situation: desert, death, thirst, lack of color, echoes of the past, sterile earth, winds. But in line 1350, the dust clouds fly against the cruel sun, covering it with black wings. One must picture the image: a sky turned red by the blown sand and black wings profiled against a white-hot sun: the United Farm Workers Union flag. The rebellion finds a symbol to oppose to the U.S. flag and eagle that flew to the moon (399-406).

The revolution immediately assumes imagery to respond to that of "Criaderos." Whereas the Rapiña had jewels and precious metals, the poet fills this newly opened space with those same elements: silver, obsidian, jeweled sky, pearls, diamonds, emeralds. Quickly, sensations are added to this oasis: colors, smells, flowers (*azahar, margaritas, cardos, geranios* [orange flowers, daisies, thistles, geraniums]—in bloom as opposed to the withered one in "Criaderos"), and the red of blushing virgins; sounds: trilling birds, pianos, harps. All the sounds are actually singing birds—no birds sang in "Criaderos." The scene is set for love.

The mythical Tonatiuh, the Aztecs' fifth sun, called here their father, assumes the form of a stallion and fertilizes nature, in the form of a mare; semen rains as earth is impregnated (1406-1417). We have known since the introduction of "Criaderos" that what was needed was a stud to turn female earth into Mother Nature. The golden age of natural harmony is gestated—and the giant sahuaros are born, sons of God, heirs to Aztec greatness (1420-1477). Nature blooms; arroyos run full. The silent voices are heard loudly. Tucson arises, a mixture of Spanish and English in friendship—Méndez' only concession to English in the text (1446-1447). The poet addresses the stranger, the reader, and invites her / him to follow the road of dreams. The tour of the enchanted city is about to begin.

The land is populated by Indian monarchs and noble knights (Spaniards); and if the strangers care to, they can talk to them. The inhabitants speak the international language of sculpture; they are "esculturas de pensamientos" [sculptures of thought] (1502). The glorious statues about to be seen—and heard through the poet's words—are those same sorrowful statues from "Criaderos," those childless parents, now transformed into the embodiment of a great tradition. The statues talk silently, "La elocuencia de los siglos / ellos la cuentan callando" [the eloquence of the centuries / they speak keeping silence] (1504–1505). Méndez creates yet another of his images of the voice of silence: "el silencio sacro" [the sacred silence] (1521).

The tour introduces us to Don Quijote, Colón (usually misnamed Columbus), Christ—a valid crucifixion to respond to the futile one in "Criaderos"—lovers, reconciled enemies, an archetypal blind poet, Lazarillo de Tormes, El Cid, Don Juan, Calixto and Melibea, Cuauhtemoc, Huitzilopochtli, Gerónimo, Father Eusebio Kino, and an enchanted green army to counterbalance the treasonous green-suited Aguijón.

The poet declares his fraternal tie to the trees; they are Aztlán, with the Indian's universal soul. Again the soul is attributed to the inhabitants. The poem ends, however, with the warning that the sahuaros will die also, but that a written text will recall them.

Conclusion

The two poems are one, interrelated piece, each inexplicable without the other. Méndez states his *ars poetica* in dramatic fashion and challenges the reader to follow him. Those who do not will remain fragmented, cut off from the sacred redemption of the unitary poem; they will misread and find fault with the works. The social realists will study "Criaderos," though they will not be content with its escapism, its individualism, and the persona's refusal to commit himself in more direct ways. The art-for-art's sake readers will prefer "Sahuaros." Méndez seems to say that the true Chicano will combine both, will see that the elements of one penetrate and inform the other. They are his ideal chronicle of an apprenticeship to the poet's life.

At the same time, the book responds to the crisis of a disappearing oral tradition. Not only does it contain an allegorical mythology similar to that of oral folktales; it also constantly utilizes the oral process of repeated questions and answers, the interchange between the old and young, and the passing on of history. In addition, and what is perhaps more significant in the context of Chicano literature, Méndez takes a new step by claiming the Spanish written heritage for Chicanos. There is no reason why Chicanos should think of themselves as a nonliterate people, when from their cultural antecedents have come figures of universal stature, such as Don Quijote or Don Juan Tenorio. Chicanos need not panic as they move into the written domain, Méndez seems to say—that is, if they still have their language. If not, then they may well be lost. In Spanish they will find a positive self-image and a code of heroic action of their own. He tells the Chicano that while U.S. society may be a foreign, and thus chaotic, space, literature is not. The written space has been cosmicized into "our world." That world will reveal that Chicano culture can draw on universal values. Méndez tries to open the limited space in which Chicanos imagine they find themselves and show them that their culture has already inhabited areas much beyond. And though the poet may die, and the ancient trees will die, the printed word may transcend.

Paradigm Charts (of the book as one text)

LIFE   vs.   DEATH

SYMBOLIC
Threat: ~~Human~~ life with ⟵—— Soullessness allows
transcendent meaning   beings to be bled.
or richness.

Rescue: Elements constituting
the community soul:
history, literature.

Response: The poem as the soul ——▸ ~~Soullessness~~.
of the community, a
richness of being.

SOCIAL
Threat: ~~Community with self-
awareness and pur-
pose.~~   ⟵— Exploitative society
that has conquered
the people and at-
tempted to wipe out
their history and
tradition.

LIFE   vs.   DEATH

Rescue:	Allegory of history of conquest, enslave-ment; images of a literary tradition of universal value.

↓

Response: Poem as symbolic his- ——→ ~~Lack of history and tradition.~~
tory and a Chicano
literary work within a
humanistic tradition.

PERSONAL
Threat: ~~Poet as meaningful participant in Chicano Movement.~~ ◄——— Poet's alleged irrele-vancy to social issues; charges of aloofness and irresponsibility.

↓

Rescue: *Ars poetica* of responsible commitment and
participation in efforts
to free oppressed peo-
ple.

↓

Response: Poem as the poet's ——→ ~~Poet's irrelevance, aloofness, irresponsi-bility.~~
contribution to the
analysis of the Chi-
cano Movement and
his commitment to the
liberation of oppressed
people.

7. TIME, DEATH, AND THE OTHER VOICE OF SILENCE
Tino Villanueva

Lo abierto en verdad es el silencio
Pero en ti era una voz
y ahora se levanta y canta
—Juan García Ponce, *Réquiem y elegía*, p. 4[1]

Hay otra voz Poems displays one essential vision: certain oppressive forces in life threaten to relegate people to a silent, invisible, anonymous state of nonexistence. In its most fundamental manifestations, the oppressive force is time, and nonexistence is death. Time's apparently unalterable flow sweeps humans unknowingly into oblivion; death envelops life, converting human beings into unconscious, anonymous victims. However, though time and death may be undeniable, anonymity is remediable; life can be an assertive, identity-creating space. The key is to turn the constant dying inherent in life into the lived experience of intense feeling that makes each moment distinct in its worth. In this way the present is fulfilled, the past made memorable, and the future bright; time's flow is rendered meaningful. Villanueva centers the conflict on the word's creative power; he himself, his people, and humankind in general struggle to break their silence and express their particular reality. Silence essentially characterizes life's victims, while sound pertains to the oppressors. Human silence searches for expression, yet it must not become empty sound, noise. Time, death, and silence in constant conflict form the dynamics of this poetry, the voice of which is faithful to the silent essence of life's victims with whom the poet identifies. Finding a voice of silence, he makes it his own.

The book is Villanueva's *ars poetica*, as I explained in a 1979 article, "The Other Voice of Silence: Tino Villanueva" (*OVS*).[2] While considering the human situation, the poet also questions the role of poetry in society and the poet's role vis-à-vis the community. The book records that aesthetic and social *consciousness taking*, and it contains and *is* the response.

Analysis of *Hay otra voz Poems* will reveal the many forms its basic elements take in transforming into a code of imagery; the author's techniques, especially that of irony; and the book's structure as a total unit. For the sake of analysis, each of the book's three sections is treated individually, and the poems of sections I and III are discussed out of sequence; but the collection forms a unit and should be read as one poem. Some poems, analyzed in detail in *OVS*, will not be discussed again here.

I. Por ejemplo, las intimidades [for example, intimacies]

The first section (the largest, with seventeen of the thirty poems) contains the exposition of the dynamics explained above. Though all the poems express the persona's personal vision of the struggle with time and death, four categories can be established, according to the focus:

    1. Infrapersonal: The human being against time.
    2. Intrapersonal: This man against time.
    3. Interpersonal: a. Love poems.
                          b. Poems of literary reference.
    4. Extrapersonal: Society.

1. INFRAPERSONAL

"Camino y capricho eterno" [Eternal road and caprice]

> Detrás se asienta el polvo con certeza,
> y barre toda huella que has dejado.
> Un eco vago vibra del pasado
> Y aviso da que el tiempo con presteza
> al fin te vence, fuga, y no regresa.
> Un campanario se oye alejado
> que llora un ritmo seco y ya cansado;
> y tú con obvio tinte de tristeza,
> con paso incierto hacia un ignoto sueño
> caminas débil, quedo y reducido.
> El sino entonces ciñe y se hace dueño
> de tu alma inerme con aliento herido;
> y sobre sombras cae tu yerto empeño
> de no morir del todo en el olvido.[3]

    Villanueva's dynamics are clear: time defeats the victim's desire to avoid being forgotten in death. The present moment is marked by the bells' steady rhythm and by the man's unsure steps as he walks, weakly, bent in silence. His past erased and his future unsure, the man cannot rise out of anonymity, his soul helpless and breath wounded. Breath is one of Villanueva's key images. This vital life function appears in the book as a soft sound, an audible passing of air that could be turned into a word if the strength, the opportunity, or the will were present. It is a silent sound, or perhaps more specifically a sound of silence, that, though not yet a word, eloquently incarnates meaning. (In "This the Place," analyzed in *OVS*, *moans* and *groans* are added to the nouns of eloquent silence.) We hear the silent voice of an imperiled man and sense that his fate hangs on a more forceful voicing of that silent breath.

The man's effort to avoid oblivion is modified by the adjective *yerto*, which underscores the central conflict with its apparent clarity and underlying ambiguity. It means to be rigid and unmovable due to cold, fear, emotion, or death—hence, defeated effort. However, *yerto*, from the Latin *erectus*, still connotes the erect and firmly vertical, even steadfast and proud. Thus the man's resistance to death is vain, yet firm, in defeat.

The struggle with time focuses on the present moment, reflected in the exclusive use of the present tense; time obliterates the past and obfuscates the future. The "vague echo" only emphasizes the past's invisibility into which the man will disappear if permanence evades him now. His failure is symbolized by the image of fate gripping him, bringing life's end to the present moment. Death usurps life's space. The poem's vision mirrors the process, centripetally drawing to the singular man in one moment, and then centrifugally out to the past and future. Eventually, the eye reaches a distant perspective from which time itself is the only distinguishable entity, the man and his particular series of moments having melded into the undifferentiated totality of the ongoing cycle. That perspective lies in the word *eterno* of the title, which generalizes the poem into a perception of the human existential situation, an example of Villanueva's penchant for titles that expand a poem's meaning.

"Somos un momento" [We are a moment] (p. 23) and
"The Inebriate" (pp. 22–23)

The conflict between time as particular moments and as undifferentiated flow is the theme of "Somos un momento." The moment expands toward the past and future, blurring indistinctly into a mass. The question, however, implicitly arises: how can one hold the moment?—for if *we are a moment*, to accept its disappearance without resistance is to accept our death.

In "The Inebriate" the situation is repeated. Being "a punctual drunk'' blinds the man to a measured succession of repeated actions. He is "the eternal caricature / that / in the dead weight of silence / leans / against the sprawling midnight." *Eternal* again generalizes the experience temporally. *Caricature* also generalizes, while adding anonymity; caricatures feature a type's most generic outlines. It also dehumanizes the drunk. This anonymous figure stands, weighed down by silence, at midnight, time's prototypical dividing moment. The eternally generic is focused in the singular instant. While in stanza 2 the past weighs on the drunk, stanza 3 shifts to the future. The present moment is symbolized in his equilibrium, which chokes on years of labor. The past sickens him, ruining his present, and the future promises the same.

He does protest: "soliloquizes / impromptu obscenities." Yet a soliloquy is a monologue spoken in solitude to oneself, often to give the illusion of unspoken thoughts, as in the theater. Tending more toward silence than speech, it fits perfectly the category of voiced silence. The obscenities, therefore, are not screams of protest. Even in his most intense moment of anguish, the drunk silently waits to disappear into another tomorrow of yesterdays.

"This the Place" and "Forest Lawn Cemetery," discussed in *OVS*, also fall into the infrapersonal category.

2. INTRAPERSONAL

"My Certain Burn toward Pale Ashes" (p. 8)

This poem deserves its place as first in the collection as one of Villanueva's best and also because it exemplifies his dynamics with some of his key imagery. The present is again conveyed through the use of present tense in the first three stanzas; then in stanza 4 the past appears, with a swing through the present into the future coming in the last stanza.

The first three stanzas balance the conflicting elements of flow versus moments within the flow.

> My certain burn
> (a)   toward pale ashes, is told by the
>   hand that whirls the sun; ⌈each⌉
>
> (b)   driving breath beats with the quick
>   pulsing face.

My falling stride
(a)   like sand toward decision,
        drains heavy with fixed age; ⌐each⌐

(b)   ghostly grain a step in time that
        measures tongues.

My ruddy sea
(a)   that streams to dryness, bares
        bewildered its clay bone; ⌐each⌐

(b)   vessel's roar at God's speed drowns
        by force.

Sections *a* contain time images: sun, draining sand, flowing water. The *each* introduces images of the moment: breath, grain, vessel's roar. *Breath* we recognize. *Grains* are points in a flowing-hourglass image of life as undifferentiated past and future on each side of a focal point called *now*. The "measuring tongues" can allude to the moment's dependence for value on verbalization. The *roar* occurs at "God's speed," eternity, an inhuman nontime equivalent to death, within which drown belated expressions of existence.

The present tense in these stanzas generalizes the action temporally, thus suspending the outcome of the conflict. Stanza 4 breaks the equilibrium:

My waking light
    began when the fertile lips spun
    my pulse; and I, with muted tongue,
    was drawn destroyed from the making-
    mouth into this mass.

We plunge into the past, repeating the pulse image from stanza 1; the tongue image from stanza 2; and, with the last two lines, the stream and sea imagery from stanza 3. In addition, the "waking light / began," a birth image, implies an eventual darkening; birth is the start of death. The birth is undermined by its link to day and sun, both time's agents, and by *spun, pulse, muted tongue*, and *drawn destroyed*, which recall time images from above. At the same time, life originates in the instrument of language. The Creator imparted life to the persona through his lips, perhaps by *speaking* him, in the Judeo-Christian tradition: "in the beginning was the word." Life and the word are equated. Yet the Creator's act also *spun a pulse* as one would spin the clock's hands in a race of time, recalling the hand whirling the sun in stanza 1. And the victim's tongue is muted, which destroys him, making him part of an undifferentiated mass. The power of creative speech is exclusively the Creator-Destroyer's; humankind is silenced by life-death.

Stanza 5 swings back to the present and on through to the future.

> And held below
>> by nature, the sweeping hand now
>> turns my dust-bound youth; tell the
>> world that I was struck by the
>> sun's grave plot.

Nature, in league with time, grips the persona—this is a motif of time's oppression. The sweeping-hand image joins that of time (stanza 1) with the hourglass (stanza 2). The last lines ask the reader to announce a message, shifting to an implied future when the act would be completed. Apparently, the message is the poet's demise at the hands of time. However, *struck* is ambiguous, referring also to the persona's realization of the central importance of time's plot against humankind and the need to resist it, to hold the moment, which would necessitate a remedy to the muted tongue. Again a word of apparent clarity and underlying ambiguity, used at a strategic point, subtly reaffirms the central theme of struggle against overwhelming odds.

"El mismo patio" [The same patio] (p. 10)

Though nature and time seem to move hand in hand, Villanueva demonstrates a feeling of nostalgic kinship with certain natural elements. In "El mismo patio," a man sits in a blooming patio, its fresh renewal of life revealing life's linear progression. In contrast, the flowers bloom their *firm essence*, the permanence of their cyclical rebirth emphasizing the man's ephemeral quality, an inversion of the usual values attributed to flowers and human beings. In the end the man looks up to the sky, where we know the sun marks time, while the dazzling grass "abarca todo tiempo y espacio" [embraces all time and space]. Nature transcends our temporal and spatial limits.

Two key words help us understand the poem: *silencio* [silence] and *suspiros* [sighs]. Silence is said to swell in the greenness of the grass, finding a surface in which to express itself. Nature communicates in a nonverbal language, and its message is equated to the child-persona's sighs, strong or prolonged breaths, expressing fatigue, sadness, or, conversely, relief from worry or a burden. The sigh is an eloquent expression not yet a word. Its relation to silence is clear, but the link to childhood is more difficult. The child is to the adult what silence is to the word, a prior essence that should reach expression if allowed to mature freely. The child's sighs resemble nature's silence because the child, like nature, is unaware of the divisive categories of rational thought, such as time, space, and the permanence of death. He is still closer to reborn flowers than to the mature man. He moves through the garden as one with it. The adult persona misses that freedom; with his precious identity to worry about, time becomes a problem, and nature the reminder of it. The passion may be the same, but he never will be.

"Inquietud" [Restlessness] (p. 20)

The next two poems to be discussed share the image of falling leaves as the signifier of change and possible death. In "Inquietud" the persona senses an imminent change in his life because the wind has blown some leaves silently to the ground. As in "Somos un momento," the moment initiates a change now that will only later be completed, and the disturbed persona fears the unknown future. The hourglass image of time (filtering through the persona's wrinkles) is repeated with all its significance. In the last stanza, the sun traitorously withdraws its warmth, and the persona's tree is cold to the roots. Time, he feels, will crystallize in some future moment when it will be too late to affect the outcome. The persona intuits a message from nature, but cannot understand its silent language, which is his own at a point deep within him. The cyclical change in nature means death. The moment slips by in silence.

3. INTERPERSONAL: A. LOVE POEMS

"I Saw the First Leaf Fall" (p. 14)

The sun marks the changing season by snapping the leaf. The poem, however, now assumes the perspective of the message's revelation, when the moment of change is finalized. At the end of stanza 3, we learn that the leaf marked the beginning of the end of a summer love, that died because the lovers' dreams were never voiced—they were left to the future rather than lived in the present. Their "dumb dreams" fling the leaf, which is "hued with a heavy hush." Autumn finds the fallen leaves gathered in a "rustle," a word similar to *breath*, *gasp*, or *moan*. The soft rustle is overwhelmed by the sounds and sense of autumn singing through the stripped trees, mixed with the sun's breath. Time is not silent; its voice is harsh, that of death burying the lost "flameless memory" of love's presence when the persona saw the first leaf fall. We realize the importance of that pivotal moment that was allowed to slip away in silence. Only in retrospect does the persona grasp the need to speak. The poem belatedly attempts to remedy the loss.

In the last three poems discussed, the persona fails to comprehend nature's silent message about the need to live in the present. Perhaps in "El mismo patio" he comes the closest, but he still does not move or speak at the time. Meanwhile, a difference is established between the message that would have awakened him to the present moment, and the voice of oppressive time, which reveals itself only when it is too late. The present moment of life is silent; the present in the grip of death is quite vocal. People, Villanueva seems to say, must not lose touch with the silent language of their own nature, though they must also learn to voice the message.

"Tú (yo)" [You (I)] (p. 13)

We now view love in the present as the man urges his lover to fill the moment before it passes into endless yesterdays. He seeks unity through communication and recognizes the need to act now, but unity is not easily achieved. Space and time impede good intentions, as the grammatical structure shows: "Aquí allá / tú eres yo" [Here and there / you are I]; "Allá y aquí / yo soy tú" [There and here / I am you]. Language itself is divisive, as are the lovers' individual consciousnesses. Love must transcend the separation inherent in the image of the complete poem, proving the unifying quality of poetry's irrational language. Poetry can make language say the ineffable, creating a voice for silence. Transcendence is symbolized in the title: "Tú (yo)," which constitutes a play on words that is completely lost in the English translation "You (I)." Tu (yo) creates the oral offering to the loved one of the persona's self: *tuyo* [yours]. Yet, visually, it maintains the separation of individual personal pronouns. The silent separation is transcended when the poem's *sign* is spoken or heard, but not when it is seen or read.

It is noteworthy that in the interchange between the lovers, the lover gives *confianzas* [confidences], implying the telling of private feelings and thoughts; while the persona offers his *resuellos*. The word comes from a verb meaning to breathe, sometimes with an audible sound, due to such reasons as fatigue. Often used as a synonym for speech, it technically refers only to an unspoken answer, as when a person does not even breathe a reply. Its other use is to refer to making one's presence known after a period of silence. *Resuello* is imbued with silence to an even greater extent than the other terms Villanueva utilizes for the sounds of silence. Most significantly, he attributes this silence to the persona, while asking the loved one to speak.

"Cycle Bound" (p. 11)

The lovers, themselves inert, reflect the love of others as the moon reflects light. The others express their desires in breaths. Love, like time, is a raging, undifferentiated flow that selects particular beings to manifest itself in at the present time. The lovers are one more couple in the anonymous string of lovers, fulfilling the strict cycle of love. As the cycle closes out, the waning light is distorted in the lovers, signifying the change and death of their moment. Yet the light carries "metaphors of reality," reality being love itself that the lovers lived anonymously, rather than personally. Love becomes another element that can be experienced personally or impersonally. The reference to "moon lovers" connotes the cycle as well as silence, and even death. Their love is a distortion, a pale mirror of the real thing.

"Love Taste" (p. 11)

This poem bridges into the literary-reference poems with its use of D. H. Lawrence as a stimulus to love-making. The persona comes into being through reading; literature provides a model for action that responds to the fleetingness of superficial sexual encounters. Unlike the "cheap paper-backs" which sensationalize sex without serious purpose, Lawrence's works explored the erotic as a possible path to spiritual transcendence. Lawrence's search for order in a world devoid of God and traditional socio-religious absolutes mirrors Villanueva's. With respect to time, Lawrence avoided anonymity through his writing; thus he is a positive model in terms of the search for a voice for time's silent victims.

3. INTERPERSONAL: B. POEMS OF LITERARY REFERENCE

"Catharsis" (p. 9)

The persona studies all night for final examinations, caught in the "ritual" of fall and spring. He reads Lorca and Whitman, poets who survive anonymous death through a literary voice. He underlines "paragraphs of future," finding models in the written word.

The morning sun brings the exam day, and the persona "yields to nausea," as time reaffirms its hold. *Catharsis* emphasizes literature's redeeming possibilities, a purification or renewal via the contemplation of art. The persona's nausea could be the product of fearful anticipation of the test when he will have the chance to distinguish a moment as full or let it slip by. The key to success is his understanding of literature, which underscores its function in the creative process of identity.

The references to ritual and catharsis allow us to expand the concept of the time conflict. Ritual is an action designed to make the sacred appear; it is repeated at set times for the benefit of the believers. By transcending linear time with its evocation of a mythical present, it gives life a sense of consistency, projecting order into the past and future. On the one hand, ritual is impersonal in its exact repetition, though the participants change.[4] In that sense, it is like time. Yet, paradoxically, ritual cannot exist without the individual. A particular body must become the sacrificial object for the ritual to be visible. The body makes the impersonal into a particular, visible event capable of cathartic intensity. This duality of focus in ritual is like that inherent in the moment and the word itself. Consciously or not, Villanueva affirms that to distinguish the moment is to ritualize the present—time and the individual harmonize for the cathartic benefit of the people and the individual. Ritual would render time's flow meaningful. It requires the voicing of a ritual code for the participants, one denied by the silence of life's victims. However, ritual and catharsis appear here in direct reference to literature, implying that literature can be the redeeming voice of the silent ones. The voice is equated to sperm ("This the Place"), desire, and birth, so literature could be the fertilizing agent for the people, their creator. This brief excursion into ritual reveals a key factor in Villanueva's dynamics.

"Antes de acostarme" [Before going to bed] (p. 24)

In a variation of the gripping-time motif, the persona's wristwatch strangles the pulse. Life's inner time battles exterior mechanical time. The skin becomes another of those zones of personal expression or impersonal surrender. The persona has been reading at night again, this time the Apocalypse and Dylan Thomas, as well as answering letters and listening to the radio. The news features an assault on an old man, the 365 Holy-Week fatalities in Vietnam, and rain for the next day. At exactly 3:34 A.M. the persona yields to nausea. The focus of time has revealed the absurdity of life. The enumeration of his actions and the news reflect the absurdity in that there is no qualitative order to the elements. Moreover, in the enumeration the persona's personal expression is limited to answering letters, a weak secondary expression greatly overshadowed by the other voices. The nausea with which the poem ends emphasizes the persona's silence in the face of different possible modes of expression. Time has won, controlling the moment.

4. EXTRAPERSONAL

"Antes de acostarme" began a shift toward the fourth category, in which the focus is on society in two specific areas of international activity: space exploration and war. Villanueva can catch society at its best or worst; the following poems swing from one extreme to another, but at both extremes the judgment is negative.

"Redeemed" (pp. 16–17)

This celebration of the moon landing treats the flight as a possible turning point in history toward a new reality, symbolized by the Sea of Tranquillity. Therefore, the moment appears twice, once in earth time and then in flight duration time. Yet, with all the sincere admiration for triumphant humankind on the surface, there is an undermining irony.

Villanueva isolates the moon walk from earthly reality. The sun is not up *yet*, indicating a suspension of time's flow; but it will come, and with it the usual order of things. References to television and Buck Rogers frame the walk, lending it a tinsel, filmland unreality. The astronauts are "far from taxed humanity" on a "plaster of Paris moon." The trip creates a sense of unity on earth, "a mood international"; but in the end, the crew returns to "old reality" of "Mother Earth / and / private love," implying the rapid dissipation of the unity. The ultimate criticism is related to time. By listing two types of time, the poet places the event both in and out of this world. Duration time has no earthly specificity, while the earth time is given in Eastern Daylight Savings, an artificial time itself. Thus a moment of great achievement is both ambiguous and unnatural in relation to humanity.

"Live, Die, and Live" (pp. 18–19)

Time and the sun sink and decay at "a dying man's pace" in the Vietnam war. The sounds of death overpower life, while men become just numbers in casualty books. Not even the dove of peace can speak. In the last stanza the sounds of society mourning the victims are heard. Yet in the midst of all this noise, the voice of the victims only manages a halting question voiced by the poet: ". . . But . . . why? . . ." The silent ones have spoken, and the reply is the only one possible—silence, for no words can explain the pointless waste of war.

"Peace Talks" (p. 12)

Again, the oppressors control sound and the word. While prisoners suffer, negotiating diplomats, dreaming of promotions, turn words into meaningless promises, verbs into false sounds, and the voice into an abyss. The stagnant air fills with invented, therefore incomprehensible, languages. The title ironically contrasts with the poem, because the last thing that *talks* at the peace talks is peace. It is the silence lost in the noise.

In these last two poems, humanity has been divided into classes —the oppressors and the victims, the former taking on the characteristics of time and death; the latter, that of humankind in the previous poems. The oppressor controls sound and the word, though they are empty; and he holds silent humanity-the-victim in his death grip.

In section I the poet has identified with the silent victims of time and society. Those victims are the silent ones who express themselves with sighs, gasps, breaths, groans, and silence itself. The battle between the person and time / death concentrates on strategic points, which can be won or lost according to the expression of life. The moment must become a ritual of particular identity, expressed in the voice of silence, not in meaningless noise.

II. Pausas de ayer y hoy [Pauses of yesterday and today]

With the conflicting elements clearly set forth, Villanueva pauses to consider his role in the world. He shifts from a general human vision to a consciously poetic one, beginning with a poem in which he states that his chosen role is that of a poet. The section is divided into the days of the week and becomes a rite of passage, a maturing process from which he will emerge into the world to practice his art. His use of *pauses* in the title could be explained by Ramón Xirau's commentary on musical pauses. "There exists a silence that musicians call pause. Interval between word and word, phrase and phrase, gesture and gesture, this silence is not yet essence-silence, even when it can become the *expression* of an essential silence. And it is not because the pause derives from a silence which is incarnated in the words itself. The pause expresses silence, but it is not the flesh of silence."[5] Villanueva's pause, between opening and closure, arises from the silence inherent in his poetic dynamics, a resonant pause, vibrant with the poetry which surrounds and forms it—it is the image of eloquent silence.

(Sunday) "The Process of Myself" (p. 28)

The poet has a means of *becoming*: to lose himself in the "duration" of poetic images, in literary space, outside of worldly time. His being originates in silence, the state prior to the word. Writing is a "desperate game of discovery" in which words and sounds compete. In finding the word, "illusions become real." But the image receives the emphasis: "To think in images is to be mature." Maturity connotes an ordering of one's existence, while the image renders time meaningful, ritualizes it; thus, poetry asserts one's existence. "Myself" and "I" frame the poem in solid personal expression.

(Lunes) [Monday] "Sentir" [To feel] (p. 28)

Time is; one feels it and carries it with one, as a blind man wears a handless wristwatch (death's gripping hand). There is no escape, not even in blindness.

(Martes) [Tuesday] "Autolaberinto" [Autolabyrinth] (p. 29)

A jailed man requests a dictionary and Borges' stories. Borges, ever preoccupied by time and existence, is a metaphor of Villanueva. In "The New Refutation of Time," Borges abolishes time through logical discourse, and counterposes an atemporal ideal world, as Villanueva could do at this point. Yet Borges' essay ends with a painful declaration that is at the heart of Villanueva's evocation of him. "*And yet, and yet*. . . . Time is the substance I am made of. Time is a river which sweeps me along, but I am the river; it is a tiger which destroys me, but I am the tiger; it is a fire which consumes me, but I am the fire. The world, unfortunately, is real; I, unfortunately, am Borges."[6] Borges incarnates modern humanity's best refutation of time, a direct reply to "Sentir," while ironically denying any escape.

(Miércoles) [Wednesday] "Espera" [Hope] (p. 29)

Unable to refute time, the poet falls into a silent impasse. A predawn fog engulfs both the poet's fingers and the modern towers of Babel, the skyscrapers, while the poet waits for a new day. Time's agent, the sun, will burn away the amorphous transcendence and reveal the persistent conflict.

(Thursday) "The Space of Death" (p. 30)

A concise statement of the essential dynamics shatters the impasse.

> Let's imagine in our own space,
> and how we go dying
> at every
> instant.
> With time, Death becomes so boring.
> But it's the shock of each moment,
> the anonymous screams
> that go undying—
> only to brace ourselves again.

Life is a dying at each instant; but in time's flow, "every" is drawn to infinity—such a distant perspective makes death not fearful, but boring. To the infinite *every* is opposed the particular *each*; to *boring* is opposed the horror of disappearance. "Anonymous screams" are a permutation of the "vessel's roar" image of belated protest from "My Certain Burn." Life must be a constant living, as if death were *now*; each moment requires full expression.

(Viernes) [Friday] "Nevadas en Buffalo, Nueva York"
[Snowfall in Buffalo, New York] (p. 31)

Words spread across the page to create the visual image of a snowfall. The snow desires to return to the sky to avoid the sun's destructive heat. After the "Space of Death," the poem may seem trivial, but it creates a literary space in which time's flow is held to preserve beauty. Death cannot be denied—and the poem includes it —but poetry can open spaces for life to manifest itself in its beauty, beauty made more significant by juxtaposition with imminent death. This is a ritualization of the world.

(Saturday) "Of Age" (p. 32)

Like a prophet from the desert, Villanueva emerges from the meditative pause. He holds onto his "unspoken silence," because it is the origin of his art and the common sign tying him to oppressed people. Yet "unspoken" implies "spoken silences," prefiguring his poetic voice. The personal and social seemed to compete for his art; but he steps into the world, indicating his decision to enter the social area of conflict. He affirms the poet's social responsibility, while intending to make his personal life into a social project for his people. The two no longer compete, but fuse in the next section.

III. Mi Raza

The six poems—two in each category: Pachucos, migrant workers, individual rebels—share the common theme of Chicano struggle against the forces of society and life. Nothing changes in the dynamics, though the content is now obviously ethnic; but the victims of life finally voice their resistance. However, the oppressor still controls words. When society's victims, the silent ones, protest, they do so with the voice of silence. This may change, as indicated in two poems; but in the end, Villanueva reaffirms his commitment to the silent ones as their voice.

1. PACHUCOS

"Pachuco Remembered" (pp. 40–41)

Pachucos,[7] depicted as precursors of the Chicano Movement, employed nonverbal methods of resistance: a knife; distinctive styles of dress, hair, clothes, walking and standing; consistent defiance of school rules. High school principals, recognizing their threat, attacked them; their voices ring violently clear in the poem: " 'Take those taps off!' 'Speak English damn it!' 'Button up your shirt!' 'When did you last cut your hair?' 'Coach, give this punk 25 licks!' " The Pachucos held firm, "Emotion surging silent on your stoic tongue." Anglo principals replace time as the oppressors. Schools become a metaphor for assimilative death in which conformity is imposed; self-expression is limited by the need to be anonymous to survive. The Pachucos, however, are remembered because they once made an eloquent, though silent, statement.

"Aquellos vatos" [Those dudes] (pp. 42–43)

In "To a Dead Lowrider," Navarro asks if one remembers the Pachuco,[8] and Villanueva answers in "Aquellos vatos." "Simón [yes], / we knew him," the poem begins, with a Pachuco slang term of affirmation opening its space, followed by a plural verb to generalize the voice's representational value. The knowledgeable, familiar tone leads us to believe that the speaker is a Pachuco; therefore, the subculture is remembering itself. This is entirely consonant with Villanueva's decision not to sing his own concerns, but to make his poetry the expression of the forgotten. Following the initial affirmation appears an enumeration of Pachucos, each with his animal nickname—Caballo [Horse], Chiva [Goat], and so on—and a quick characterization in animal terms. Conejo [Rabbit] had women everywhere; Bear was always polishing his Cat's Paw shoes, like a bear licking its paws. Each one is depicted in his own terms.

One Pachuco, however, is almost forgotten. The persona states, "I don't recall" him. Nevertheless, since it does not serve the poet's purpose to eliminate him without explaining why he merits oblivion, the persona adds a dubious epithet of rescue: "they tell me he was / a chavalón que se curaba con las gabas" [a kid who fooled around with Whites]. Obscurity is justified by the accusation of cultural betrayal, while his presence is relegated to hearsay information.

"Aquellos vatos" might have been a simple response to forgetfulness through mere enumeration and evocation, had Villanueva not transformed it into a conflict between different cultural codes of life perception, and essentially a poem about language in which the language and the poem's space become conflictive. The vital, aesthetic code of the Pachuco subculture, in which language and dress are used to enliven one's environment, is counterposed to the rational, cold, dull, and restrictive code of the Anglo American culture, as represented in the school system, one of Villanueva's —and the Chicano Movement's—favorite whipping boys. As in "To a Dead Lowrider" there are different ways to view a bull, in "Aquellos vatos" there are opposing codes for animals. In the last stanza the persona speculates about what has happened to the Pachucos.

> They're probably married by now
> those cats,
> and their kids try to comprehend culture and
> identity by reading "See Spot. See Spot run,"
> and by going to the zoo on a Greyhound bus with
> Miss Foxx

The school system, Villanueva's image of forced assimilation, imposes its own code of animal signification. Animal life is reduced to abstracts, restricted to cages by the school, while the Pachuco's animal code is depicted as vital, immediate experience. Moreover, the former isolates humans from nature, as if they were not part of the animal world, while the latter harmonizes humans into a total animal world. At the same time, this is a conflict between the school's written language and the Chicano community's oral tradition. And these codes of language (culture) dispute the future, the children. Which will predominate?

The poem may seem an ambiguous response in its apparent

abrogation of the future to the school. The children are steeped in the other code; they try to find identity in and through it. However, the last stanza states the threat which must be responded to; that is to say, the poem contains its own catalyst and reason for existence. It is the response to the threat it states itself. The vital animal code, usually found only in the oral tradition, is transposed into written media, to stand and compete with the Anglo American code. The poem challenges the dominance of the latter within the area, written language, so long closed to a Chicano presence. The Chicano oral culture is rescued by writing it. However, to write it, though necessary, is a betrayal of sorts, since it goes against its oral nature. Villanueva responds by making the persona a Pachuco and the language conversational. Actually, Villanueva turns the poem over to his persona, ceding his voice and his space to the Pachuco, who in ''Pachuco Remembered'' was silent. In this fashion, Villanueva stages the cultural struggle within the poem's framework; and the Chicano, though apparently losing on the anecdotal level, with its social reference, wins the battle for the poem, capturing the aesthetic level. The poem, which is the Pachuco's voice, convinces through its success as an aesthetic object; and at the same time, it infiltrates the system which threatens its source.

2. MIGRANT WORKERS

''Day-Long Day'' (pp. 38–39)

The migrant is locked into an unalterable life dictated by time: ''Third generation timetable.'' The sun beats unmercifully; the boss blends with the sun, and time's voice rings clear: ''I wanna bale a day, and the boy here / don't haf'ta go to school.'' The elders dream of escape for the children, but they ironically place their hopes in the school system which rejects them in other poems. However, it is significant that the elders speak their minds instead of remaining silent. We are approaching a voice, though the mother still *moans* her lament, a verb similar to *breathe, gasp, sigh,* and *resollar* in its quality of silence.

''Que hay otra voz'' (pp. 34–37)

''Hay otra voz que quiere hablar'' [There is another voice that wants to speak]. Locked into the circuit, the farm worker wonders where he is going. As a transient he is rooted between *el ser y el estar,* indicating his total alienation from society. *Ser* is the verb *to be* for essence: *estar,* that of location; he is neither, and no change is foreseen. Yet migrants seek a different future. The children in school ask for *pencils with a future*, because another voice wants to speak. But the school rejects them again.

In the last stanza, change occurs: a shout rings out from the United Farm Workers. Like Elizondo and Méndez, Villanueva attributes the first sign of the Chicano Movement to César Chávez' union. This first shout blares, echoing with the sounds of silence that preceded it.

3. INDIVIDUAL REBELS

"Chicano Is an Act of Defiance" (pp. 45–46)

The poem is dedicated to Rubén Salazar, a Chicano reporter killed during an antiwar demonstration in 1970.[9] Salazar's memory *survives* death because his shout—his use of media to state his ethnicity —remains, a historical proof of Villanueva's message. Ironically, Salazar still must be saved by the poem.

"Escape" (p. 44)

Villanueva dedicates the poem to his grandfather, a watch repairman who dedicated his life to the instrument that measures time. Villanueva has established the watch's negativity with the gripping-death motif. Yet while living in the jaws of death the grandfather is miraculously unaware of time's flow. He sets the springs to the beat of his pulse, in contrast to the image of the springs squeezing the persona's pulse in "Antes de acostarme." With his magnifying glass, he holds seconds, expanding them beyond their allotted space—the way poetic images do in "The Process of Myself." The grandfather humanizes and personalizes time instead of submitting to it. He dies, as all men do, but the last image is of his visible wrists. No watch grasped or hushed his pulse; he won the battle against time and remains visible in death. Villanueva seems to say that, even in the most dangerous situation, one can assert one's personal identity. It is highly significant that the only words the grandfather speaks are the question "What time is it?"—asked punctually, as if time depended on his concern for its existence. At the same time, the question emphasizes his independence from it.

The title does not mean that the grandfather ran from time, but that he escaped anonymity by ritualizing time into a human element. He is the most memorable individual in the book. One feels that he, much more than Lorca, Whitman, Dylan Thomas, or (certainly) Salazar, is the poet's model. Silently he forged an enduring image; yet, again, we know him only through the voice of poetry.

Conclusion

Confronted by a world of empty words, realizing that his people have been silently anonymous, Villanueva finds a voice between meaningless sounds and silence. His poetry is *unspoken silence* now written, but still essentially silent. It becomes the language of ritual for his people; in it they begin to transform into themselves. But always Villanueva is faithful to his silent origin, hence, his reticence. He speaks in metaphors, often hermetic, though always consistent. He employs ambiguities on many levels. He expresses through images, because they communicate with life's original silence. If his poetry feels soft, quiet, it is because like silence it can seem to disappear if one does not listen closely, silently. He does not wish to outshout the world. Yet his poetry is consistent, firm, enduring.

Finally, I will quote what I have written elsewhere regarding the book's general structure as the *ars poetica* of the author:

> The structure of the whole assumes an hourglass shape. The personal, though general, Section I narrows into the compressed space of Section II, draining through individual temporal units, highly magnified under the poetic lens, and then bursts out into Section III on La Raza. Section II is the battleground, and like the cadaver ["This the Place"] the poet can represent a single personal body, or the impersonal surface of totality. He chooses to be both at once and seeks to maintain the state of tension between them. His writing will be, on the one hand, an impersonal space, so that his people can speak through him. Hence the language becomes interlingual in Section III, while in prior sections the usage is bilingual.[10] Hence, too, quoted speech—the words of other speakers—appears more and more often in III, underlying the poet's effort to become a more than personal voice, even to the extent of completely yielding "Aquellos vatos" to a Pachuco's voice, which then quotes still another Pachuco. On the other hand, the writing remains his own particular voice, so that a carrier for the other voices can be assured. In this extremely precarious equilibrium between the personal and the communal, between silence and the word, Villanueva carves out his position as the other voice of silence. (*OSV*, p. 140)

Paradigm Charts

	LIFE	vs.	DEATH

SYMBOLIC
Threat: ~~Memorable existence.~~ ⟵ Dead silence.

↓

Rescue: Images of the lives of
the forgotten.

↓

Response: Book as a voice of ⟶ ~~Dead silence.~~
and for the forgotten,
preserved as
memorable life,
though silent.

SOCIAL
Threat: ~~Chicano existence.~~ ⟵ Voices of imposed
assimilation and ex-
ploitation.

↓

Rescue: Chicano life images.

↓

Response: Book as a voice of af- ⟶ ~~Alien voices.~~
firmation of existence
and resistance.

PERSONAL
Threat: ~~Human fulfillment~~ ⟵ Time, death, and
~~within a social con-~~ silence; poet as
~~text.~~ escapist.

↓

Rescue: Images of personal
confrontation with
time and death, and
of social responsibili-
ty.

↓

Response: Book as a breaking of ⟶ ~~Time, death, silence,~~
silence, as poet's ~~and escapism.~~
duration as an image,
as the declaration of
social responsibility.

8. A VOICE AGAINST SILENCE
Ricardo Sánchez

Silence knows no history.
—George Steiner, *After Babel*, p. 24

Silence is also essential to Ricardo Sánchez. Against the threat of exclusion by a silent world, he shouts loudly for attention. Like Villanueva, he refuses to go unnoticed, or let his people become society's forgotten; but, unlike Villanueva's, his voice is anything but quiet. A *song and shout* of his freedom he called his first book.[1] Silence—the world's or his own—is the enemy.

His writing originates in "Soledad," in the "sheer feeling of aloneness," of "identity's lost," of prison (*Canto y grito mi liberación* [*CG*], pp. 27–29). To prison's degradation is added the abandonment by the outside world, his friends, and relatives: "no one seems to give a damn" (*CG*, p. 45); "Two years / and you sent me four letters" (*CG*, p. 76); "i made hectic love with my wife . . . still trying to bring about a redress for the emptiness of prison" (*CG*, p. 83). Returning home, he encounters "frigidity and indifference" (*CG*, p. 77): no one will employ him; or if he finds a job, his parole officer gets him fired. Eventually, he is forced to wander the country, working here, receiving a grant there, reading his poetry at universities, teaching at others, never in one place long, returning intermittently to El Paso. And always he takes a prisoner's consciousness with him, seeing and writing about society as a massive prison for all human beings.

Reading Sánchez' writings, one wonders if anything outside of himself—and perhaps a small circle of relatives and close friends—is positive. From the prisoner's perspective, the world is hostile and dehumanizing, rigidly limiting human fulfillment; modern culture propagates anomie on all its participants, mainstream or marginal.[2] Hence Sánchez' vituperation of the bourgeoisie and the rich as vacuous beings amid their material goods; hence his importuning of the marginal to actively seek change. He insists that the latter suffer more because society relegates them to invisibility—"an unswerving

/ monster called / social obscurity"; "i boil inside / knowing full well the consequence / of inconsequential existence" (*CG*, p. 115). The threat produces what Sánchez calls his *schizoid self*. "I looked toward past, toward school authorities, and in return they looked down at me. I looked inwardly—but i really hated being me, for my eyes were brown, my hair black and my voice modulated sing-song accents that did not meet the criteria set by gringo society" (*CG*, p. 151). Society's definition of values produces self-hatred. As in other Chicano works, school is the Other's space. As profane society's agent, school teaches conformity; and without an opposing center of self-definition, one is lost in chaos. "The profane experience," Eliade says, ". . . maintains homogeneity and hence the relativity of space. No *true* orientation is now possible, for the fixed point no longer enjoys a unique ontological status."[3] Sánchez would probably agree, insisting that everyone in modern society suffers to some extent the same malaise.

Chicano literature, in great part, attempts to fix a unique ontological center for Chicanos. Yet, though Sánchez would accept that Chicanos can resist anomie through traditions of "humanhood" and survival, he sees that Chicano resistance and protest follow another tradition, that of being "mainly an unvoiced protest / indictment" (*CG*, p. 32). Chicanos avoid confrontation by retreating to the barrio, considered by many writers, and nonwriters, both a type of walled city which keeps the Others at a distance, and a *fixed point of true orientation*. Sánchez again agrees, to an extent; but his prisoner's perspective prevails, and the barrio looms as a permutation of the prison image: isolation and distance, but at the mercy of the ubiquitous jailer.

"Homing" (*HechizoSpells* [*H*], pp. 144–148), Sánchez' version of Raúl Salinas' "A Trip through the Mind Jail," treats both his barrio in El Paso and The Barrio as literary images. The poem comments on Chicano symbols and ideals, as it explores Sánchez' existential / literary orientation.

The poem (containing 207 lines) has a seemingly superfluous introduction (lines 1–43) to the main subject matter, the poet's old barrio. Further on we will understand that it is inextricably related to the main body, while purposefully set off.

The repetition of the words *Homing* (lines 1, 34, 44, 57) and *cruise* (12, 45) creates a centering movement to the origin of being. And since the home is a microcosmos, we can expect to be privileged with Sánchez' world vision through its recreation.

As early as line 46, we are advised that the barrio is "crumbling ruins." Self-destruction is evoked in barrio youths who "used to slice up life and hope" and escaped with heroin, because "life is hell / within poverty & self-hate." True to his anti-idealism, Sánchez leads us home through hell—ruins, wasted lives, and death. The home itself is a mere *skeleton*, a bleached-bones image in stark contrast to the "blueridged veins . . . brown flesh" of the heroin addicts mentioned a few lines earlier, and at the same time the image of their fate. Life has been, and is still being, annihilated; and, as in Salinas' "Trip," the implications are shaking. However, there is not the same urgency, because the introductory verses show the poet among family and friends; this trip begins from the continuity of life, despite destruction of the *axis mundi*. We are here to understand the why and wherefore of survival amid chaos.

The poet associates himself with the house—"that home that saw me grow / at 3920 Oak, later avenida de las américas." By placing himself between *home* and the address, he locks himself into the structure; as his witness and the refuge of the "voices of the past," it can reveal his origins. We are asked to "listen closely" to receive answers to our questions.

The reader hears a tale of constant efforts to break out of a series of limiting brackets. Death images frame the home—heroin and La Llorona, abductress of wayward children.[4] La Llorona is located by "algodonales del ayer" [yesterday's cottonfields]: thus heroin and La Llorona, metonymically linked through the color, form a white-death frame. Both are exterior forces which the Chicanos interiorize, the first through injection, the second through cultural symbolism. They mirror each other, though one is Mexican and traditional, and the other (apparently) U.S. urban and contemporary. Both symbolize death for the wayward.

La Llorona haunts rivers, introducing the Río Grande and locating the barrio on the Mexican / U.S. border—it is a microcosm of Chicano space, an international zone. Sánchez emphasizes the *inter*-countries image when his memories drift to an island, to which he and his friends used to escape to dance freely to *Chicano* music, a geographically *between* space and an image of defensive isolation. Once Mexican, it passed to the United States in the Chamizal border adjustment in the 1960's. Even land is subject to national whims, and barrio youths are caught between two countries that can decide their fate and invade their *island* with impunity. This exchange reminds one of the similar change in the home's address: the street went from Oak to Avenida de las Américas. The poet's typically cynical irony is at work; what seems a balanced exchange is anything but. The Chamizal Treaty was heralded as a return of land to Mexico, but here the island has been taken by the United States, though its name remains the same. In the address change, only the names are altered, going from a simple, strong, monosyllabic English noun to a hyperbolic, idealistic Spanish phrase with connotations of the debunked U.S. Panamericanism of the Good Neighbor Policy. The poet comments, thus, on the Chicano framework of delusion with respect to land ownership and imperialism, creating two supporting images for the death frame of Heroin / Llorona. The three frames are metonymically joined through the river, shared by La Llorona and the island, and the Spanish language shared by all three. And in the center stands the home, encapsulating the poet.

Yet he persists in escaping. Sánchez creates a concentration-camp effect: "we used to slip over or under the fence"; and later, "we used to slip through the fence." Whether entering or leaving, the youths escaped into music, dancing, marijuana, food, and sex. But escapades signal danger, because La Llorona stalks wayward children. This introduces the poem's longest segment (lines 90–140) and the character of Doña Chuyita.

First reaction to Chuyita associates her with La Llorona. A centenarian hag, with brown, wrinkled, clawing hands, and "dark stained bits of teeth," she chased the boys, daring them to stop. But unlike La Llorona, she let them go. The superimposition is purposeful. La Llorona's metamorphosis into Chuyita represents the confronted and humanized threat, the transformation of traditional fear into traditional strength. Chuyita's concrete reality (brown earth and hawklike eyes) contrasts with the superstition's whiteness and invisibility. The two women share Mexican tradition; but whereas La Llorona is fear, limitation, restriction to the old, Chuyita is movement, freedom, adaptability. She tells "stories / of life in those mountains / when there existed no cars, / just burros and tired people / who knew how to dance and sing / and live off the land." Her fearful mouth is the door to the Chicanos' past, the *patarrajada* [poor and ragged] Indian ancestors Sánchez opposes to the Aztec-Mayan nobility of some other Chicano writers. In her stories of a nontechnological world, the people lived harmoniously with nature, humanly, but not ideally (though a bit romantically); an alternative image to modern chaos. Yet Chuyita is in the city, surviving with dignity—she can adapt.

She also teaches the lesson of honesty. Chuyita catches the boy-poet smoking and asks if his father knows; he lies, saying maybe. When Chuyita refuses a bribe for her silence, the boy fears disclosure. She calms him by saying that anything done in the open is not a secret. The lesson takes: live openly and you have nothing to fear from revelation, and, thus, nothing to escape from.

The flashback ended, the present barrio is an archeological site "full of shards." An old Mitchell's Beer can bespeaks another ingested poison, an escapist liquid drug, itself a limitation. Chuyita's lesson begins to clarify the poem—escapism imprisons. The can is found next to the "crumbling wall / of that home my father had painstakingly built"; poison besieged the walls of the *axis mundi*.

As shards do, the can sends the poet back in time. The house repeats the expansive movement beyond limits, going from one room to several, then out to the cinderblock wall. The poet grows along: four years old to eight, and finally to military age, only to be brought back to the same edge through the image of his dead brothers, who used to sit on the wall, playing guitar and singing. The passage is devastating. The father's handbuilt home and his sons are both reduced to dead remains, introduced by the beer-can *shard*. Moreover, this home resembled Chuyita's images of hard work, harmony, and joy; what could have gone wrong?

A glance at the sequence shows that the wall and the beer can form frames. Life's expansion ends in the limiting structure and death, represented here by the can. In Chuyita's ideal world there was no technology; the barrio, however, is controlled by technological products. The wall itself was made of cinderblocks, a mass-produced, modern material; the can represents consumerism and liquid drugs. The wall, meant to keep out danger, represented the threat in its substance. In other words, provincial utopia, when transported into the Chicanos' technological environment, becomes an impossible dream. The limiting forces are everywhere, and Chicanos interiorize them. In Chuyita's world there was no mention of walls, nor of threats that make them necessary. Sánchez creates a subtle, yet deadly image of contradictions within the Chicano life style that mirrors the conflict of modern life. The house truly has proved a microcosm of the *imago mundi*.

The present reappears, and the poet has once again returned to his home town, to "a barrio dead." The poet now must reside in the "alien worlds" of other barrios and is no longer blind to the barrio's susceptibility to the world. There follows another image of bracketing death. In a devastating image vis-à-vis the Mexicanism of so much Chicano literature, the home is looted by Mexicans from Juárez, who take "any goddamn thing that can be marketed"; while on the other side a superhighway is being built. Between the two, the barrio's old order crumbles. The poet focuses on the house's epicenter, the "doorframe / from what used to be the doorway to our kitchen," the familial nurturing room, a traditional cosmic axis.[5] Its disappearance "cut my soul / and severed forever / my linkage to my barrio." By what mythology tells us, he should be cast into chaos; but his reaction is ambiguous:"[I] realized / that barrios must make way for progress." Then, as he leaves "to file another parole report," he hears "soft voices of the past . . ." To understand this calm ending in the face of chaos, we must return to the beginning.

In the three introductory stanzas, a new *axis mundi* is established. Stanza 1, with such words as *amidst, embraces, hovering over*, is a family reunion. The mother hovers over "her returned children," like escapees from La Llorona. The home's essence is love, not a material space. The mistake was to synonymize *house* and *home*, a tendency for interlingual Chicanos, who know that in Spanish *casa* is both. But if we reread, we find that from the start, between home and its location was the poet's human *me*. Without that presence it becomes a skeleton. But any house can become a home, even in the "alien worlds" of other barrios. In truth, as he travels through another barrio, we see that it is the same as his, with the destructive forces at play. To recognize the barrio as *alien* is to see it with enlightened eyes, the prisoner's eyes for which all the world can be a trap.

With friends he founds a Chicano publishing house—a new home, a new *axis mundi* from which chaos will be ordered anew, changing "the horrid imagery / that has ever haunted us" (lines 32–33). Creating positive Chicano images becomes the new centering love act. Ironically, the poem is full of horrid images; change does not mean escape. One confronts reality, like Chuyita, and turns fear into strength. This new family is "the nether world / of causa [the cause]" (lines 35–36). Like veterans of a war, they regroup underground. The family has survived, the new house / home has been founded, and a cosmicising principle has been found in writing. Order is renewed, which explains the poet's calm acceptance of the barrio's destruction. It has *made way for progress*, Chicano progress. The barrio's negativity must be left behind; the positive, like Chuyita's lessons, rescued. The latter are the soft voices the poem leaves suspended (suspension points end the poem) in literature. There, too, is the conflict between forces, because life will never be free of conflict—that is, if it is not escapism. The poet utilizes Chuyita's lesson of not hiding.

To emphasize non-escapism the poet introduces the parole officer, another exterior threat. At the end the poet must pay him his due by writing a report. The liberating activity, writing, also links him to prison. This is not strange, because the vision developed in prison has helped him see more clearly that his barrio was always a conflictive space of imprisonment and escape and reimprisonment. He actually has been a prisoner all his life. Realizing it allows him to live in joy despite the parole officer. Life is a constant struggle with limitations. Returning to his origins has taught him that there is no escape, but there is survival and self-order.

This world vision imbues all of Sánchez' work. The scope may expand, but death and human life are the basic antinomies. At a national level, "Death is Amerika. . . . The ultimate tragedy must be to have lived furtively, never to have protested nor raised one's voice and never having been in defense of human-ness" (*H*, pp. 26–27). At the international level: "Seeing the Chicano struggle within a broader scope, as part of a global push for human liberation . . . realizing that we, too, must participate creatively and thoughtfully, I find myself propelled to write and write and write" (*H*, p. xv). And at a universal level: "To live is to define one's humanity within the . . . humanity of one's people and to have sought a universal thread with all humanity with one's particularized expression of human-ness" (*H*, p. 27). The response is constant—writing, to express himself and his people. "And i strive only to express myself / in order to determine my own course . . . / and this then is my aloneness, / my being confronted by a vacuum / and / I write of my people—LA RAZA." (*CG*, pp. 55–56).

His people's everyday life must be expressed loudly through him. He is the microcosm of the Chicano Movement (*CG*, p. 152). So he writes his life—reaching back past prison to an even more fundamental experience of entrapment—in the style of the Pachuco. Pachucos believe that if they can stake a claim—scribble a *placa*, or personal graffito—on a surface, it is theirs. Sánchez fills pages with his activities, fictionalizing, creating, verbalizing himself, his friends and enemies, his surroundings in hope that they will transcend fleeting time. Even if one manages to humanize the world, life itself is ephemeral. The ultimate silence is death, that takes all equally: "all victims victimizing each other; seeking answer and respite for and from the basic insecurity of man—short span of life that goes puff before one knows" (*CG*, p. 159).

Sánchez responds by asserting himself in a more lasting space—the written word: his life as literature; his voice as more than the traditional quiet retreat into isolation. He will be heard; he must be remembered. One wonders, however, at his faith, considering his cynical image of the fate of the *placa*. Upon viewing graffiti on tenement walls, he comments, "I smiled at all the different bids for eternity and immortality made by unknown people of the night; pachucos, sensing the loss and hurt of their humble yet rebellious lives, striving to impress their names and histories on crumbling tenement walls, hoping against hope that somehow these same walls would last and become the eighth wonder of a society falling apart at the seams all around them" (*CG*, p. 103). Even the wall built by Sánchez' father was destroyed by and for progress.

Sánchez seeks to inscribe himself in the written language and tradition of the society he pictures as chaotic, hopeful that his voice will survive, though mindful of the futility of relying on others and the eventual destruction of the page itself. Dreams fade, *axes mundi* are looted, and publishing houses go broke, as did the one Sánchez and his friends founded. No escape, just constant conflict.

Sánchez writes so much because the act of writing, not the product, cosmicizes his life. While he writes, he lives; while he talks, there is no silence. Perhaps someone will read it.

Yet one gets—I get—the impression of insecurity, of over-compensation in the boisterous assuredness—of fear of silence. Sánchez fills every possible space. His books contain several introductions; poems are prefaced, annotated, explicated, and introduced, as well as dated and located in place. It is as if he were filling an empty wall with graffiti, and any empty place is a lack of existence, a dangerous silence.[6] The next moment may thrust him back into Soledad, as devastated as his barrio. As long as he writes, he forestalls the eventual silence. But there is no escape, and as his writing tied him to the parole officer, it also ties him directly to the enemy waiting after each period.

Paradigm Charts (of Sánchez' Work in General)

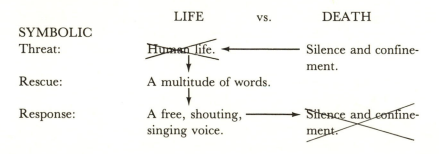

	LIFE	vs.	DEATH
SYMBOLIC Threat:	~~Human life.~~ ⟵		Silence and confinement.
Rescue:	A multitude of words. ↓		
Response:	A free, shouting, singing voice. ⟶		~~Silence and confinement.~~

	LIFE	vs.	DEATH

SOCIAL
Threat: ~~Communal order and purpose.~~ ←——— Exploitation and alien values limit movement and destroy a sense of cosmic order, chaos.

Rescue: Tradition of human values and survival; images of negative traits to be eliminated.

Response: Writing as creation ——→ ~~Chaos.~~ of new *axis mundi*.

PERSONAL
Threat: ~~Human existence.~~ ←——— World's and his own silence.

Rescue: Images of the writer living a meaningful life for and with his community.

Response: Writing as a constant ——→ ~~Silence.~~ forestalling of silence; a never-resting voice.

9. RITUALS OF DEVASTATION AND RESURRECTION
Bernice Zamora

L'intimité est la violence . . . Si l'on décrit l'individu dans l'opéra-
tion du sacrifice, il se définit par l'angoisse.
—Georges Bataille, *Théorie de la religion*, p. 69[1]

Having been born into a family that can trace its presence in
Southern Colorado and New Mexico back some two centuries; having grown up among rural, traditional people who practiced the
centuries-old religious rites of the Penitentes and treated land as
sacred, it is no wonder that Bernice Zamora would preoccupy herself
with the state of the cultural spirit. That it, like the spiritual condition of modern society in general, is not at its best explains in part
why the ancient religious symbol of the serpents is *restless* in the title
of her book, *Restless Serpents*. These mythical beasts want their due;
the cosmic order is out of phase, and something must be done. This
sensitive artist, the child of the people of sacred land, feels a special
responsibility to consider the situation.

Having been born into a culture of male-chauvinistic traditions
predating even her family roots; having grown up in a country that
still withholds equal rights from women, it is no wonder that Bernice
Zamora preoccupies herself with the status of women. This concern
intrinsically relates to the spiritual one. Society cannot be spiritually
sound if women are repressed. Zamora's search for new spiritual
centering coincides with her zeal for a sexually unbiased society.

Zamora confronts a maelstrom of social and moral chaos;
nonetheless, society is structured by rigid propriety, now often out of
touch with changing life styles. Her own culture—her regionally
distinctive form of Chicano culture—has a traditional religious
system, that of the Penitentes. The Penitente Brotherhood functioned "as an integrative social power in isolated communities,"[2]
governing matters from political to religious. They conserved
culture in the nineteenth and early twentieth centuries when New
Mexico was being taken over by non-Hispanics in both politics and
religion. Marta Weigle's book *The Penitentes of the Southwest* summarizes their importance: "[They] formerly served as the nucleus of

a folk religion in the fullest sense'' (p. 3). Modern life has eroded the sect's power, which, in turn, has weakened the communal social cohesiveness, since no ''new mechanism has yet developed in the villages to fulfill the social or the religious functions of 'Los Hermanos Penitentes.' ''[3] Again, Chicano culture serves as a microcosm of the general society; with appropriate substitutions, the above statement could be made of Occidental culture. Zamora responds with a personal ritual of aesthetics. *Restless Serpents* chronicles her arrival at the response, while being the space in which it is tested and proved.

Ritual is of central significance in Zamora's work, seeking, as she does, the reestablishment of an *axis mundi*. However, she questions the validity of extant rituals, starting with those of her own culture. Her skepticism is that of the would-be believer, of the nostalgic heretic, but skepticism nonetheless. Hence her undermining irony through which ritual is tinged with injustice. Moreover, she sees humans as fabricators of meaning through interpretation or verbalization of reality. Thus how other poets have responded to the malaise draws her scrutiny. She considers those who treat the issues that concern her, incorporating them into her poetry through humanizing parodies—a type of sacrificial ritual of tribute and consuming communion. Often she agrees with these other poets except in their aloofness from common people and their male chauvinism. Her aesthetic ritual will poeticize the down-to-earth common life and the woman's plight.

In a society devoid of a centralizing ritual system, people resort to other practices to order their life. Zamora sees these as ceremonies, customs, habits, mores that hide profound beliefs beneath surfaces that seem insignificant. Zamora focuses on them, steadily, until an epiphany occurs—the poem's image. This is part of her ritual, but it is also a method of debunking ingrained repression, especially that of men over women or of the United States over minority people. And her own culture's sacred cows are put to the block as well.

Restless Serpents contains fifty-eight poems, in six sections. Framing the total are two poems of ritual, both featuring the snake image. To understand the movement and change between the first and last poems is to grasp the book's meaning. The analysis seeks to explain exactly that.

An overview shows that Zamora traces the move from sacred to profane structuring of society and attempts to find relief from the concomitant loss of meaning and alienation which that change produces. To begin with, she establishes an image of the old sacred society as a reference for the rest of the book; from here, society falls apart at the center and the proverbial seams. Recovery is sought through law, social customs, personal alternatives, and even established religions, but nothing satisfies her. Through parody she confronts the same issues within the writings of other poets. One, Robinson Jeffers, highlights her nostalgia for natural harmony, actually present from the beginning, and a determination to espouse the human, the personal, and the common. In the section called "Situation" (pp. 54–63), she turns to those interests, achieving the high point of harmonious imagery. Yet in the last section, as if applying to herself her indefatigable cynicism, she returns to a world of conflict. Finally, from the center of her zone of mastery, art, she considers two basic paths open to her: to serve modern society—*mad masters*—or to try to renew the sacred in some contemporary sense. We will analyze this movement in more detail.

On Living in Aztlán (pp. 7–17)

"Penitents" (the first poem) establishes the reference image of the sacred, focusing on the Penitentes' Easter Week rituals in the *morada*, their ceremonial gathering place. The rituals followed Catholic tradition, but included flagellation, self-abuse, and, at times, mock crucifixion.[4] The rituals were the central event of the communal year.

The poem's first words, "Once each year," convey traditional repetition; rituals occur at specific times to insure temporal continuity, past and future, and render it meaningful. Verbs in present tense are used because ritual also repeats an identical now;[5] it is this sameness that insures the meaning of past and future—within this culture nothing will change. The ceremony has already begun; the brothers wear their mailshirts to travel to the *morada*, following "arroyos Seco, Huerfano" [Dry, Orphan]. The arroyos do exist, but the names transcend geography; the brothers travel along defining adjectives: the land is *dry* and *orphaned*, a characterization of the environment, as well as the culture's status vis-à-vis the larger society. Moving along arroyos ties the brothers to water: like that life source, the Penitentes course through the land's arterial system, heading toward the heart.

Zamora immediately conveys the sense of ritual, both temporally and spatially. Arroyos are dry streambeds that fill when the rains come; these common, everyday spaces transform during rainy season into areas of life's intense, even violent movement, affecting everything around them—as common objects are transformed by hierophanies. The Penitentes will bring a similar change in similar fashion. Finally, their coming is a centering action in itself; they centripetally gather, like energy lines, to perform rituals that invoke the sacred, which, in turn, irradiates meaning. This movement is mirrored in the poem.

> Brothers Carrasco, Ortiz, Abeyta
> prepare the Cristo for an unnamed task.
> Nails, planks and type O blood are set
> upon wooden tables facing, it is decreed,
> the sacred mountain range to the Southwest.

Individuals perform the rite; without the particular presence, the impersonal, invisible holiness cannot appear in the world. Yet at the mention of that force—Cristo—which may be a carved statue but more probably is one of the Penitentes who will represent the divine personage, the verse loses all specificity in the *unnamed* task. This refers to the ceremony's secretive nature, obviously; yet it presents the ritual process. As with the arroyos, a real object is made other through the invocation of the sacred, becoming all-presence without ceasing to be its particular self. This is the mystery of centering transcendence.

The last three lines quoted above enumerate objects placed in strictly patterned location. Ritual demands exactness, repetition of the *same*. Moreover, the world is being ordered: we center into blood (life source, again) of universal type *O*, the sacred centering sign. From there the focus expands to the table, then out to the "mountain," which immediately expands into a "range"; and, finally, with "Southwest" (the direction becomes more through capitalization), the whole area Chicanos call Aztlán is enveloped. The same lines move from specific to vast generality, pivoting on the *word*—"it is decreed." Note that the objects are common ones: nails, planks, wooden tables—society's building materials and synecdoches for that society. They are to be ritualized into impractical, irrational objects.[6] Together with the man, who also must transcend his practical state, they will form the sacrificial rite of crucifixion. Yet the objects are still objects, metaphorically functioning as the building materials of the protective social *home*, the *axis mundi*.

At the center, however, in the *O*, something is amiss. Zamora subtly undermines the whole structure. Universal blood, a particular that is also everyone's, is a perfect ritual image. Perfect, also, is the coincidence of circle and letter; the natural sign and sacred symbol meld with writing to prefigure Zamora's ritual of writing. But the mention of blood type is incongruous; through that small hole at the very center, theatricality seeps. All ritual is show, certainly, with no pejorative connotation; it is sacred play. The real problem is that *blood type* allows the modern world to tinge the play with science, with rational discrimination that undermines religious faith. The danger of its presence is implicit, and the book will support the modern world's undermining presence. This confrontation is of essence to Chicanos, and the question remains: does modernity negate the traditional, or can traditional ways incorporate it and transcend? (The *O* as sexual imagery is discussed below.)

Within the dark *morada* average	*9*
chains rattle and clacking prayer wheels jolt	*10*
the hissing spine to uncoil wailing tongues	*11*
of Nahuatl converts who slowly wreath	*12*
rosary whips to flog one another.	*13*

The third stanza returns to the center, where the ritual is in progress. In the center (line 11), the snake lurks, hidden within two items, but *hissing* and *uncoiling* its *tongue* for those who seek it. Only at the end of the book will the beast come forth openly. For now, fear rules. The chains and prayer wheels are associated with the *tinieblas* [darkness] ceremony, which reenacts Christ's momentary disappearance from life. The lights go out in the *morada*; the world is in chaos, in danger of remaining in darkness, and the participants wail in grief and uncertainty. The ritual will bring back the light—if efficacious. This moment mirrors the world situation Zamora confronts; her task is to find a new ritual to insure the return of light. And at the center the snake will reappear.

From the mountains *alabados* are heard:	*14*
"En una columna atado se	*15*
hallo el Rey de los Cielos,	*16*
herido y ensangrentado,	*17*
y arrastrado por los suelos."	*18*

Stanza 4 is part of an actual *alabado*,[7] except for line 14, which shifts back to the mountains in another centrifugal burst. This expansion reverses, however, when the *alabado* focuses on a single column, to which the King of Heaven is tied. He is wounded, bleeding, and has been dragged on the ground. The poet creates a pulsing movement: mountains→ column→ heavens→ body→ ground.

And the ritual is again enacted: a man, who can suffer bodily, is transformed into an omnipresent God, while nature is centered around an *axis mundi*. Moreover, by using a real *alabado*, Zamora renews a tradition within her new ritual, establishing continuity within this sacred space.

The poem has been leading up to the climactic sacrifice: after the scourging at the pillar (stanza 4), the crucifixion should follow. But there is a sudden shift to the persona's relationship to the ritual.

The irresistible ceremony	*19*
beckoned me many times like crater lakes	*20*
and desecrated groves. I wished to swim	*21*
arroyos and know their estuaries	*22*
where, for one week, all is sacred in the valley.	*23*

Through similes the centralizing ritual is diffused. To explain her attraction the persona compares it to two sacred places in nature, both images of violence and beautiful tranquillity coupled. She admits a desire to explore the same paths the men followed, but in a different way. Whereas they walked or rode horseback, she would swim, and not to the *morada*, but to where the arroyos feed into rivers, and by extension to the ocean. She wanted to do this within the sacred time-space created by the Penitentes, though she locates the effects in the valley, a general, abstract, but limited area. Though refusing to center back into the *morada*, the persona credits it with sacred power.

The ritual is also thrust into past tense vis-à-vis the persona, though its effects on nature stay in the present. It is no longer efficacious for her, because it does not bridge time. In fact, it was not completely efficacious for her in the past. Though attracted, she could not participate; she cannot say what went on in the *morada*, outside of common knowledge or by quoting an *alabado*, because women were not allowed in the sacred center.[8] She must resort to similes of the sacred, which are female: lake, grove, valley, with the first two violated. Whereas the men are sporadic streams, mountains, and constructed wooden objects in their imagery, women are more stable units that gather the sporadic flow and conserve it, that produce the wood for the objects, and—yes—lie under or at the feet of mountains. The traditional male-female imagery is nature in harmony. Yet the persona wants to travel the male route, though she would turn the intermittent flow into a sustained, far-reaching one.

The desire to invade the male space is implicit in at least two images in the male ritual. The converts make "rosary whips," thus flagellating themselves with a sign of the Virgin Mary, mother of Christ. Hidden in the whips is the female source of the central male figure. And type O blood is implicitly female, *O* symbolizing the vagina, which also bleeds. Women infiltrate the space from which they have been excluded, reclaiming the center. Yet Zamora is not for the exclusion of men, but the harmony of the sexes.

Like many of Zamora's poems, this one has an underlying eroticism that cannot be overlooked. The separation of sexes in society leads to frustration and violence. She would have mutual rituals in harmony. She would extend the man's violent, soon-spent flow into the longer-lasting female orgasm. Instead of blood sacrifice in death images, she can offer the natural source of life blood, an allusion to reproduction. Zamora seems to desire a complete sexual union that would render life significant, a metaphor for social stability based on equal, though different, roles. At the same time, words are to play a key role in changing the world, as they do in the poem. This is an attack on the male bastion of writing, for which the poem could be an allegory. Zamora wants changes in all these areas because in the traditional systems they are not fulfilling.

The sacred center of traditional life breaks down when the environment changes. Commercial-technological society strikes at the *O* in "Penitentes." In the next two poems, "A qué hora venderemos todo?" [When will we sell everything?] and "When We Are Able," the family falls apart, stripped of its sacredness by modern utilitarianism and labor exploitation. The woman and man no longer harmonize; unable to control his environment, he uses her without regard for her natural purpose or desires. He strikes at her, and she strikes back. In "A qué hora," he—no longer a brother but a *citizen* of another society—tells her to abort; her traditional *utility* is now *inutility*. Her refusal is a withdrawal into the sacredness of her body and an "indifference to the [new] world," as well as the title's accusation. Since he is the citizen, he must be the one selling out everything but what is hers to protect.

With reproduction negated, marriage becomes meaningless in "When We Are Able." The woman refuses to get legally married as long as they live in an oppressive society that turns her lover into a stranger to himself and even in bed. Again the *O* is vitiated, the central sexual ritual undermined. The stranger "ravish[es] what is yours," she tells him, ironically revealing a double possession of herself in which no one gets anything. The bed-center is a social microcosm—they live in a devastated *colony* exploited by strangers, but the vice is possession. The same thing that turns this woman into *his* allows the living-working space to become *His*. From colony to bed to meal table, fear flows, negating the sacred energy that should radiate from the bed and from the *O*. That center, however, refuses to participate legally in the society. The only expression of freedom is her rejection of marriage.

Zamora's poetic world often centers, especially in a structural sense, on the sexual act which could be the transforming ritual of the world—yet she does not develop the possibility. In this poem it is the only element that the man could influence immediately; it might form a family unit out of a split couple (coupling). A truly erotic relationship, one in which neither possessed nor used the other, might be the first step to that balanced participation Zamora seeks, and perhaps give the man the strength to do what she requires.

As a unit the first three poems demonstrate one of Zamora's favorite techniques, the juxtaposition of idealized visions of life and the grim view. In their clash and eventual blending, within the poem or book, perhaps a realistic balance is achieved.

Her traditional role denied, the woman retreats into the celebration of herself alone in "El último baile" [The last dance]. Menstruation separates her from men, allowing her to dance to the moon in an ancient night ritual. Irony and foreboding undermine the escape to the *sea of tranquillity*, however, the moon's inhumanity being as sterile without the sun as female bloodletting without the context of both sexes. This is a ritual of isolation, not harmony. Zamora prefigures the temptation to aloofness which profane society imposes on one. This is a trap and a warning.

The persona seeks an outlet for her *utility* by becoming the "Progenitor" of her people, male and female. She will resurrect them through her *resurrections*, a metaphor for poetry clarified in "Restless Serpents." Highly significant is her choice of ancestors: an alcoholic, macho, incestuous father; the mother of a suicide victim; and a whore. Not a pleasant heritage, but effective for emphasizing that she refuses to idealize; she will rescue society's discards. And again sexual connotations are present; behind each incident lies sexual frustration closely tied to social or religious taboo—eroticism in the offing.

"Pueblo, 1950" and "Bearded Lady" are rites of passage into sex and love; the first, a traditional socio-familial rite; the second, an asocial alternative. In the first of the two, everyone, including the persona herself, blamed her for a kiss when she was twelve; but no one said anything to the boy who *gave* it to her. Though the male instigates it, he remains outside the rite, which is performed by the mother and teacher—family and society—and the persona. Structurally, the male seems to frame the ritual, appearing in the first and last lines—in traditional society, women's rituals are legitimate only within the men's larger context. Irony lies, however, in the verb *remember*. Zamora now betrays the lesson by naming the boy and saying the word no one said when she was twelve. Moreover, she, not he, frames the poem by remembering and speaking the word.

"Bearded Lady" is important for its definition of *strokes*, a key word in "Restless Serpents." When the young woman asks about love, she is sent to the bearded lady. Having to go to a social freak to learn about love is not as ironic as it might seem. Love is taboo; marriage is a social ritual, only incidentally related to love.[9] The lady speaks in mysterious terms, but leaves the clear image of stroking her beard. Somehow love is that hermaphroditic stroking; the balanced female/male participation in the enjoyment of the sign of power, wisdom, and tradition; that self-sufficient masturbation. Once again the poet has invaded the traditionally male area; once again sexual pleasure lies at the center of the key image.

In "Asunto de principio" [A matter of origin], the sexual act is directly treated. Though sex succeeds here, the implication is that society restricts woman from being herself, except in bed; and then it is something attributed to *savage women* who stir *prehistoric bones*. The title supports the comment above that healthy erotic relationships could be the beginning of liberation.

"Gata Poem" [Cat Poem] is an idealized, and I suspect ironic, vision of the Chicano as a *bronze god*. He calls her to take her to a solar paradise, as false as the moon's tranquillity ("El último baile"). Woman assumes a subservient role—though cats are never completely possessable—that of an adored, weak pet, dependent on man. Zamora is laying a trap, into which woman can fall for the sensations granted her in the previous poem. When she says, *I went*, it is the past tense of a previous self ("Pueblo, 1950"), who accepted the double standard.

"On Living in Aztlán" responds to "Gata Poem" and summarizes the whole section:

We come and we go
But within limits,
Fixed by a law
Which is not ours;

We have in common
the experience of love

—*after Guillevic*

Law could be the Anglo American's, but here it is also the Mexican tradition of Chicanos. This law is and at the same time is not *ours*, the image of a system of order still binding, but no longer appropriate. Could Zamora be using irony again? Love according to whom? Is this the frustrated experience or the fulfilled one? She leaves it ambiguous.

The poem succinctly presents the underlying structure of her thought. Life traps humans, who attempt to render the trap meaningful through communal experience. The conflict is between social law and personal life. Authentic social rituals should allow a person to feel significant in society. Zamora would like that society to be Aztlán; and she has a ritual in mind, love. In the end, however, she settles for poetry.

The reference to the poet Guillevic is the book's first open intertextuality. She uses these to relate her work to that of poets she admires, even though she differs from them. Guillevic is both admired and accepted: a Marxist who bares his indignation at society's injustice and lack of human meaning, but who does not refrain from personal imagery nor from a deeply religious, even mystical sense of the world. He also comes from an ethno-linguistic minority in France: he was a Breton from Carnac, who also lived in Alsace and spoke Alsatian and German.[10] He learned French in the classroom. Yet he uses French like a native. His typical poetry is sparse, pared to the minimum to convey essential images with ever-expanding significance. For all these reasons, Zamora chooses to incorporate him into her poetry, creating an intertextual relationship of significance to her work and, perhaps, to his as well.

Girded Us (pp. 19–29)

The second section is framed by an image of floating in liquids within a contained space, a pond for the dying ("Having Drowned") and a barrel of dung ("Girded Us"). The poems in between reflect the structure of entrapment and/or exclusion from ritual life centers. From the bloody corral in "California," to the temple of mythology from which Chicanos are excluded in "Unattended" (in spite of their pre-Columbian mythology), to the feast of fools looked down upon by "the higher minds of things" ("Supping on"), to the separate beds—the wife's and the prostitute's—of macho subculture ("Mirando aquellos desde los campos" [Looking at those guys from the field]), to the boxed-in reflection of an alcoholic's face in the mirror ("Morning After"), to disappearance of a totally ritualized life and the domination by strangers—who now inhabit the center of the palace ("Moctezuma's Treasure")—there is a constant movement from one closed space to another, with the ever present reminders of a vaster space somewhere outside (the view of wonderous nature from the perspective of youth and a country bar).

Only César Chávez's hyperbolized figure transcends common life ("The Sovereign"). Though he towers like a giant, he is not lost in the cosmos—like the female moon-dancer or the Chicano God of the first section—but rather *sustains the world* with *love* and *justice*. His "head is directed / toward a heart promiscuous" with those qualities. His love exceeds the social norm. Instead of the suffering heroes, Sisyphus and Christ, Zamora pictures him as Atlas, sustaining life on his shoulders, the *axis mundi* of his people.

Chaff (pp. 31–40)

The third section explores alternatives to entrapment, forms of personal order, especially through the word, literature, and sex. The poems are placed in mirroring pairs. The second member of each pair repeats the first in parody fashion, bringing it down from an idealized plane to the common, or worse, usually through irony.

"Pico Blanco" and "Martha" are about individuals who structure their world through words. The persona is "in awe" of both, of Robinson Jeffers for the magnificent characters in his poetry, and of Martha for her repeated obscenities. Yet both are refuted to an extent. Jeffers' character Cassandra, whom the persona appropriates as her own, contradicts him, claiming to be achieving a worthwhile goal. Martha claims that no one, including the persona who is shining Martha's shoes, knows "shit from Shinola." The irony is obvious. In both poems someone pontificates from an elitist position divorced from reality. We may find Martha's repeated phrase trite and vulgar, but it is the mocking parody of Jeffers' repeated deprecation of humankind's ability to rise above its irrational destructiveness.

"Re: An Egyptian King" and "Orangethroats," which occupy the middle of the section, deal with sex. The first begins as an idealized tryst under an elm. The poet cannot resist an animalistic counterpoint: flies that, in the heat of the humans' passion, are allowed to "defecate / on a knee, a hand, a breast." The noise of their wings precipitates intercourse. Sex culminates in an exclamation of "My Lord!" But the poem ends on another metaphorical counterpoint: "one fly alights on another." Sex is only ideal through language, Zamora seems to say, but should be seen for what it is. Yet language serves also to degrade the ideal. *Homo poeta* can do wonders with the most basic materials. "Orangethroats" has fish breeding in an aquarium, and the persona sickens at the sight. "Bolting gurgles within" her, ironically mirroring the gurgles and swishes in the aquarium. The sex is impersonal, violent: "Torn fin swills are half-sucked / By vacuum." Breeding has the ghost image of abortion: vacuum-torn swills, *burying proof* of spawning, and the bolting within the persona. Sex sickens when seen coldly from the outside as nothing but a violent, biological process.

So Not to Be Mottled (pp. 41–52)

The fourth section opens with a search for the past of the poet's grandparents' mountain society, "an age *ya mero olivadado*" [almost forgotten]. Not finding its end puzzles her; she gives in to the seductive nostalgia, to the sense of sacredness of their life. The end, though almost gone, eludes her because she is its continuation. She explores herself then, recalling her failed participation in Catholic religion. "From the Vestibule" and "Among the Ordained" proudly proclaim her exclusion from the church. In the former she comes to understand the church only as an excommunicant, and what she sees is misery. When still inside she used to think about natural wonders, like the volcanoes, crater lakes, caves, sacred times of day. The poem is ambiguous in that, although she claims to see through the farce now, when she was in the church she did feel the sensation of the sacred—perhaps as much as one can ask of religion. Moreover, the world was structured into meaningful units—with her in the choir loft! As with the Penitente ritual, she was relegated to peripheral participation. The poem, however, fails because the lasting image is of the Church. "Among the Ordained" is more powerfully stated. The *miscreants*—the truly ordained—keep crumbling structures together and are the just among the people.

In "As Viewed from the Terrace" and "Widow's Barter," established, rigid rituals are rejected in favor of natural processes. In the first, flaunted promiscuity always becomes a representation of preestablished categories of *sacred* or *profane*. Once again the distant perspective reduces sex from freedom to entrapment. In the second, death is accepted, but the funeral ritual rejected. Life should return to the natural acceptance of events, instead of falsifying itself through preordained ceremonies.

"So Not To Be Mottled" reminds one of the shattered-mirror scene in Hesse's *Steppenwolf*, where the character learns that he is infinitely fragmented. "You insult me / When you say I'm / Schizophrenic. / *My* divisions are / Infinite." *Mottled* connotes one color, with blotches of another. She, however, is so many that they become again one, a perfect blend. Zamora revolts against imposed, limiting structures. As a metaphor for Chicanos, she advocates a synthesis of many sources.

This section contains two poems of intertextual play. The first, "Sonnet, Freely Adapted," parodies Shakespeare's Sonnet 116. Juxtaposing the two is useful.

Sonnet 116

Let me not to the marriage of true minds
Admit impediments. Love is not love
Which alters when it alteration finds,
Or bends with the remover to remove:
O, no! it is an ever-fixed mark,
That looks on tempests and is never shaken;
It is the star to every wandering bark,
Whose worth's unknown, although his height be taken.
Love's not Time's fool, though rosy lips and cheeks
Within his bending sickle's compass come;
Love alters not with his brief hours and weeks,
But bears it out even to the edge of doom.
   If this be error and upon me proved,
   I never writ, nor no man ever loved.

"Sonnet, Freely Adapted"

Do not ask, sir, why this weary woman
Wears well the compass of gay boys and men.
Masculinity is not manhood's realm
Which falters when ground passions overwhelm.
O, no! It is a gentle, dovelet's wing
That rides the storm and is never broken.
It is whispered, secret words that bring
To breath more hallowed sounds left unspoken.
Men, sir, are not bell hammers between rounds
Within the rings of bloody gloves and games.
Men, sir, aught not rend the mind round square's round,
Spent, rebuked, and trembling in fitted frames.

So I return, sir, worn, rebuked, and spent
To gentle femininity content.

On first inspection Zamora seems to drift far afield, turning a poem about constancy of love between "true minds" into a polite harangue against machismo. It might be more appropriate to compare it to Shakespeare's Sonnet 129 on lust; but no, *compass, storm, never broken*, and the *O, no!* reference it to 116. Zamora attacks machismo, not Shakespeare, reiterating his point that love is a matter not of physical endurance, but of constant affection. Aimed at Chicano machos—boxing is one of the macho rituals most admired among Chicanos—the stroke is devastating; she prefers homosexuals. Again she employs an enclosed space to signify entrapment in a code of violent competition, one that excludes women from the ritual. The difference is that now she denies it sacred power. Yet boxing is a gross—profane—parody of the Penitente ritual, just as football or hockey parody once sacred games of bloody competition. Zamora attacks this cultural vice and retreats from it, preferring Shakespeare's marriage of true minds.

The parody functions to bring the parodied poem down to earth from its ideal plane. Whereas Shakespeare boldly defines love, the eternally undefinable, Zamora explains that one cannot even begin to discuss love while machismo eliminates the encounter of true minds, or any minds. Whereas Shakespeare's love is a star above earthly storms, Zamora's masculinity is a dovelet's wing "never broken," but caught in the tempest. His love escapes time's compass, while she is inside it; and though she wears well, nonetheless she wears. And while Shakespeare, in a grandiloquent flourish, stakes his writing on the truth of his statement; Zamora simply retreats. Perhaps here lies the essential difference and the key to the parody. Shakespeare is so absolutely sure of his systems—stellar, amorous, divine—that he can act as their high priest; in his centered world the ritual of the poem is unquestionably valid—it is a metaphor of a world with a firm *axis mundi*. Zamora's systems have been sorely shaken, in great part by men professing Sonnet 116 but practicing Sonnet 129. In her excentric world the poem's ritual needs support—but socio-religious props have crumbled. She seeks exterior support in Sonnet 116. By relating to it, Zamora calls on the only heritage a writer has in the final instance, literature. She relates, but changes the sonnet to renew it, to give it contemporary life. After all, she is *not to be mottled*; her influences are infinite.

Poems of Intertextual Reference to Robinson Jeffers

The section ''So Not to Be Mottled'' also contains the third of four poems of intertextual reference to Robinson Jeffers, to be discussed now as a unit. They demonstrate the book's movement and reproduce its main themes. Jeffers (1887–1962) was one of the most read and most controversial U.S. poets of his time. With such long narrative poems as *Roan Stallion* (1925) and those in *The Women at Point Sur* (1927), *Dear Judas* (1929), *The Double Axe* (1948), and other collections, he made known his concept of Inhumanism: a transcendence of humanity, which he considered essentially and hopelessly flawed and fated for extinction, through an immersion into inhuman nature. In his words it is ''a shifting of emphasis and significance from man to not-man; the rejection of human solipsism and recognition of the transhuman magnificence. It seems time that our race began to think as an adult does, rather than like an egocentric baby or insane person. . . . It offers a reasonable detachment as a rule of conduct, instead of love, hate and envy. It neutralizes fanaticism and wild hopes; but it provides magnificence for the religious instinct, and satisfies our need to admire greatness and rejoice in beauty.''[11] It was ''based on a recognition of the astonishing beauty of things, and on a rational acceptance of the fact that mankind is neither central nor important in the universe.''[12] He insisted that good and evil were indistinguishable from an objective, aloof perspective. War, crime, violence, and hatred were part of a great plan, though the human factor in the universe was so small as to be meaningless. Man would destroy himself, leaving nature the better off. Thus he could decry human folly—and in his political anti-war and pro-ecology poetry he did so with a bluntness that got him censored—but insist that one should not get involved or try to help the unfortunate. The Inhumanist was to be a kind of mystic who, through the contemplation of nature, would transcend personal vision and become one with the total, inhuman perspective. In ''The Loving Shepherdess,'' he calls it ''the eye that makes its own light and sees nothing but itself'';[13] in ''Carmel Point'' he advises us to ''uncenter our minds from ourselves . . . unhumanize our views a little.''[14] However, since one is human, the Inhumanist has to learn to endure the situation and survive with a moral integrity. Jeffers particularly detested the saviorism of organized religion and politics, denouncing it in several works. Nature was sacred, all of it; and religion—including ritual—fragmented nature into good and evil, outsiders and insiders, leaders and victims.

Zamora disagrees with Inhumanism, but chooses to lock

together Jeffers' poetic world and hers. They share love and awe for nature, pessimism about the United States, antipathy for organized religion, a sense that something must be done to show humankind its folly, and faith in poetry's didactic and cathartic power. Their essential differences are that Zamora believes that humans can improve, that they are not doomed, that humankind is significant, that the aloof perspective is wrong, that one should maintain individuality within a communal context, and that ritualized living is a positive alternative to modern chaos.

In four poems Zamora addresses Jeffers directly: "California" (p. 21), "Pico Blanco" (p. 32), "The Extraordinary Patience of Things" (p. 50), and "Phantom Eclipse" (p. 59). She borrows Jeffers' poetical material, but turns the poems into refutation of, or at least a challenge to, Inhumanism.

"California" begins with the last two lines of Jeffers' "Roan Stallion."[15] Zamora evokes the poem that made Jeffers famous as a preface to hers. "Roan Stallion" tells the story of a mestiza woman, California, who lives with her young daughter and despised husband. The husband uses her as chattel, even paying debts with her body. California has a vision of God and then transfers it to a stud horse her husband has won at gambling. She offers herself to the horse as a rider and a victim to be trampled, since she cannot have sex with him. In the end the horse kills the husband, and California shoots both the man's dog and the horse. For Jeffers the poem ends with an Inhumanistic liberation from the oppression of a man—who used the woman as a god might, arbitrarily and harshly—and from adoring another god. Killing the horse also frees him from the role of Savior that keeps him from being just himself. The corral is the space of studding and arena of the gods' death. California and her child remain outside of it in their freedom. Zamora assumes California's point of view, implicitly accepting the plot, except that she changes the ending by adding one more shot, "one that plunged / my wailing will to the center of this bloody corral." She has not been liberated, but encompassed by the corral's significance. The meaning is ambiguous; she could be trapped by responsibility, a concept Jeffers would reject. However, the shot is *another* one so it must be the one fired by the poet in placing her into the poem. Zamora seems to protest California's being primarily a sexual being. The bloody corral becomes part of Zamora's ubiquitous sexual imagery, another bloody *O* being misused by men. California has been shot down by the poet, who limits her "wailing will" to sexual actions that end in death. Zamora's imagery of entrapping spaces coincides with Jeffers', but she protests his mistreatment of the woman.

In "Pico Blanco" Zamora adopts the persona of Cassandra, from the poem of the same name,[16] and also draws from Jeffers' "Return," "To Death," "The Inquisitors," and "Roan Stallion."[17] The poem-collage pays tribute to Jeffers' impressive characters, but rejects their Inhumanism. They are Jeffers' *stewards*, but she says she will search for her own. She even redeems Christ, whom Jeffers called a cousin to death, by stating that "He will / rise above America's adoration for / blood in the corners." The direct confrontation comes in the last stanza. Jeffers' Cassandra is a truthful prophet, who, unlike poets, Jeffers says, refuses to lie. She will "still mumble in a corner a crust of truth to / men / And gods disgusting. —You and I, Cassandra."[18] Zamora's Cassandra denies that she is mumbling to the people about her gods, implicitly accusing Jeffers of doing that and nothing more. She, in contrast, is "chipping the / crust of the Pico Blanco." Zamora combines a famous line from "Roan Stallion" with an image from "Return." In the former, Jeffers defines the Inhumanists' precepts: "Humanity / is the start of the face; I say / Humanity is the mould to break away from, the crust to break through, the coal to break into fire, / the atom to be split."[19] *Pico Blanco* is the image of inhuman, natural magnificence, with all the connotations it carries, and Jeffers asks us to stop thinking and return to it in "Return." By combining the lines, Zamora inverts the meaning; she calls for a chipping away of Inhumanistic coldness and aloofness and a return to human concerns. The crust to be broken is that of *Pico Blanco*, not of humanity.

"The Extraordinary Patience of Things" is Zamora's parody of "Carmel Point."[20] Lamenting the ravages of suburban housing developments, Jeffers takes refuge in his concept of transcending the limits of the personal perspective: "the image of the pristine beauty / Lives in the very grain of the granite, / Safe as the endless ocean that climbs our cliff.—As for us— / We must uncenter our minds from ourselves, / We must unhumanize our views a little, and become confident / As the rock and ocean that we were made from." Zamora's parody reads: "—As for us: / We center our minds on our minds; / We humanize the unknown and become confident / As the very grain of the granite housing fossils." Zamora's staunchly reactionary defense of rationality and the individual even contaminates with traces of human (we presume) remains Jeffers' image of pristine beauty, the grain of granite. Zamora wants human presence everywhere. Jeffers' uncentering corresponds to the elitist, escapist perspective that she denied in other poems; Zamora's centering ritual humanizes the world. While she and Jeffers share the diagnosis—decadence, alienation, misguided religious structures, and human weakness—they differ diametrically on the cure.

"Phantom Eclipse" (in the fifth section of *Restless Serpents*) responds to the mystical-vision segment of Jeffers' "The Loving Shepherdess." It is significant that the seer in Jeffers' poem is a Chicano, Onorio Vásquez, the final product of racial blending on the California coast. His dream begins with the Indian migrations from Asia to Alaska, and south to "Mayan and Aztec Mountains."[21] The vision of Inhumanistic totality becomes the climax of Chicano evolution in Jeffers; Onorio sees that humanity is insignificant. The universe draws together into one light that Onorio worships: "The eye that makes its own light / And sees nothing but itself"; and later "the fire-studded egg of heaven."[22] Zamora eclipses the *eye* with the moon, the female symbol, giving it something else to see while calming its fury. By bringing the sun and the moon together, she also couples the sexes in a balanced, human image. The union implies that man can change and reach a sacredness with nature if woman is an equal. Note that the image centers the moon within the sun—"It gleams in the morning sun / like a temple on a friendly planet"—not fully eliminating it, but quieting its "spastic" movement. Another female centering brings order to the sacred cosmos.

In this series of intertextual confrontations, Zamora develops her own voice, drawing more and more away from Jeffers. Their meeting is brilliantly played out, like the sun and moon image above. Zamora creates a ceremony, a ritual of encounter and destruction, changing the meaning where there was one that displeased her; she humanizes Jeffers through parody.

Situation (pp. 53–63)

Having explored different alternatives, Zamora turns to the commonplace to ritualize everyday *situations* in the fifth section of her book. "Derby," about a man racing the undertaker's hearse, is a trite poem that sets the tone for the section. It summarizes the contemporary situation—our flight from death has become our life—with the image of being chased by a menacing enclosure. It also locates the reader in a more traditional world, the hearse being a carriage, not a car. The section's *old-fashioned* ("At Hand") quality must be kept in mind lest the reader misunderstand why the poet cannot remain in this setting as a response to the modern malaise.

"Pueblo Winter" repeats, metaphorically, the dynamics of unwritten law of "On Living in Aztlán"; within the limited space of a yard, birds interact with a purpose lent only by the poem's words. The movement has meaning, though *what* is not clear. In "41 Trinkets" an Indian adjusts to nature and tourists equally, surviving through movements rendered meaningful when held in the poem's space. "El Burrito Cafe," "Denizens," and "State Street" are less successful, not because of the low-life subjects, but because the poems lack memorable images.

"At Hand" parodies blood sacrifice. A toilet handle pinches a man's finger, and he sucks the blood. The common, necessary act of urinating, a centering and biological catharsis itself, is exalted to an epiphany through language. The toilet is "old-fashioned," connoting that traditional ways suddenly have impinged upon the man to remind him of his precarious existence. One can easily imagine that the handle is connected to a chain as they used to be, creating a parody of the whips and chains of the Penitentes. The blood centers through the mouth in an image of circular, self-contained communion with one's own body.

"Anton Chico Bridge" is Zamora's best-realized poem of natural harmony within a Chicano-cultural context. With "Phantom Eclipse," discussed above, it occupies the section's center like an altar; they form a hierophany of total cosmic order.

In "Anton Chico Bridge," Zamora returns to the flowing-water metaphor for cultural life. A shallow, macho stream represents the Spanish explorers who sought the fabled land of El Dorado. Utilitarian pursuits, which have characterized the macho, again lead him to ravage the female environment to which he is indifferent. She bleeds uselessly. This stream "stops short in Kansas," an allusion to the Spanish explorations, but also an expression (common in Colorado) for worse than nowhere. Zamora condemns people who pretend to be Spanish, the self-referential term used by many Chicanos in Southern Colorado and New Mexico. The other flow, deeper and wider, is a mestizo one that "knows itself to be muddy with adobe," a metaphor for cultural consciousness. Hence its self-assurance. The Chicano stream's location is *under* the bridge; thus it is *here*, remaining like a lake. This image represents Chicano life as movement through a permanent structure—the culture—that conjoins and orders the movement and space of that life.

The bridge becomes a classic *axis mundi* in the poem, a permanence capable of radiating meaning because it is a hierophany. Once again an everyday object is revealed, transformed by the literary selection into a sacred *something else*. Between the bridge and the river bed there appears a vertical circle, an enclosure that does not limit, but orders life. The horizontal plane is marked into four directions by the tranversal lines of movement over the bridge and that of the water under it. The extension of the bridge's lines creates a vertical axis that joins the levels of existence: celestial, human, underworld. Through this spatial mandala, traditional life both flows and stays in a permanence that is movement, or perhaps it is better stated as a movement within permanence. This is a metaphor for traditional culture, but also for literature.

Vis-à-vis the book this image also conjoins much of the essential imagery. Zamora has been searching for a harmonious, balanced participation of elements in ritual. In the first poem, man constructed and woman was the natural material; here, the two harmonize, uniting in an embrace; through the *O* flows a stream-lake, the combination of the female and male waters of "Penitents." As in "Phantom Eclipse," which adds a sacred celestial event to this space to activate the ritual, two elements adjust themselves perfectly. And since sexual equality is sought, in one poem the man covers the woman, while in the next she covers him. These are metaphors of sexual union and cosmic harmony; the bed is reclaimed through a sacred erotic act. The persona also achieves her desire of following the male flow to discover its essence; as promised she gives the usually sporadic ("Penitents")—or *spastic* ("Phantom Eclipse")—male an extended duration. This is the book's sublime moment.

The significant thing, however, is that the real ritual is the poem, or poems, which hold the image in such a way that the *objects*—the words, not the things they represent—become a hierophany. Zamora's poetry, not water, flows through the sacred *O*.

The final poem in this section takes up the undertaker character from the first one; yet, unlike the fearful man of "Derby," here the female persona comes to an accord with death. Neither minds the other's profession: undertaker and midwife, celebrants of birth and death—not high priests, however, but common ones, non-elitists. Zamora again harmonizes man and woman, maintaining the signs of life and death that they have had since the first poem. She is not really changing their traditional function, but insisting on equal participation in any ritual. And the two again join to frame life; between them it flows. Give life order, a frame of reference that allows it to move with purpose, without fear, and you have performed the ritual of cosmic centering; that is what Zamora does here.

This harmony attracts the weary, modern citizen. Why not stay here, end the book with this section? Zamora deliberately framed and toned it in old-fashioned, rural images to place it in a nostalgic space. The section represents escape into the past, not a responsible response to the present. It also represents an escape into literature. The sixth and final section returns to *reality*, in Zamora's view.

Restless Serpents (pp. 65–74)

The last section recapitulates the conflicts before closing with the poem "Restless Serpents." As she is wont to do, the poet frames the section with an image, here the *serpents*. The first poem, "Stone Serpents," reestablishes the situation of class and economic inequality. The "castle of the weary wealthy," from which life is restricted, is a sealed box, cut off from the outside and life. *Castle* evokes the feudal system; an elite center from which law and order radiate, and into which flow the products of the scattered individuals under the castle's protection. Inside, the man and woman are separated. Each receives approximately five lines forming one sentence; both are introduced negatively, "No man . . .", "No woman . . ." The men are metaphorically blind, unable to see life around them; the women are afraid to move. The latter share their space with unconceived children. What saves this stereotypical exaggeration is the imagery.

The serpents are of stone, carved into the balustrades surrounding the castle. They frame the poem as well, forming the castle's sustaining pillars and ordering element. Because the man cannot see them, he is blind. They could teach him a lesson of *balance* in life, especially through their bisexual imagery, but they are stone, like lifeless religious icons. If they came to life, the castle would crumble; if the people could reclaim them, the society would be reordered. The political allegory is obvious, as is the cultural. Zamora's task is to reclaim those serpents.

The poems that follow initiate a reclamation process, especially vis-à-vis female-male relations. "Propriety, 1972" restates the conflict of sex roles. A rural scene seems traditionally ideal, but the characters actually are entrapped by an old propriety that, by 1972, no longer has the sacred-communal base. The "valley" is not isolated, as in "Penitents," but dominated by the "castle of the weary wealthy"; woman's *utility is inutility* now, though she is expected to continue as if it were still 1872. The poem opens with common images of rural family life: after the meal, Loretta says the rosary and Juanito chops wood; Teresa, the oldest daughter, enters the outhouse; Loretta decides to kill the goat in the morning. An air of ritual, of eroticism, of traditionally suppressed life threatens to explode. We are left to deduce meaning from the images. After the customary family gathering for dinner, the members separate according to the female role of praying and the male role of worker. The girl triggers violence. Zamora creates three focal points: the sky-blue crystal rosary, prayer instrument for honoring the Virgin Mary, an image of purity reflected in its circular shape, round beads, color, and material; the chopping of wood, man's splitting of nature for utilitarian life and a sexual metaphor; and the outhouse, an enclosure where biological functions reclaim central importance, a flow of life's waters, a passing between life's gates—inside is Teresa, the oldest girl, thus first to be married and delivered to a man. The tensions are obvious. Teresa's purity will be violated. The juxtaposition of rosary and axe exemplifies separate visions of life inculcated by culture. That urinating is as natural as sex, and as necessary, is irrelevant here because it does not inform the situation. What dominates is the cultural code of woman as passive, pure; man as active, violent defiler of purity. And the same culture insists that she be sacrificed to him and, yet, remain pure. The woman responds by killing a *macho*, probably with the same axe. Blood will soothe the pent-up frustration of being entrapped. Yet even that act will follow propriety. The poem holds the incident in another light, however, one that allows it to be repeated—like a ritual—until its significance comes almost clear, with the clarity of a mystery revealed; and the world is centered, for the reader at least.

In "Sin título" [Untitled], a simple question, "What if we survive?", introduces the last two poems, "A Litany for Mad Masters" and "Restless Serpents," alternative responses to that question. In "Litany" a woman artist serves the Masters. Somewhat mad herself, she is forced to struggle through harsh landscapes, still another allusion to "Jeffers' country." She even works in a corner, like Cassandra. She milks the bloated cows and paints a mural of "moon beaches and sinking cliffs." Serving the masters seems futile, insane, despite the great effort. In comparison, the main character of "Restless Serpents" is more productive.

In "Restless Serpents," the protagonist, who apparently had turned away from the sacred, is summoned by serpents resentful of neglect. The protagonist's relationship with them is antagonistic; they are spiteful, perhaps because, as *neglect* implies, they have not been given their rightful attention. "Humbling strokes" also implies that the snakes' master must be brought back from proud aloofness. The bite draws "bounded resurrection," soothing to pain. This may seem rather hermetic; in effect, one must have experienced the book in order to understand what is being said.

Between the first and last poems, the book's persona time and again has found the limits of social intercourse, the world's limiting nature. The old sense of sacredness cannot be recaptured, and new alternatives are either escapist or maddening. Withdrawal to aloofness, as in poetry, tempts her; but social responsibility constantly draws her back, while her sensibilities push her in the same direction. *Resurrection* was defined in "Progenitor" as the creation of the memories of her people through her own life and work. History and culture flow through her veins; but she has withdrawn to a corner, like Jeffers' Cassandra, from which the serpents recall her. Having rejected serving the Mad Masters of the previous poem she is now her own master, alone with her art, with her serpents. Their bites, like the toilet handle in "At Hand," impose an epiphany of personal life in communion with itself; but in this case we know that the flow is also communal. Through the puncture flow the resurrected images of the people.

Stanza 1 closes with, "Lyrics / lyrics alone soothe / restless serpents." Her response to responsibility and her proposal for a new ritual is writing, the only act she has faith in. Of course, writing is a refinement of the word's sacred power to transform reality seen in her poems since "Penitents." But now she purifies it of the male dominance that denied her participation.

Stanza 2 repeats the familiar centripetal-centrifugal movement associated with ritual. Cassandra's isolation is broken when from four corners poetry's elements—rhythm and sound—flow into the persona. She then "laps / about the droppings / of disregard," a circling movement around society's rejects, the subjects of her poetry. She takes them into her mouth in communion; that this implies destruction is in the nature of ritual sacrifice. She must liberate them from oppressive life to resurrect them into poetry's timeless, permanent movement. To do so she becomes one with them, humbles herself, and bleeds. The ritual is a permutation of prior ones, at once a continuation of tradition and a new ceremony. The serpent and the woman are still at the heart of the ritual, but now free from synecdochical disguise to participate fully.

Radiation follows centering in the last lines, which repeat the "Lyrics / lyrics" lines from stanza 1, but add, "strokes / more devastating than / devastation arrived." Having learned from the serpents, the persona now has strokes of her own. The lyrics aim strokes of devastation at herself and others. *Devastation* connotes ruination over a wide area, opening a wide circle in which others are sacrificed, whether they are Chicano or not. And as the serpents delivered her from suppressed tensions and aloofness and forced her into self-realization, the strokes of her poems are meant to do the same for her people. Keep in mind that *strokes* were defined as love by the ''Bearded Lady''; devastation is motivated by the poet's love for humanity. She deals harshly with anything she finds unconscionable, especially male dominance; but to be resurrected for the better, things must die.

The image of the serpent is a sexually balanced one, representing both sexes in mythology. Zamora rejects the separation of the world into female-male poles through deities and mothers of deities, etc., and concentrates both sexes in one, ancient symbol of vast significance. ''The symbolism of the snake is somewhat confusing, but all the symbols are directed to the same central idea: it is immortal because it is continually reborn, and therefore, it is a moon 'force', and as such can bestow fecundity, knowledge (that is, prophecy) and even immortality.''[23] It would be difficult to find a more appropriate symbol for what the poet Zamora strives to be.

Paradigm Charts

	LIFE	vs.	DEATH
SYMBOLIC			
Threat:	~~Penitente ritual.~~ ←		Castle of modern society.
Rescue:	Of positive and negative alternatives.		
Response:	Serpent ritual of → poetry.		~~Castle.~~
SOCIAL			
Threat:	~~Community unity.~~ ←		Male chauvinism and disintegration of society.
Rescue:	Community images in world relationships.		
Response:	Poetry as a means of → self-awareness and preservation and improvement of culture.		~~Chauvinism and disintegration.~~

LIFE   vs.   DEATH

PERSONAL
Threat: ~~Women's equal participation in community.~~ ←—— Machismo and discrimination.

Rescue: Images of women's assertiveness and rejection of male dominance.

Response: Poetry as a new ——→ ~~Machismo and discrimination.~~
                 cultural and personal
                 expression of a
                 woman's major con-
                 tribution to Chicano
                 literature.

10. PATRICIDE AND RESURRECTION
Gary Soto

> **Women are imprisoned in the image masculine society has imposed on them.**
> —Octavio Paz, *The Labyrinth of Solitude*, p. 198

In Gary Soto's *The Elements of San Joaquin* (1977) the world struggles to survive disintegrating forces, from natural, to social, to human, that grind on in cyclic fashion. While one line of energy seems bent on reducing the elements to stasis and nothingness—entropy[1]—another tries to structure the elements into combinations of living units. Even the writing of the text is a struggle between the word and a silence that would confirm human isolation and social chaos. Yet there is no reassuring idealism or even optimism in Soto. He reduces things to bare elements, speaks of them coldly, as if from a distance. Yet this is not the clarity of objectivity. The metaphor for his life-vision can be found in "Field Poem." From a bus for migrant farm workers, the persona looks back and sees the cotton field "From the smashed bus window" (p. 23). Soto and his persona look back at what they know intimately as participants, victims, and their vision is fragmented, shattered, though still a related and framed whole.

We should, however, distinguish between the author and the persona, though it is difficult. The latter, the *I* who seeks the origin of his personal dilemma, the negativity undermining his existence, travels the limited paths accessible to migrant farm workers. With his alter ego, Leonard, he shares the poverty of youth and, in the present, a nostalgia for the lost past. Leonard, an alienated worker, perhaps a rapist, an inmate of a mental asylum, and a drinking friend, also shares the persona's loneliness. Through Leonard, Soto establishes a social perspective of the urban worker. Thus, whatever affects the persona is generalized to a class of workers, both urban and rural. Moreover, the persona's ills are societal. That the book is to be representational of Chicanos is made clear when the persona's grandmother's migration from Mexico is said to have passed through "The places / In which we all begin" ("History," p. 41).

The resolution, however, is reserved for those, probably few, who manage to escape.

Leonard and the persona coincide in another element: they attack women. This should not surprise us; if Soto is sincerely depicting society, and specifically Chicano culture, then how else could he present it? He exaggerates, surely, but then we must discover why his persona would exaggerate misogyny. The essential truth, nonetheless, is that in our society female-male relationships are unstable. The journey back to the source will reveal why the persona mistrusts and hates women; a careful reading must also explicate the function of misogyny in the text, as well as a final transcendence.

The author differs in that he *chooses* the perspective, but lives outside of it; the persona exists only in the text. Yet Soto includes the question of writing in the text, as a possibility for the persona, making the journey a poetic search as well. The author and the persona coalesce in some characteristics making the book seem somewhat autobiographical and the persona a poet. This adds a dimension which becomes very important in turning the book from negative to positive, for there will also be a difference between the persona and the persona-poet. And like the difference between author and persona, what distinguishes the persona-poet from the persona is the former's ability to move away from the text per se, to establish a perspective outside the text's commonly accepted limits. Whether at that point the persona-poet and Soto are one is impossible for me to say.

The author chooses structure, movement, symbols, and realizes the text. He sets up the persona's negativity, the constant undermining of joy or beauty, the shattering disintegration of everything into basic elements, the chaos; and he transcends it by giving the text coherence and order. His faith in the word's power to reveal significance contrasts strikingly with the persona's mistrust and hatred. Soto may share the smashed-window perspective, but he also knows how to fit the frame so the glass stays together, giving the world a sharp, menacing look at first glance; but since the frame holds it steady, when it is seen as a whole, from a certain distance, there appears an intricate design. In the end it is from the book as experience, both as reading and as writing, that order and purpose derive; because the life placed before us is insistently negative.

Elements resembles T. S. Eliot's *The Waste Land*. Society is sterile, about to collapse, with God the Father and the father as god absent, leaving no absolute in their stead. The *axis mundi* has disappeared, though nature recalls its old presence. But order is a façade, a vain effort to hold back entropy, or, in colloquial terms appropriate to the book, to keep the bottom from falling out. Just behind or below the surface lie the sewers. From this situation the persona begins a pilgrimage to the source, a motif of regeneration; but, as in *The Waste Land*, the shrine is deserted. The trip, however, retains the capacity to order life; this is a poor substitute for the return to the sacred, but we live in an ersatz time. At this point the text itself becomes the possible substitute; and we confront, once again, the text as *axis mundi*—which is a question of reading.

Elements suggests a wasteland. Winds erode everything to dust, which, in turn, permeates whatever survives. Clouds cover the sky; gray predominates. Violence is ubiquitously imminent; life's underside threatens to collapse or explode. Soto accents this with offensive details, from several rapes and at least one murder in section 1, to a drowned baby in section 3. In between, the world is one of unflushed toilets (pp. 3, 5), boredom (p. 26), and hunger (pp. 34, 48), where life is a series of burnings (pp. 3, 26, 38, 54) and children salt slugs to death (pp. 45, 55). When beauty or peace appears, negative elements arise to counterbalance or deny it, usually in the last lines. There is a propensity to focus on sensually offensive images: armpits (p. 16), blisters (p. 22), gutted and noosed chickens (p. 27); even the rain has broken fingers (p. 22). This is not a pleasant land.

This vision is obviously that of the persona's limited experience, because the area described is also the milk-and-honey land of the American Dream—California. Soto implicitly contrasts the affluent paradise with the world of the migrant worker. The *axis mundi* connects heaven, earth, and hell; the last is Soto's choice of route back home. As such, his literature represents the invasion of middle-class America by an undesirable element; but we should remember that life at the margins reflects the center.

We must distinguish, also, between the author and the persona vis-à-vis the negativity of the imagery. Soto lays waste to the world for artistic purpose; his persona sees the world as wasted because he can see it no other way. Part of the book's venture is to reveal why.

Elements' thirty-eight poems are distributed into three untitled sections. We can categorize them as (1) the present urban situation; (2) a journey through the migrant farm workers' rural ambience on the way to another urban center; (3) return to the persona's childhood home. In geographic terms, the poems create two circles. The first goes from ''San Fernando Road'' (p. 3) to ''Braly Street'' (p. 54), implicitly moving from Southern to Northern California; but since it is a return home, it forms a circle. On another level, that of social setting, the movement's closure is symbolically in the South. When the persona arrives in the north, ''Braly Street'' has become the same as "San Fernando Road." This is purposeful. While the persona-poet follows the first circle, which closes at the old home, the persona is caught in the second, a *same-thing* cycle of deadly labor. Also, circles are a key motif in *Elements*, enclosing the world and, for the most part, locking it into a hopeless cycle.

Circles culminate in the image of tree rings, and life in the book is a series of experiences similar to the rings of the chinaberry (*axis mundi*) at the center of the persona's childhood garden. However, besides growth rings, there are oppressive rings, like the "bracelets of burns" (p. 3) on workers' arms, slave bracelets of scar tissue; or the tightening belt of hunger (p. 20); or a rapist's encircling arm (p. 5); or a Pontiac's scorched valves (p. 21); or the noose around a gutted chicken's neck (p. 27); or the dirty rings of an unflushed toilet (p. 3). The odds heavily favor the restrictive rings, and in the end the text itself must combat its accumulation of negative imagery to prove itself a positive cycle.

Tree rings are a metaphor of the book; each poem, a ring of experience. We move from the bark to the center, to the original core. A peeling away kills the tree; or do we see the tree as a whole again? Another obvious metaphor functions the same way: the elements, which can stay fragmented, or be united. Careful reading reveals binding motifs, but binding depends on the reader's ability to overcome the negativity of the imagery and surface. In the end the persona faces the same challenge, but in his case it involves patricide.

Section 1

Four of the six poems refer to rape (pp. 3–4, 5, 8–9, 10); one (p.11) and possibly two more (pp. 8–9, 10) to murder; two to drugs (pp. 3–4, 11), another to drunkenness (p. 10), and one treats mental illness (pp. 6–7). The first five are set predominantly at night, and when morning appears in the sixth it brings violent death. The setting is urban, with one reference to a vineyard.

The first and last poems frame the section in contrasting, but complementary, images. The first portrays Leonard, the poor, homeless, physically weakening manual laborer; the last, a barber-drug pusher, with a wallet stuffed with money and surrounded by material comforts. Yet the latter is killed violently. In truth, society preys on both, the difference being that the second loses in spite of having played the corrupt game, while the other is a loser, dying more slowly. Both are victims of their work. *Drifting* frames the section, with dark clouds drifting overhead (p. 3) and Tony Lopez drifting through the dark earth (p. 11); both relate to death. At the start dust penetrates Leonard's body as he tries to sweep it; at the end, Lopez's body penetrates the earth. Death wins either way; the time it takes differs. Between the two poems, the prospects for survival are not much better.

The first poem, "San Fernando Road" (pp. 3–4) also frames the book with the other pole of movement, "Braly Street" (pp. 54–56); in that role it establishes many of the central motifs. The first one is the journey; we are placed on a road, with the traditional connotations of movement to and from somewhere. The road is "of factories / Gray as the clouds"; natural and artificial objects reflect each other in grimness, trapping the persona between. The clouds will remain constant, although the factories will reappear only in the last poem, creating the circle effect discussed earlier. Leonard, the persona's alter ego, will appear in two more poems in section 1, and possibly one other, then disappear until section 3. As Leonard represents the alienated worker's side of the persona, however, the experience of section 2 can be attributed to both of them. As we will see, Leonard and the persona have similar epiphanies, which set them on the journey homeward.

Lines 5–30 of "San Fernando Road" introduce several more motifs:

Leonard was among men	5
Whose arms	
Were bracelets	
Of burns	
And whose families	
Were a pain	10
They could not	
Shrug off.	
He handled grinders,	
Swept the dust	
Of rubber	15
The wind peeled	
Into the air	
And into his nostrils,	
Scrubbed the circles	
From toilets	20
No one flushed.	
Young Mexicans	
Went into ovens	
Squint-eyed	

And pulled out the pipes   25
Smeared black
With tar.
Far from home,
He had no place
To go. . . .   30

The ambiguous images relate to motifs developed further on, such as
the arm bracelets that mark these men as slaves, which are part of
the circles-of-life motif. *Burns* is another. In "Summer," a child
"Burned his first book of matches. / Maybe the burn is disappearing / Under the first layer / Of skin" (p. 26). Apparently there will
be more burnings under more layers of skin. In "Braly Street" the
persona lists primal experiences, and among them is that "matches
flare." Bracelets of burns are to arms as rings are to trees, the image
with which the book ends. The persona moves between ringed symbols of tabulated experience; but whereas burns scar the body, slowly killing it, the tree's rings are outward-growing life. So he moves
from slavery-death to naturally free life.

Families are defined as unshakable pain; we will find that the
persona's family pains him, vitiating every experience. He carries it
like a scar; and like a ring, it locks him in. The road home will reveal
the pain's source; but the home is far away in the first poem, and
Leonard has no place to go. The characters, like many in Chicano
literature, find themselves lost outside the home space. The difference is that the memory of home brings no joy here; the plural *men*
makes the pain, and the journey, exemplary. Soto is altering a
nostalgic motif, as he does when he refuses to romanticize field labor.

Dust entering the nostrils is the first of twelve images (pp. 3, 15,
16, 17, 24, 26, 30, 33, 39, 46, 52, 54) in which natural elements
penetrate the body, reclaiming it before death. Life forms
disintegrate through infiltration and abrasion. Leonard works at
order, sweeping, smoothing, scrubbing, and making pipes; yet his
actions stir up dust, wear away with grinders, erase the tracks of
filth. The unflushed toilets—perfect example of Soto's penchant for
the unpleasant—form another ring that marks the human passing of
experience, another inward-clogging ring. Throughout the book the
rings and natural substances resist efforts to counter them.

Toilets allude to the netherworld underlying society, held at a
distance through technology and stoop labor. The potential return to
the amorphous that they represent threatens society. The reader
voyages through those dark regions. In the first poem, the toilet
locates Leonard at the bottom of the social heap, charged with

keeping that bottom from offending the upper levels. (Perhaps this explains Soto's delight in vulgar imagery—he rebels against having to clean it up, putting it back in front of the readers, most of whom come from the class of people Leonard cleans up after.) Workers, who have no place in society, maintain and protect it. Leonard even walks into hell to make the pipe that channels away waste, or delivers gas. But society remains oblivious to the worker (pp. 8, 22). As long as toilets are cleaned, pipes produced and laid, and heat and food delivered, nothing will change.

It is tempting to interpret the ovens of "San Fernando Road" as a clichéd allusion to Nazi crematoriums; the context allows such a reading. However, in the book's overall design, the ovens are more appropriately a Hades image, the opposite pole to the tree of paradise in "Braly Street," with which they form yet another piece of the general frame. Leonard enters hell to begin the book's journey; and, in effect, the persona is also as close as he can come to death without dying. His trip home through hell (section 2) will be a resurrection, in part. This interpretation is supported in two poems, "Photo, 1957" (pp. 44–45) and "Spirit" (pp. 50–51), which establish *south* as the direction of death, and in "In December" (pp. 37–38), when the persona states that he left his home town to go south. In returning north he comes from death, from hell, into which Leonard enters in the first poem.

In Leonard's hell, night brings respite, but only "once / While watching / The stars / And what might / Have been a cloud." Then he is rescued from thoughts about his "cousin / Spooning coke"—the family burden—and "the woman / Opening / In her first rape"—perhaps family, but more probably his victim. Leonard is allowed to withdraw into himself, the poem centering on his "weakening body." There is, nonetheless, no spiritual transcendence in Soto. He deals with surfaces, not souls. This is the land of the walking dead. Yet he implies activity below the surface: tensions unseen, but almost heard—like the plumbing of an abandoned hotel (p. 32)—or felt—like the burns absorbed by the skin—or smelled—like stinking sewers. He creates metaphors for the tensions of socially and sexually repressed society, routing the journey through the hell of the psyche. Those tensions will be felt, like a disturbing presence intuited somewhere—like the rapist perhaps lying in wait in "The Underground Parking" (pp. 5–6). Meaning will surface if the reader faces the implications of letting it come to light; just as the persona has to face why he is trapped in negativity.

Leonard's epiphany is sparked by the night, stars, and a possible cloud. The *might have been* modifying *cloud* implies that it could be something else, and the book will reveal what. The surface images assume significance, explaining why the persona's alter ego is allowed the epiphany. In "Stars" (p. 18) the sky transforms into a pasture, and the stars into sheep, when the moon is compared to a shepherd who leads them toward dawn. The image symbolizes the old order of a lost garden of nature, which the persona, like many readers—and so much of Chicano literature—seeks. It is a momentary revelation of nature's order, what a religious person would call its sacredness. The cloud's meaning is revealed in "Spirit" (pp. 50–51); the persona recalls when, as a child, after his father died, he sensed the disappeared parent watching him from behind a cloud. Thus the cloud also symbolizes the lost order searched for. Shepherds and fathers both guide their gentle, innocent charges, protect them, and lead them home. We should note, nonetheless, the irony involved, especially in "Stars." The vision—exaggeratedly ideal, deliberately clichéd—should alert us to an ironic level. The exaggeration distances earth from sky, or more appropriately, Soto's twentieth-century vision of life from that of pastoral poetry. Thus the father / shepherd is relegated to an absence whose continued presence is manifested through signifiers that are out of reach, though visible: moon, clouds. Father, shepherd, moon, and clouds are all metaphors for God. Moreover, once familiar with Soto's propensity for the negative twist in the final line, we might ponder the irony of the "dawn" to which the shepherd leads the star-sheep-children. The first inclination is to read it as "home," coinciding with the persona's journey home. But could it also mean *home to the slaughter*? Dawn makes the stars disappear; it also brings death to Tony Lopez and slow death to Leonard. Should we not be alerted to the possibility of home not being the ideal paradise of pastoral poetry? Can the shepherd mask the butcher? Can the God being followed be God the deceiver? Perhaps. But for now we can understand that in the text the night-stars-cloud cluster represents the nostalgia for a lost order and serves, however ironically, to lead the persona home.

In "San Fernando Road" momentary revelation of lost order leads Leonard into the only home left to him, his body, producing an epiphany: he is dying. Perhaps this self-awareness is what raises Leonard above the anonymous workers: he knows he is being threatened. This could catalyze a flight in search of reasons. He must do something to escape, because dawn means death. Appropriately, the persona also first mentions going home during the night ("In December"); and in "Copper" (section 3), Leonard and the persona meet again.

One last element should be noted, although at this point in a reading it may seem marginal: "Leonard was among men." This is a man's world; women are included only as rape victims. The text declares immediately its misogyny. The persona's closest relationships are with Leonard and his brother. He relates sexually to a female only in "Piedra," where he refers to "my woman," and perhaps in "Sadako."² As will be seen in the discussion of "Piedra," the poem contains images of key importance that mark the union as profound; but the persona turns away, back toward the social realm of fear and mistrust. In section 3, the grandmother will figure prominently, but not as a sexual figure. The mother and sister, on the other hand, are implicitly denounced as traitors. Why, will be seen in section 3. At this point the misogyny surfaces in Leonard's only reference to women. The startling callousness of *first rape*, which implies a second, etc., is sustained in the book. Leonard may well think of sexual relations openly in terms of rape, an attitude which would be consonant with the misogyny revealed later on. Certainly the sympathetic defense of the pathetic rapist in the next poem does little to deny this interpretation.

"San Fernando Road" introduces us into contemporary society from the underside, through hell's gate. In the following poems, Soto shows how middle-class security is a sham which could disintegrate at any moment. A rapist "waits for your wife" (p. 5), the reader is told in "The Underground Parking"; and again in direct address, a woman is warned not to think that her door can keep out the man "who hugs and kisses / His pillow / In the corridor of loneliness" (p. 8). When God has disappeared—not even the Bell System can reestablish contact ("Telephoning God," p. 10)—and Tony Lopez had the world in his hands "When they entered through the back door . . . and shot [him] once" (p. 11), what can the defenseless middle class expect? Soto makes his obviously middle-class reader, the *you* he addresses,³ look into the hellfire ovens and toilets of "San Fernando Road."

In blatantly stereotypical fashion, middle-class society is described as purposeless and alienated. The members are separated, even when together, be it in the home of drunken parents (p. 10) or in the "County Ward" (pp. 6–7) for the mentally disturbed. Society's security is based on artificial ordering agents, which Soto attacks as impotent. "Because there are avenues / Of traffic lights, a phone book / Of brothers and lawyers / Why should you think your purse / Will not be tugged from your arm," begins "After Tonight" (p. 8). The phone book is Soto's metaphor for technological society: the gathering place of a community whose members are joined by wires;

without it isolation would reign completely. Brothers must be looked up, and the law's representatives can be called by phone—but criminals are just outside the door. Tony Lopez had no time to think, much less phone the police before dying. Death appears, and worlds crumble. The structure of Soto's poetry underscores the precariousness of life, the last lines tending to introduce images that shake the stability of those established earlier in the poem.

The lower world may revolt. "The heat rising toward the ceiling" (p. 8), or the gas in the stove may stop if something goes wrong in the unseen world. It is no coincidence that the rapist lurks in "The Underground Parking." In that poem Soto inverts the social order, putting the woman "under the heaviness of a toilet not flushing," or under "arms of tattoos," both signs of Leonard, the would-be rapist. Violence is explained as a revolt of society's oppressed, and Soto sides with them.

Soto sympathizes with the rapist and tries to sway us by emphasizing the man's fear. It is compared to lung cancer, a disease no one favors. According to this ingenuous logic, one is supposed to pity the rapist. Soto tries to displace our sympathy from the real victim, the violated woman, who receives no expression of condolence. He would apparently have us believe that the victim is the class the rapist represents. This is not the place to enlist the feminist disproof of this defense. We need not accept the ideology expressed in this poem—which, fortunately, will be seen to be deliberately misleading—but understand Soto's imagery and its implications for the text. Fortunately, Soto avoids this ideological pitfall by associating it with Leonard—and by revealing, in the end, the source of the erroneous perception of values.

Although not inconsonant with a class-conflict explanation of violence, Soto's use of sexual frustration is too pervasive for it to be taken as a mere metaphor for economic tensions. It is, in itself, a driving force in the book. As there is a socioeconomic underground, so there is a psychosexual one; and both are turbulently unstable.[4] The journey back to the source can be expected to divulge the cause of the persona's sexual imbalance, which has nothing to do with class conflict.

Finally, Soto raises the essential question of the journey as a poetic quest; that is, the writing of the text is established as a necessary venture within it. In "County Ward" (p. 7), the inmates' space is limited to their rooms; emotionally, they are limited by frustration, loss, absence, guilt, loneliness—all the pains of existence. Pain "comes to speak in a drugged voice / that ate its tongue." Once again we find an image of a silent, though eloquent voice. Outside the ward the persona's space is also limited, "Left of the neon glowing *Eat*, / Right of the traffic returning home." He too is trapped in the social malaise, far from home with no place to go. Suddenly, a chance occurrence catalyzes an epiphany. As he enumerates elements we can read as additional manifestations of the ubiquitous pain driving everyone insane, there appears "The stunned face that could be your father's—" and the enumeration abruptly ends with a dash. At this point in the reading, one can only know that a face similar to his father's has interrupted the poem. From the complete text, we know that his father was "stunned into a coma . . ." ("Braly Street," p. 54). (Note that the line is suspended here also.) *Stunned* is a euphemism for dying. Just as the stars and clouds, metonymic allusions to the father, allowed Leonard to momentarily forget society, producing in him self-concentration and an epiphany that illuminated his life-death struggle, the father's face here produces the same effect. Even the wording in the two cases is similar: "what might have been a cloud" and "face that could be your father's." Uncertainty is underscored, but the effect is clear. The face "Deepens the gray space between each word / That reaches to say you are alone." Pain's silent voice speaks sharply: the persona is no better off than anyone else in the section. Through metonymy with Leonard, we also know that the persona must be weakening under his labors. Both characters must break the inertia that submits them to the erosion of humanity and search for what gives them meaning. If it is the father, then they must go find him.

What is the persona's work that tortures him? Obviously he shares the labor experience of Leonard, but he has his own, special work: words. Pain manifests itself in the form of an absence suffered by inmates; in the persona's case it is the absence of words, the unfilled space between them—silence. His task is to turn those silences into language. He will write the journey back to the source, back to the stunned face of the father, who, after dying, disappeared behind clouds—probably gray ones, like those that drift over "San Fernando Road," or like the persona's hair that falls ("Fog," p. 21) or the frost-killed grass ("October," p. 29), or the death film on a drowned man's eyes ("Avocado Lake," p. 30); gray is the color of death, and the spaces between the words are gray. To eliminate that space, to give pain back its tongue, is the book's vital venture, on all levels. It implies giving order to emptiness, revealing what hides behind the façade of false order and then behind the chaos threatening that façade. It requires becoming the voice of the menacing underworld, that of the oppressed for whatever reason. The alternative, represented by Tony Lopez, is to lose oneself in the corrupt social game and die. Tony did not leave in time; *they*, the anonymous force, caught him before he could take the "train to Los Banos," probably his home town. He will forever "drift" in exile, as the gray clouds drift. But Leonard and the persona have had their epiphany; they know the danger of lingering in a falsely ordered, disintegrating hell. They will leave for the north, following the migrants' route through the San Joaquin Valley, through their life experience in reverse, a pilgrimage back to the source.

Tony Lopez again offers a lesson: he, too, returns to his sources in the image of his death. "You twisted the face your mother gave / With the three, short grunts that let you slide / In the same blood you closed your eyes to" (p. 11). Birth as death, or vice versa, is not a new image, certainly, but that Soto employs it here is like the ironic *dawn* with which he ends "Stars." It should alert us to the possibility that the end of the journey to the source might be a painful death—and, perhaps, a new birth.

For the persona the journey is also a movement toward his future, an adventure to discover—create—a destiny, that of a poet. Each poem will establish him as a master of words, a filler of empty space. He creates his future by turning his past into words, a classic image of the writer; although, ironically, each new word creates yet another space. The task is endless, perhaps hopeless. And if the gray spaces eventually reveal an unbearable pain, the venture might end badly. But the journey must be played out.

Section 2

Counting each part of "The Elements of San Joaquin" separately, section 2 contains twenty poems, thematically divided into two approximately equal parts. The first eleven poems predominantly treat farm work. The initial poem of the second part marks the persona's withdrawal from the fields and a return to his home town.

Two levels of time function in the section. In present time the cycle represents the farm workers' return home after the work season. Yet, on the level of the journey, we travel back from the city to a town, a temporal reversal of sorts. But again we should be alerted to Soto's negative twists; he is anything but an escapist. One may move back in time symbolically, or in the simultaneous space of the poetic image, but in "reality" there is only the cyclical "boredom" of another summer, and pain. Traveling in two different times allows Soto to maintain his distance from sentimentality, and, in the end, to split his persona into two characters.

The first part of the section shows us a world of intense labor to produce goods from a thankless valley, for a thankless public. The farm worker is devoured by the dust and elements that erode everything. The "Wind" (p. 16) reduces tremendous masses to insignificance: mountains are no less susceptible to erosion than the social order. The small mounds built by ants from the dust left by erosion also get washed away ("Rain" p. 20). One might try to read these as images of life in constant evolution, but Soto's typically negative imagery belies that panacea: "The wind picks up the breath of my armpits / Like dust, swirls it / Miles away / And drops it / On the ear of a rabid dog, / And I take on another life" (p. 16). Through a cliché of human offensiveness, body odor, the persona is reincarnated into a lower species; the latter is also fatally ill, unable to control its body, as disabled as the County Ward inmates. Nothing consoles Soto's persona, who knows that in one hundred years "There should be no reason to believe / I lived" (p. 21).

"Field Poem" (p. 23) foreshadows the withdrawal from farm work. The persona waits in a bus to be taken from a field in which he has been working. Between him and nature is the "smashed bus window," the metaphor of the book's vision: fragmented, shattered, distant. But through distancing, nature is personified: "I saw the leaves of cotton plants / Like small hands / Waving good-bye" (p. 23). This is a reversal of the human-into-dirt images. Disintegration reappears in the very next poem, where the persona is again in the field. The point is that "Field Poem" demonstrates the possibility of the text itself; that is, of escaping the erosion and enslavement of this type of life, and life in general, through literary vision—withdrawal, observation, and the humanization of nature through an ordered viewing. The persona and Soto respond by turning to literature. But to do it, one must escape the fields.

In "Summer" (p. 26), now in the second part of the section, the persona assumes the role of oral historian and teacher, repeating *once again* stories about work. The poem's question-answer format implies that distance now exists. Though the poem is about labor, it is not set in the labor situation. Thus, when the persona cannot answer a question about "the Projects in the Eastside," because he does not know them, he supposes that life there must follow the same basic patterns; he calls upon his own experience, projecting in on the unknown to structure it into a meaningful code. A child possibly burned "his first book of matches. / Maybe the burn is disappearing / Under the first layer / Of skin" (p. 26). Later the persona will reveal that he burned himself as a child. The last question asks about the future, presumably in a work context, and the persona again draws on his past: the future will be boring. The farm worker's life is a cycle of exact repetitions—boredom

"Piedra" (p. 28), as stated above, is the only explicit reference in the book to an intimate relationship with a woman, and the encounter produces significant imagery. "A piece of the night rising from within us / And spreading among the cottonwoods / The dark water wrinkling / Like the mouth of an old woman whispering *Lord.*" They have left both labor and society at a distance. The night's epiphany rises from them, and the water reflects it with its own sacredness, that speaks in a woman's voice. Everything points to a moment of discovery through the mediation of female agents. Yet the persona "pointed out carlights," distracting attention from the dark, asocial space, to where rat-race traffic illuminates a road that "narrows / Toward the collapsed bridge," another metaphor for Soto's idea of society. The persona draws back toward the journey, though it signals disaster. The woman responds by showing him a "card of bark" (stripped from a tree, perhaps) and "smashed bottles flaking back to sand." In context, the woman is a traditional muse, revealing to the persona the book's basic image: life breaking into elements. She presents, also, the duality of life: the natural and the artificial elements, both caught in the disintegration process. Moreover, the sacredness of the space indicates the possibility of harmonizing the elements. But the persona turns away again; there is a gap in the line—"And farther away   near the road"—and someone, that anonymous menace that killed Tony Lopez, approaches from the direction of the road, provoking imminent violence represented by the persona's clenched fist. Once again Soto uses the technique of the interrupted line to introduce the call of the unknown; but since we now recognize the motif, we associate it with the father. The paternal search draws him away from a revelation in the offing; highly significant are the female source of that revelation and the fact that the interruption prevents its fulfillment. The persona is recalled to the journey because something must be found before he can turn to the full pursuit of sacred harmony. The conflict is between the stranger who approaches, the one associated with the masks of God the would-be butcher ("Stars"), and the *Lord* of harmonious nature. For the present, the former wins.

"October" (p. 29) is a simple nature poem about preparation for winter, the traditional season of death; in "Avocado Lake" (p. 30) it arrives: a young man's body floats in a lake. Again, birth and death join in a reference to the mother, life, which here drifts beneath the surface (an image of death itself) and draws the man back into prenatal existence. The poem ends ambiguously, with a young woman skipping stones over the water. Does her friend's death mean nothing to her; did she play the same kind of surface games on his life? Or is she putting a last touch of movement into what remains of him? We cannot be certain, though Soto's penchant for the negative leads one to interpret it as callousness.

Section 2 ends with three urban poems, with the typically negative images: cold, or humid heat; fires in the street; an abandoned hotel; neon; blind beggars; the smell of ox tripe and rotting fruit; drunkenness; a dog biting a woman, who kicks it in return; spiders; a dust-filled throat. In the last poem (p. 34), middle-class America (cars, homes, newspapers on porches, coffee and eggs, and a "radio saying / *It's 6:05   this is the music of America*") is juxtaposed to hungry young people. Yet the sun will shine on all of them alike. The persona is back in town and ready to visit his old home.

Section 3

"In December" (p. 37) opens the twelve-poem final section with the persona recalling two images of his home town—barking dogs and a rosary-muttering midget. Soto avoids pathos by introducing home through less than pleasant images. We should note, however, that whereas the dogs of section 2 were rabid or ran loose and attacked people, in his home town they were fenced. It is the first image of a world, now lost, of order imposed on nature; the persona's first memory is of that order. The rosary signifies order, also: a closed system representing a socio-spiritual absolute within which one knows one's place and relationships are determined by rules of conduct and promises of an afterlife of rewards or punishment. These values of order are almost lost in the imagery of aggressiveness and grotesqueness, but they are there nonetheless.

Simultaneously, the persona recalls his first departure: "From town I went south / Beyond the new / Freeway, searching" (p. 37). He is returning through an inversion in temporal sequence, giving another image of change, the freeway, a standard motif of small-town destruction.

Instead of going straight to the center of the home space, however, he evokes another house, a metaphor for his own. It has been abandoned; the broom, an ordering tool, stands unused. The house is being invaded by the forces of nature and eroded back to nothingness. But "So long ago / the yard was gardened—" (p. 38), and the evocation of human ordering of nature for a personal harvest from private property produces, like magic, a flash of that past order: "Like small red globes / And carrots poking / Into the kennel of earth; / On the line clothes lifted / With a slight wind. / And a child, perhaps, / Shaded by a cottonwood / And nailing on nailed two-by-fours / Or burning a shoe box / He imagines a hotel / And a lobby of people / Wanting out" (p. 38). The first six lines here portray an ideal order of nature and humanity in harmony. The earth is a kennel, another enclosure for controlling nature; the image gives the vegetable world animal life, connoting the need for human control, lest it go wild, like dogs. The clothesline image is that of nature assisting human efforts to live; the sun and wind did not destroy the former world. Yet the sixth line ends with *perhaps*, similar to the *maybe* of "Summer," the *might have been* of "San Fernando Road," and other such terms that indicate a projection of the persona's own past. By now we should have learned to expect the Sotoesque twist signaled by that perspective, the vitiating images. The persona injects negative elements, just as he distracted the focus from peace in "Piedra." The burning, discussed previously as a motif, not only destroys the imaginary hotel and kills people, it also destroys the memory of human-natural harmony in the poem. Perhaps if one were to read the poem separately, the image could be dismissed as youthful innocence; but in context it assumes sinister significance, the sign of an early-present resentment against the kind of people who might go to hotels. In a grown man this might be the attitude that would lead him to pity a rapist. Most important is that this attitude appears in the garden—of another home—implying that its source lies in the experience prior to the garden's destruction, in which, perhaps, a burning played a role.

The last stanza informs us that the persona has "started home," at night, with stars overhead. He sees a nest outlined against the sky and feels the sensation of night within him. Once again the night has brought an awakening related to a homing movement.

This first poem mixes times: the present, in which the house is abandoned, and the past of the garden. Soto maintains this dual level throughout the section. Eventually, he leads the persona to another home, his own, framing the section with images of homes seen simultaneously in the past and the present.

"Emilio" (p. 39) is also about going home; but this time an old man returns to Mexico and to his wife when she was young by slipping into the night of death. Like the persona, he is being infiltrated by dirt, but his comes from his own garden. His boots smell of "crushed chinaberries," the aromatic berries of the persona's tree of paradise. But though he seems to have maintained the garden home the persona seeks, Emilio dreams of another which he left to come north. Soto generalizes the significance of the journey motif, while evoking the closed circle. The old man is heading south, to death, in his deep sleep. In this poem, also, Soto juxtaposes time levels. The old man represents order as the gardener—a dying breed—while "kids" represent the disorderly present, rolling worn tires through the streets, or scarring their arms with initials. Those scarred arms are the first step towards the braceleted arms of alienated workers.

"Copper" (p. 43) recalls when the persona and Leonard were the young men walking the streets looking for cars to strip, before they were locked into the limiting rings of work. The symbol of past happiness is the copper they used to sell; it signifies technology broken down to serve their needs. Again they are a part of a system of destruction working with rings—"coiled tubing / And the short-throated pipes / Furred in oil." Those were happy days to which both of them would like to return. The poem has them in the present, together, which resolves their loneliness of section 1 and places them in the home setting of section 3, solving the place-to-go problem as well. They have found the way back to each other and shared memories.

"History" (pp. 40–41) and "Remedies" (p. 42) evoke the ordered world of the grandmother. "History" begins with a stereotypical image: the old woman cooking traditional food in the early morning. The time is the 1950's, and she lives in a house with her husband, who still works. They have sons who paved a walk for her; and she buries money under a chinaberry tree. Hers is an ordered world. The third stanza begins to divulge her experience as a migrant worker, passing then to her physical ailments, as if to tell that all was not well in her world. After a dash, Soto's punctuation mark for sudden revelations, we are told that "Her second son / Dropped from a ladder / And was dust" (p. 41). The reader recognizes the motif of the sudden collapse of security from section 1; what the persona projected into the lives of the middle class comes from his own experience.

The poem ends by evoking the stories of the grandmother's immigration "From Taxco to San Joaquin, / Delano to Westside, / The places / In which we all begin." As mentioned above, these lines generalize the personal story into a history of Chicanos.

"Remedies" recalls the grandmother's home-medicine cures, another traditional form of security that can collapse suddenly. Her mixture of superstition and folk medicine, a rosary and natural products, cured everything—except that the ending once again undermines that order and peace. "It won't / Be long before the pain / Napping in you / Yawns and blinks awake." The patient is still sick, in spite of Grandma's remedies. Soto is preparing us for a complete collapse of the home order apparently so reliable. It comes in "Spirit" (pp. 50–51), with the death of her son, when the rosary will be a useless recourse.

"Photo, 1957" (pp. 44–45) focuses on the mother. In a photograph, probably taken by the father, the mother holds the persona's sister and looks toward the sky. All along, Soto has captured scenes just before the disintegration of security. The mother is caught in a moment of security just before death leaves her with a manless house that will "tick like fire / The cat circle / A table and refuse to lie / Flat" (p. 45). The sexual connotations cannot be ignored. The poet emphasizes the burning tension and the catlike restlessness of the young widow. There follows the persona's reaction in another sinister image of death: the boy salts slugs to death. Again the context rules out childish innocence; the motivation is too obvious. His trauma was not only his father's death, but his mother's continuation of life. The poems that follow explain the trauma in more detail.

The use of the photograph allows Soto to create several absent presences, as well as establish relationships and perspectives that reflect the book's structures. That the father probably took the photo, and that now the persona describes it, superimposes the two men into one vision, one eye looking through the lens. Yet the father's plane of vision is not exactly the same, because the son has both reduced and expanded it according to his own vision. The picture is torn in half. We can only speculate that the lower half included the persona and his brother. It would be reasonable to expect the proud father to include the whole family; later, someone would violently divide it. Not the father, but perhaps a son who resented his mother. Significantly, the tearing leaves the women isolated from men, a structural division of the persona's adult world as well. The tearing also cuts the upper part of the mother off from the lower, specifically sexual part of her body—an attempt on the son's part to "purify" her? The expansion comes in the persona's addition of events after the father's death, events and reactions to them that are actually impossible to attribute to the father. Nevertheless, through the metonymy of perspective, the two are one, and the son's reactions become the father's. In "Spirit" the son invents a ghost to which he attributes his own resentment. In other words, the persona comes to believe that his emotions come from the father's, when actually it is the opposite. In addition, it should be noted that the mother is looking up, "Smiling to a cloud perhaps." Leonard looked up at what might have been a cloud, and the persona saw what could be his father's face; one was the other, as explained above. In "Photo" the mother looks at the father taking the picture and at a cloud, the two coinciding as they have throughout the book. But the cloud-father is absent from the photo, hidden behind something, but watching, as if from behind a cloud. Yet his presence-as-absence still determines the structure of the relationships as they are presented by the poet-persona; although the father's determination has now been changed to include violent division of the family.

What is encapsulated in "Photo," the death and its aftermath, becomes two separate poems. The death is remembered in "The Evening of Ants" (pp. 48–49), but only as a fact that interrupts the boy's life. It is not described in detail. The first stanza mixes the boy's fantasy world and the false-security motif. He sits in the chinaberry tree with a play telephone, calling a taxi, a plumber, and his mother: they can resolve his problems quickly and simply. No wonder the adult persona-poet singles out the telephone as one of the prime symbols of false security; it is closely tied to the trauma of his father's death. Note also that taxis drive on streets, and plumbers fix toilets, both of which were also elements in section 1 in association with false security and oppression. This leads to the third person, the mother, who by association becomes another, perhaps, the major, purveyor of false security.

The second stanza focuses on imminent death down on the ground, where no fantasy intervenes. Soto utilizes an overlapping temporal perspective to present what was happening at the moment and tone it negatively with the knowledge of what would happen later. The moment of death becomes the moment between security and collapse. The chickens may die from pecking glass, and cats will be killed by cars; the Italian who lounges on his porch will roll his car "A month later." The dividing moment, "the moment our father slipped / From a ladder . . . was the moment / I came down from the tree." Childhood and its happy fantasies die, and he enters the ugly world of want and lack that we have come to recognize. In the tree he was hungry; when he enters the house, "ants / Swarmed for the rice   the cupboards   the stove / Carrying off what there was to carry." The home is ravaged, revealing its insecurity. The usually unseen underlings revolt when crisis gives them an opening; and in this case, they strike where the mother was expected to satisfy his needs. These lessons will not be forgotten by the persona, who then projects them into every poem we have read.

"Spirit" (pp. 50–51) treats the aftermath of death. The grandmother resorts to her rosary; the grandfather turns and faces death, the south. The father's ghost haunts the house, or so the persona says, wanting to destroy the family photograph—which is probably why it appears torn in two in "Photo." When his "wife slept / With another," the father watched until they fell asleep, and then set traps for them in the house, or left the "garage light / On and burning silent / As your jealousy." The persona identifies with his father, searching for him in nature, and locates him behind a cloud, in "God's limbo." Limbo, neither heaven nor hell, is the realm reserved for innocent babies who die before they can be baptized. The persona puts the father in an unresolved state, like an innocent spirit betrayed and in need of vindication—revenge—before he can rest. The betrayal is obviously the mother's remarriage, significantly referred to as "sleeping with another" to give it an illicit connotation.

If anyone resented the lovers it was the persona, and he has never overcome it. He spied on the newlyweds, perhaps even from the edge of the bed, and set traps. If burning jealousy existed—another and perhaps the first *burning*, the one that destroyed the garden of paradise—it was the son's burning, which he attributed to the mother as a burning sexual drive. As in "Photo," the persona adopts the father's perspective; but it is his, as projected onto a dead father incapable of feeling or seeing anything. In his father's name, the persona invokes a vengeful, embittered, negative spirit; he projects it everywhere, undermining all life. We have arrived at the source of the negative life-vision in the poems and of misogyny: an *axis mundi* of death, of vitiating absence, of a Hamlet-like delusion.

The comparison of the two poems entitled "Moving Away" (pp. 52, 53), one addressed to his brother and the other to his sister, demonstrates the Manichaean division of the world under the vengeful spirit of the invented father. While the first is a recollection of shared actions, the second pictures the sister as completely separated from the boys. She is resented, possibly for identifying with the surviving parent, or perhaps just because she is a woman. Three times she is told to remember, as if she has to be reminded of her roots; while the persona seems sure that his brother will never forget anything. Though both siblings are moving away, the sister is admonished for leaving "our family some distance / From your life," as if there were a solid family unit displayed somewhere in the book that she could leave at all. Even her dolls are said to have been blond, an inchoate sign of her *treasonous tendencies*. Obviously there is no understanding of, or empathy for, the sister, as there is none for the raped women. The misogyny began with his family and became a predominant vision. That is why he turns away from the woman in "Piedra" and could never remain even if he wanted to: he must follow the invented father as long as he exists.

The brothers might be thought to share love, but in reality their close bond is hate. Though he claims to remember the quiet moments "before daybreak / And you next to me sleeping" (the most intimate image in the book), this poem, as well as the book in general, is dominated by the negative imagery of a macho world. It is their hatred for the *white* stepfather that really unites them: "But what troubled us has settled / Like dirt / In the nests of our knuckles / And cannot be washed away" (p. 52). This pattern of returning to dust, of being eroded by the world, is not a product of farm labor, but a result of the trauma of a supposedly betrayed home. The persona sees farm work this way because he sees everything this way, through the lens of hatred. He is psychologically, spiritually, scarred. No wonder he compares life to burning, to unflushed toilets, to justified rape. And the text is so much his vision that we can see that the persona has become the interior narrator, a poet writing the text we read. Soto has created this possibility for a purpose—or unconsciously saved his book through it.

Finally, we reach the lost home, "Braly Street" (pp. 54–56). The dual temporal perspective continues; memories of the past are juxtaposed to the devastation in the present. The site was "bulldozed" sixteen years before, an action telescoped onto the father's death. The neighbors are gone; factories, warehouses, and asphalt cover everything—except the lot where his home stood, which is empty, an "oasis of chickweed / And foxtails." *Oasis* is not far from *garden*, and in a hell of asphalt and cement, a lot full of weeds is a relief. The home, even in the present, can function as a space of natural encounter. Yet everything is gone.

Briefly the persona recalls his uncle's death in 1957 and the father's in 1958; but he returns quickly to the present of sweat shops and smog. Memories are no escape; the sacred spot has been found and nothing exists. He even repeats twice that he comes back every summer, undermining the security the reader has built up by this point in the journey's specialness. And, as was seen in "Summer," summers are boring. The persona is debunking the book's spiritual venture; Soto cannot bear anything that seems positive.

The poem's last image, and the book's, is of the devastated lot. We have traveled with the persona since "San Fernando Road," tolerating his negativity, for this moment:

> When I come
> To where our house was,
> I come to seeds
> And a sewer line tied off
> Like an umbilical cord;
> To the chinaberry
> Not pulled down
> And to its rings
> My father and uncle
> Would equal, if alive.

The journey through death and hell, begun in the pipes and toilets from "San Fernando Road," brought us through the umbilicus. Now that it has been tied off, perhaps the persona will finally separate himself from his excremental mind-set. The chinaberry tree still stands, the tree of his mythological garden of paradise. As trees in the center of paradise, this one joins the three zones of heaven, earth, and hell, or past, present, and future. The tree is equated, however, to the years the uncle and father would have lived; that is to say, the persona sees it as their life and their ongoing presence after death. The final revelation is that what is at the center of the persona's life, what determines his world, is death, specifically the death of these two men. His *axis mundi* is death imposing itself on life. Hence his negative perspective. His garden of paradise was inexplicably shattered, and he came down from the upper level of the tree to the lower level, into hell, and has lived there ever since.

The search culminated, one wonders if this is all. Is the discovery of reasons for a negative view of life enough? It certainly does not satisfy us. We can look back on the work as a carefully structured path, as a poetic success in terms of craft; but the results are still unsatisfying. The chaotic world cannot be denied, the garden is devastated, but the journey itself can give structure to life —yes. This is the lesson of *The Waste Land* and essentially that of *Elements*, though the latter seems more negative in outlook. What of misogyny, ugliness, fear; do they become the affirmed elements of life? Do they define culture?

Yes; and we must live with Soto's vision, in spite of its horror. In social terms the condition of the lower economic class has not changed at all since the writing of *Elements*. Life is no less perilous. What the book achieves on this level is to force its presence upon a segment of society that usually ignores the reality the poems express. It rapes the reader; admittedly, the metaphor is poor, because in spite of the ugliness of many images and the violence of the constant undermining of particular hopes and beauty, the collection is more of a seduction than a rape. It convinces because of its well-wrought structure, the craft, the coherence of its totality—because of its overall beauty. Yet it also represents one more invasion of the U.S. literary establishment by Chicano culture; it forces the reader to travel a route not usually chosen by the literate public. This is a social as well as a literary achievement.

On the cultural level, Soto's vision is also devastating. He has Chicanized *The Waste Land* and placed at its source a reworking of the Malinche figure from Mexican mythology. Once again, the male line is tumbled from its rightful place without justification. The father's death was an accident. Later, nothing is known of him; his absent presence remains a determining factor, but not a liberating one, rather a bond to revenge, distrust, hatred. His presence becomes self-destructive. He is a false god. Once again the mother gives herself to a *white* usurper, and the male children are dispossessed of their rights. The hated stepfather sits under a tree, watching the brothers hoe the garden ("Moving Away"); later in life, he is the foreman in the fields, or the night attendant in the County Ward, or the complacent, self-secure husband waiting for his wife to return home. The Malinche becomes all women, not to be trusted. One may love them, bed them, feel transposed beyond oneself through them; but, according to the persona, one can never trust them. "Reality" proves trust fatal. This is the message of "Piedra." The persona prepares a fist because a stranger approaches, and his greatest fear is that "his woman" will go with the stranger. It has happened to him before. Only men are to be trusted; but not always, because they are potential strangers when women are present. Thus they gather among themselves, excluding women. This is Mexican psychology at its commonest, an academic cliché and a popular-culture constant. One finds it in the best—Samuel Ramos, Octavio Paz, Salvador Ramírez—and in the *corridos* or *rancheras* sung in cantinas. Soto's utilization of the Malinche figure is another return to origins achieved by the book. Mexican culture's garden of paradise has its Eve, and Chicanos have inherited Malinche. The serpent is the stranger, Spaniard or Anglo American. But the important personage is the mother, who repeats her betrayal with every man. (Ironically, the return south means death in Soto's code; this return to the Mexican source of myth is a southerly turn.)

The real wasteland is that of the persona's spirit, devastated by his childhood trauma. Certainly urbanization has turned ethnic neighborhoods into industrial blight, but it is *his* perception of every scene in terms of betrayal that determines the negativity of *his* text.

He takes the smashed window along wherever he goes. He is locked into his personal history, fated to repeat it just as a farm worker is fated to repeat the boring cycle; he is held by the rings of experience. But Soto and the poet within the persona, are they also held?

No. Whereas the persona is forced to repeat the cycle of the text forever, Soto is now beyond it. True, it could have formed a slave bracelet around his writing hand; but when we go back through the text, employing the technique of withdrawal he advises in certain poems, we are granted our own epiphany: Soto uses those elements not to enslave but to transcend.

The challenge to both the persona-poet and the reader is to read the collection into a creative unit and transcend its forceful entropy, to find Soto's transcendent epiphany that takes one beyond the painful limits of the present. To a withdrawn reader, the significance of the text becomes increasingly clear. Whereas the persona, or perhaps the Leonard alter ego side of him, is trapped by the rings, the poet-persona travels the journey only once. When he writes it, the trip becomes new, forming an expansion beyond the rings that lock the workers in. We return to the metaphors of the rings and the elements. The tree standing at the center of creation, joining the realms of time and space and centering the four directions, as well as the elements of matter, is the source; but the persona has misread his source.

The persona's vision, and the one the reader adopts to be able to follow the persona, is negative because he fixes it at the point of death. Like a photograph, he freezes life and expects it to remain exactly the same. Change is betrayal to him; but change is life. Yet the chinaberry is still alive; its rings have augmented. The persona has fixed the wrong sign at the center, and the tree tells him. The uncle and father are not alive, but the tree and the persona are. To be the true extension of the father, he must find not invented symbols, but the one his father planted, the tree. His uncle and father were not negative men, but creators of order and life.

The poet-persona, while still oppressed by this misreading and still viewing the world negatively, discovers at the end the father's living process. Moreover, in spite of the misogyny that dominates until the end, the poet-persona, turned reader of his text, discovers women at the heart of life. It is the grandmother who incarnates history; it is women who reveal the sacredness of nature. And his father knew it. His father and uncle ordered the garden and built the homesite. Death takes them, but their life work is there to be imitated. The only time in the book that we can possibly know what the father chose as the focus of his life, without the persona's disturbed psyche interfering, is in "Photo, 1957"; and we find the mother occupying the life center. The persona may have converted the father into a burning, scarring slave bracelet; but the text reveals him as an expanding chinaberry tree. Father and son share the framing metaphor for life vision; but whereas the former photographs life, the latter looks back on death. Both visions appear fragmented in the book; but it was the son, not the father, who tore the photo. Yet the text itself is finally redirected toward the mother. This product of the persona's life is dedicated to the mother and the grandmother, and in their language: "para mi Abuelita y mi Madre" [for my Grandmother and my Mother]. The persona-poet and Soto merge, leaving the misogynistic persona-macho behind, trapped within the scarring rings of repetition. They transcend by understanding the error of misreading the world as negative. At the source lies life, ever growing, in spite of devastation. At the source stands woman in her ability to survive, adapt, change, and, above all, love—and love again. Like another ring on the tree of experience, after discovering their loving essence, the poet-persona adds the dedication to women. It is one more verse, but outside the cycle of the text itself, a transcendent act of love and reintegration with the real source. Its realization constitutes an act of patricide that lays the invented, macho father to rest—and resurrects the real father, the creator of order and beauty.

Paradigm Charts

Charts for Soto's work are more difficult than those for the other poets due to the complexity of his poems. First of all, he does not direct his work mainly to Chicanos, but to the non-Chicano reader; thus social meaning is multiple. Is alienation or machismo the target? I choose alienation, because machismo is a form of alienation. More charts could be drawn, but these depict what I consider the most important points.

	LIFE	vs.	DEATH
SYMBOLIC			
Threat:	~~World as unity of elements; Life.~~ ←		Entropy; elements in disintegration; death.
Rescue:	Images of life with structure in constant struggle against entropy.		

	LIFE vs. DEATH
Response:	Book as unity and life ⟶ ~~Entropy.~~ out of apparent chaos.

SOCIAL

Threat: ~~United Society living in peace.~~ ⟵ Society of alienation, separation of classes.

Rescue: Negative effects of alienation and class oppression; images of the dispossessed.

Response: Book as introduction ⟶ ~~Class separation.~~ of alienated to other classes; transcendence of separation.

PERSONAL (Persona)

Threat: ~~Positive view of love and life.~~ ⟵ Hatred and mistrust of life because of imagined betrayal by mother; machismo.

Rescue: Negative results of hatred, mistrust, and machismo; images of the source of negativity.

Response: Book as discovery of ⟶ ~~Mother's betrayal; machismo.~~ false perspective; transcendence through order and beauty of book and its dedication to women.

Conclusion

Soto's work is of great significance within Chicano literature. It marks a new high in craft and a definite shift toward a more personal, less politically motivated poetry. It also contains a more open challenge of Chicano clichés, such as family unity, machismo, community, and others. soto shares an apparently cynical, disillusioned attitude with Bernice Zamora and Ricardo Sánchez, and with younger poets like Orlando Ramírez, whose *Speedway* is a devastating piece of antiromanticism. Yet if we go back to the center of Chicano literary space, José Montoya was doing the same thing as Soto: asking the reader to see past the negativity of death, which threatened to engulf the character, to the "class" and beauty of life. And in the final analysis, the "class" and beauty have only the poetry to represent them in life. Knowing that death has robbed life of a necessary center, both create a new center in literature. Soto's work is change and continuation, one more element in the space of Chicano literature.

11. CONCLUSION

And in the end,
The love you take
Is equal to the love
You make.
—The Beatles, ''The End''

Since the start Chicano literature has been reacting to a threat of Chaos, of the culture disappearing into something other than itself. The initial images of the major works reflect a sense of imminent disintegration. The personas in *I Am Joaquín* and *Los criaderos humanos* are lost. Death has taken the central figures of ''El Louie'' and ''To a Dead Lowrider.'' Death threatens Zamora's world in the form of abortion, Villanueva's in a lack of consciousness, Sánchez' through a lack of communication. Jealousy and a lack of self-love threaten Elizondo's youthful heroes; through the lack of materials and opportunity Abelardo's frustrated artist will self-destruct. Alurista's Chicanos are trapped in labor exploitation and a profane society; Soto's have still not escaped a decade later. Chaos is the sense of being outside of one's familar circle, of being in the Other's territory, forced to act according to rules that do not arise from one's own form of life. In that alien space, the images offered by the Other as indexes of value become dark, grotesque mirrors. That they are grotesquely deforming or simply blind for the majority of people in modern, technological, profane culture is not much of a compensation.

Chicanos feel, however, that they are not yet completely lost, not yet entirely absorbed. They see salvation from the images that begin so many works of Chicano literature.

The poets, seizing on that hope, attempt to retreat into a ''Chicano world'' to find and rescue the primordial hierophanies, the basic defining and cosmicizing actions and beliefs preserved in the collective cultural consciousness (often seen as the oral tradition). Once found and renewed, the assumption is that they will once again give Chicanos a sense of self-worth, which, in turn, will allow them to control the surrounding space and order their life. Ernest Becker says that this is asking the impossible in the context of our society, although he spent his life trying to find a way to do exactly that and proposed a very similar answer: *Homo poeta*. Mircea Eliade says that, in profane society, sacredness is almost impossible to achieve; but he recognizes that people cannot live without the sense of purpose sacredness gives, so they invent an *axis mundi* of some sort according to the traditions of their *own world*. Chicano writers, for the most part, have faith—or a strong hope—that the culture can survive; but they, too, recognize the threats. The first reaction is a strategic withdrawal into the safety of one's own circle, into the barrios, into the image of the Pachuco's recalcitrance, into history, into cultural differences at any level. But the retreat is more than spatial separation. It is hoped that within that space, given time to concentrate on oneself, one will find the primordial communal rituals among those who still maintain the tradition. Thus, *Joaquín* finds the ritual of blood sacrifice of the Other, who is often a brother; Alurista finds voluntary blood sacrifice of oneself. By retreating into the Mexican heritage, they have come across the ancient Mexican duality: Huitzilopochtli versus Quetzalcoatl, with their respective rituals through which the world can be ordered. The ancient gods are the *axis mundi*; the rituals are hierophanies to be repeated. Elizondo prefers to focus on the Southwest itself and finds familial love, not bloodshed, as the defining ritual; in his celebration of the ritual, he employs techniques from the oral tradition, humor, and satire to attack the Other. All three find in the oral tradition a wealth of self-knowledge which they try to return to, and incarnate, in their text. Others follow suit, searching on their own, finding and projecting something essential in the culture, though not always the same thing nor in the same manner.

At the same time, there appear voices that come back from the search doubtful about certain things they have seen. True, *I Am Joaquín* depicted brothers killing each other; but the killing was the ritual of survival. Others will try to justify negativity in favor of cultural cohesion. But then others still, like Ricardo Sánchez, are not ready to accept self-destruction at all. The literature becomes a meta-literature, with responses and counter-responses arising in poems and books. There is no agreement on the Chicano political structure, yet there seems to be a general nostalgia for the basic unit of the family, and most of the writers accept a return to it.

At the core of the return to the family lies a hope, an explicit or implicit belief that the family retains the cultural traits necessary to maintain identity amid chaos, that the family in interaction is a constant hierophany and *axis mundi*. However, from the start there were signs of cracks in the façade. Once again, *Joaquín* itself declares openly the tradition of fratricide. ''El Louie'' died alone, after fighting his own people. Raúl Salinas bears his barrio no grudge, but reveals the damage it inflicted. Zamora, who so much would like the family unit to be healthy, recognizes that even when it seemed to be, women were not treated as equals. Sánchez gives a brutal image of the material destruction of the home, but asserts the rise of a new Chicano family. Soto's persona asserts the macho family, only to find that the assertion almost destroys him; he switches to the female core in the end. Tradition can be a vengeful, limiting deity; but this one is "our" tradition, and most of the authors accept it. *Joaquín* and "El Louie" said it from the beginning.

Behind the façade of family cohesion, the artists turn to the primordiality of love itself. *Family* would be love returned, mutually communicated. But Sánchez knows that he has been abandoned before; Zamora depicts the marriage bed as exploitation, not correspondence; Elizondo shows his young people talking to the older generation, but never receiving answers—in the end they break tradition and talk directly to each other and form the new Chicano family; and Soto's family has become a painful legacy, a bond of hate and distrust. La Familia de la Raza is a beautiful ideal, but those who have worked with any family in modern settings know the problems involved in maintaining the ideal well enough to not even talk about trying to reestablish it. So the writers, though they may not admit it, retreat, once more, into unrequited love: the self-sacrificial rituals of Alurista, Zamora, Villanueva; the insistent love of Ricardo Sánchez or Abelardo. They reveal what was present from the beginning of the literature: *writing is the writer's primordial ritual*, her/his sacrifice of self out of love. Love remains the *axis mundi*, the structuring act in the life of the artists, even when they see hatred reflected back. Even when grim killings for no apparent purpose abound in the barrio, the depiction of those senseless murders is an act of love. The writer performs Zamora's ritual every time a page is written.

Literature among Chicanos has been highly didactic; but in the end, it is a small influence in the lives of the people. The Outsider is much more powerful—television reaches more Chicanos each hour of prime time than Chicano literature in its decade and a half of existence. The literature has always recognized that the interior strife is the result of exterior pressure—the threat defines the Chicano self. And Mexico is no help, bombarding the Chicano home with soap-opera drivel, game-show idiocy, or Spanish-dubbed U.S. fare. Sánchez' image of the Chicano house/home being razed by U.S. technology and looted by Mexicans is horrifying, but symbolically true. Chicanos are neither one; they do not control the image-making media on either side of the border. So the writers offer lessons of love and, over the years, lessons—examples—of fidelity and perseverance. Literature becomes an experience shared with those who read it, a momentary focusing of an ordered existence —the text—in the midst of the few who gather to celebrate it. The *axis mundi* is the text; the ritual, the reading. Yet the hope remains that the readers will take the lesson of self-creative love and find communal rituals outside literature in which to realize it. Literature becomes the sacred act of teaching through example.

Perhaps it is a sign of change that poets are less willing to end their works with optimistic images of communal unity than they were several years ago. Yet the fact that they are transforming their energy and talents into the reflection of their people is itself a ritual of love, a lesson in heroics, a response to chaos.

NOTES

1. Introduction

1. See Anselmo Arrellano, ed., *Los pobladores nuevo mexicanos y su poesía, 1899–1959*; Doris Meyer, "Anonymous Poetry in Spanish Language New Mexico Newspapers (1880–1900)," *Bilingual Review* 2 (1975): 259–275; Philip Ortego, "Backgrounds of Mexican American Literature," Ph.D. dissertation, University of New Mexico, 1971; Tino Villanueva, ed., *Chicanos: Antología histórica y literaria.*

2. The best treatment of the subject to date is Tomás Ybarra-Frausto, "The Chicano Movement and the Emergence of a Chicano Poetic Consciousness," *New Scholar* 6 (1977): 81–109.

3. Noam Chomsky, *Syntactic Structures.*

4. Floyd Merrel, "Toward a New Model of Narrative Structure," in *The Analysis of Hispanic Texts*, ed. Mary Ann Beck et al., p. 154.

5. "The image of a universal pillar, *axis mundi*, which at once connects and supports heaven and earth and whose base is fixed in the world below . . . can be only at the very center of the universe. . . . around this cosmic axis lies the world (= our world)" (Mircea Eliade, *The Sacred and the Profane*, pp. 36–37).

6. Gayatri Chakravorty Spivak, "Translator's Preface" to Jacques Derrida, *Of Grammatology*, p. xiv. "Under erasure" is the translation of Derrida's "sous rature." The translator explains the technique as: "To write a word, cross it out, and then print both word and deletion. (Since the word is inaccurate, it is crossed out. Since it is necessary, it remains legible.)"

7. Derrida, *Of Grammatology*, p. 47.

8. Mircea Eliade explains that mythological journeys to the center are expeditions of "victorious entry into a place hard of access, and well defended, where there is to be found a more or less obvious symbol of power, sacredness and immortality.

". . . The way is arduous and fraught with peril because it is, in fact, a rite for passing from the profane to the sacred, from the passing and illusory to reality and eternity, from death to consecration, an initiation. To the profane and illusory existence of yesterday, there succeeds a new existence, real, lasting and powerful'' (*Patterns in Comparative Religion*, pp. 381–382).

–9. *Princeton Encyclopedia of Poetry and Poetics*, ed. Alex Preminger et al., p. 215.

10. Tomás Rivera, the Chicano novelist, noted these same underlying elements and concerns, though he stated them differently: ''What I should like to discuss here is the ritual of remembering as a basis for a living culture for the Chicano of today. Chicano literature has many currents and facets, and within its complexity are contained distinct strata and orientations. In my perception, what Chicano writers strive for most is the capturing of a fast-disappearing past—the conserving of past experiences, real or imagined, through articulation. But to me the past is now, as well. There exists in Chicano literature both an external and an internal preoccupation with the past. . . . it is a ritual from which to derive and maintain a sense of humanity—a ritual of cleansing and a prophecy'' (''Chicano Literature: Fiesta of the Living,'' in *The Identification and Analysis of Chicano Literature*, ed. Francisco Jiménez, p. 22).

11. Eliade, *The Sacred and the Profane*, p. 33.

12. To *cosmicize* is Mircea Eliade's term, meaning to organize space around a sacred principle, to create an *axis mundi*. He adds that it ''is always a consecration; to organize a space is to repeat the paradigmatic work of the gods'' (ibid., p. 32).

13. Ibid., pp. 29, 31.

14. Ernest Becker, *The Structure of Evil*, p. 229.

15. Eliade, *The Sacred and the Profane*, p. 64.

16. Ernest Becker, *The Denial of Death*, pp. 4–5.

17. Eliade, *Patterns in Comparative Religion*, p. 368.

18. Becker, *The Denial of Death*, pp. 5–6.

19. Tino Villanueva, ''Sobre el término 'Chicano,' '' *Cuadernos Hispanoamericanos*, no. 336 (June 1978): 387–410.

2. Rescuing the World Center

1. ''His fame lies asleep in the shadows, / injured by forgetfulness because of the lack of authors.'' This medieval Spanish poem can be found in *Cancionero castellano del siglo XV*, ed. R. Foulché-Delbosc (Madrid: Nueva Biblioteca de Autores Españoles, 1915), 1: 153.

2. Pachucos came to national prominence during World War II, when U.S. servicemen stationed in Southern California declared open season on them, attacking them on the streets of Los Angeles, beating and stripping them. The so-called Zoot Suit Riots made international news. Pachucos were distinguished by their extravagant zoot suits: fingertip-length, wide-lapel coat; narrow-brimmed hat; draped pants that ballooned at the knees and narrowed tightly at the ankle; and thick-soled shoes. They spoke a combination of Spanish, English, and a slang known as *caló*. They were already prominent in the barrios in the 1930's; and Beatrice Griffith,

in *American Me*, talks of them coming from El Paso to Los Angeles in the 1920's. Other sources are Carey McWilliams, *North from Mexico*; George Carpenter Barker, *Pachuco*; Haldeen Braddy, "The Pachucos and Their Argot," *Southern Folklore Quarterly* 24, no. 9 (December 1960); Rafael Jesús González, "Pachuco: The Birth of a Creole Language," *Arizona Quarterly* 23, no. 4 (Winter 1967); Adolfo Ortega, *Caló Tapestry*.

Octavio Paz' controversial discussion of Pachucos as rebels who rejected both Mexican and U.S. societies, but who became criminals to enter the latter, can be found in "The *Pachuco* and Other Extremes," in *The Labyrinth of Solitude*, pp. 9–28.

The most concise summary of the Pachucos' significance to Chicanos is Octavio Romano's. "*The Pachuco movement was one of the few truly separatist movements in American History*. Even then, it was singularly unique among separatist movements in that it did not seek or even attempt a return to roots and origins. The Pachuco indulged in a self-separation from history, created his own reality as he went along even to the extent of creating his own language" ("The Historical and Intellectual Presence of Mexican-Americans" in *Voices: Readings from El Grito, 1967–1971*, p. 83; emphasis in original). This is also a good example of the use of rhetoric by Chicano scholars to dignify Chicano antecedents. The repetition of *movement* creates the impression of a unified program, with purpose and ideology. There is no justification for the usage.

3. José Montoya, "El Louie," in *Aztlán: An Anthology of Mexican American Literature*, ed. Luis Valdez and Stan Steiner, pp. 333–337.

4. In an interview in Bruce-Novoa, *Chicano Authors: Inquiry by Interview*, Montoya spoke of his admiration for Octavio Paz. He is probably aware of Paz' idea of death as a definer of life. "Death is a mirror which reflects the vain gesticulations of the living. The whole motley confusion of acts, omissions, regrets and hopes which is the life of each one of us finds in death, not meaning or explanation, but an end. Death defines life; a death depicts a life in immutable forms; we do not change except to disappear. Our deaths illuminate our lives. If our deaths lack meaning, our lives also lacked it. Therefore we are apt to say, when somebody has died a violent death, 'He got what he was looking for.' Each of us dies the death he is looking for, the death he has made for himself. . . . If death betrays us and we die badly, everyone laments the fact, because we should die as we have lived. Death, like life, is not transferable. If we do not die as we lived, it is because the life we lived was not really ours: it did not belong to us, just as the bad death that kills us does not belong to us. Tell me how you die and I will tell you who you are" (*The Labyrinth of Solitude*, p. 54).

5. Orlando Ramírez, "The Myth of the Pachuco: A Chicano Reading," senior essay, Yale University, 1977. In his chapter on "El Louie," Ramírez demonstrates that the poem functions interlingually, creating a code of meaning by harmonizing English and Spanish sentence fragments. Like Louie, the text mixes language codes to achieve its own language, i.e., *shainadas* (from *shined shoes*), *vaisas* (a Hispanicization of *vises*,

a metaphor for hands), etc. When Louie ceases to be able to harmonize the poles of his reality—fantasy and the material world—the languages split and his death appears in the text.

6. Ibid.

7. Octavio Paz explains that the zoot suit was a standard suit transformed into an object of art. "Its novelty consists in the exaggeration. The *pachuco* carries fashion to its ultimate consequences and turns it into something aesthetic. One of the principles that rules in North American fashions is that clothing must be comfortable, and the *pachuco*, by changing apparel into art, makes it 'impractical.' Hence it negates the very principles of the model that inspired it. Hence its aggressiveness" (*The Labyrinth of Solitude*, p. 15).

8. Margarita Vargas, a Yale student, observed that the music, *tan tan taran*, seems to be more appropriate to a death scene, resembling the first notes of the funeral march. A heroic entrance would be *tan tararán*. Thus even the music transcription is that of an antihero; perhaps it is also an ominous prefiguration of the *dead end* to which Louie's fantasies lead him.

9. Of the film stars mentioned by Montoya, Bogart is obviously the most important, appearing among both the U.S. and the Mexican actors, and then figuring in Louie's death. Though Montoya was unaware of it, Bogart played a black-suited, western outlaw, similar in appearance to the Mexican characters named in the poem, in *The Oklahoma Kid* (1939) and a Mexican bandit in *Virginia City* (1940). While insignificant in Bogart's career, the latter role is highly significant vis-á-vis this discussion, in that it mirrors Louie's fate. In *Virginia City* the Mexican's presence, complete with stylized cowboy garb—silver conches on his hat—and a latinized accent, unites Union and Confederate troops in the climactic scene. Enemies unite as U.S.A. brothers against the Mexicans, whose leader is killed. It is one of Bogart's few death scenes in which no emphasis is given to his agony. Bogart, famous for dying on camera, is almost forgotten in death when he plays a Mexican. In this role he is Louie's double. Parallels between the role, its costuming and function, and the Pachuco and the role he played in Los Angeles in World War II, I leave for future study.

10. Ortega, *Caló Tapestry*, p. 22, lists *vaisa* under the category of "*Peninsular Caló*. Words which have changed little in form and meaning from the original gypsy Caló," that is Spanish gypsy slang from the fifteenth century.

11. Conversation with José Montoya during Flor i Canto IV, Albuquerque, August 1977.

12. J. L. Navarro, "To a Dead Lowrider," in *Aztlán*, pp. 337–339. A lowrider is a customized car that rides low to the ground. Through metonymy, the car's driver is also a lowrider.

13. My discussion of Navarro's poem owes much to two former students at Yale. Jesse Jáuregui, though he could not specify why, insisted that the poem was not as superficial and negative as I said in class, thus forcing me to give it a closer reading. Marty Ulloa gave me the key by pointing out the use of *carnal* by the persona.

14. A similar analysis of "Stupid America" appears in Bruce-Novoa, *Chicano Authors*, pp. 11–13.

15. Abelardo Delgado, "Stupid America," in *Chicano: 25 Pieces of a Chicano Mind*, p. 32.

16. Juan García Ponce, "¿Punto muerto en las artes plásticas?" in *La aparición de lo invisible*, pp. 68–76.

17. Raúl Salinas, *Un Trip through the Mind Jail y Otras Excursions*, pp. 55–60.

18. Eliade, *Patterns in Comparative Religion*, pp. 367–387. *Imago mundi* is the entire cosmicized space at the center of which stands the *axis mundi*.

19. Ibid., p. 382. Also, Eliade, *The Sacred and the Profane*, p. 32: "To organize a space is to repeat the paradigmatic work of the gods."

20. See Johan Huizinga, *Homo Ludens*.

21. Tino Villanueva, "Apuntes sobre la poesía chicana," in *Chicanos*, pp. 48–67.

22. "Kratophanies, that is manifestations of power, and therefore feared and venerated" (Eliade, *Patterns in Comparative Religion*, p. 14).

23. September 16 is Mexican Independence Day, celebrating the day Father Miguel Hidalgo y Costilla declared Mexico independent in 1810. He raised an army, mostly of common people, to fight the Spanish, but was captured and executed. Independence came eleven years later, in 1821. May 5 commemorates the battle of Puebla, 1862, in which the Mexican liberals defeated the forward guard of the French expeditionary force brought in by Mexican conservatives. The battle was the first in a long war that ended in 1867 with the execution of Maximilian, an Austrian Hapsburg prince who had been installed three years earlier as emperor of Mexico.

24. Salinas, like other Chicano authors, severely limits the space of the anecdote, creating the impression that everything depicted happened only to Chicanos. However, although the changes he refers to *may have been* more shocking to the Mexican immigrant, it should be remembered that the U.S. population was undergoing a transformation from predominantly rural and agricultural to urban and industrial during the same period that Salinas evokes. One did not have to be Mexican to feel the pressure of rapidly changing mores brought about by urbanization, the beginnings of mass-media culture, and contemporary merchandizing techniques based on sexual fantasies. However, the insular perspective of the poem accurately mirrors the community and its conflicting tensions that Salinas seeks to rescue from oblivion.

25. Again, Salinas is simply proving the Chicano experience as a microcosm of society in general. These same sexual frustrations are the result of any social organization, as has been explained by such thinkers as Georges Bataille (*Death and Sensuality*), Norman O. Brown (*Life against Death*), Herbert Marcuse (*Eros and Civilization*), and, of course, Freud.

26. Samuel Ramos, *El perfil del hombre y la cultura en México*, pp. 72–74.

27. Salinas has written another poem, "Journey II," in Raúl Salinas, *Viaje/Trip*, pp. 10–14; also in *Voices of Aztlán: Chicano Literature Today*, ed.

D. Harth and L. Baldwin, pp. 192–196. It begins, "They're tearing down the old school," and recalls the school's role in forming the peer group. It is a companion piece to "Mind Jail," being a second journey through the same territory in his mind.

3. The Heroics of Sacrifice: *I Am Joaquín*

1. Rodolfo Gonzales, *I Am Joaquín / Yo soy Joaquín*. All quotes will be made by line number. The poem has 502 lines, over half of which are three words or less—89 lines of three words, 72 of two words, and 76 of one word. The Bantam edition contains both English and Spanish versions of the poem. I am quoting the English except when the Spanish is of particular significance.

2. Walter J. Ong, "Literacy and Orality in Our Times," in *Profession 79*. Ong calls primary orality "the pristine orality of mankind untouched by writing or print which remains still more or less operative in areas sheltered to a greater or lesser degree from the full impact of literacy and which is vestigial to some degree in us all" (p. 3). According to Ong, writing is necessary "for the analytically sequential, linear organization of thought. . . . which is unknown to primary oral cultures, where thought is exquisitely elaborated, not in analytic linearity, but in formulary fashion, through 'rhapsodizing,' that is, stitching together proverbs, antitheses, epithets, and other 'commonplaces' or *loci* (*topoi*)" (p. 2). The author of *I Am Joaquín* directs the poem at people of this type of oral culture; yet Chicanos live in a society no one would call pristine or primary, and what the author attempts to convey—history, culture, ideology—is, according to Ong, only possible through writing and the kind of mind that a writing culture creates. "Without writing the mind cannot even generate concepts such as 'history' or 'analysis,' just as without print, and the massive accumulation of detailed documented knowledge which print makes possible, the mind cannot generate portmanteau concepts such as 'culture' or 'civilization,' not to mention 'macroeconomics' or 'polyethylene' " (p. 2). The poet attempts to create a work that functions without the analytic characteristics of written media, but with the benefits of print. The printed product functions like oral tradition in its use of the characteristics Ong enumerated above; but it was created by a mind capable of formulating the concepts Ong attributes to print, a written-media mind.

3. See the discussion of "inhabited territory" and "our world" in Chapter 1.

4. Heroes: lines 38, 46, 47, 90, 108, 109, 110, 137, 158, 164, 206, 216, 217, 218, 224, 232, 234, 244 (two named), 245 (two). Villains: lines 43, 49, 203, 204.

5. Rodolfo Gonzales' organization is called the Crusade For Justice. *I Am Joaquín* is sometimes considered its manifesto.

6. Ironically, the appeal to a higher moral order, under which "all men are equal," was and is a basic principle of the United States. That there is inequality no one would deny. However, that the ideal and its

realization are much more a U.S. reality than a Mexican one is also a fact.

7. An adequate study of the influence of Jewish liberals and radicals on the Chicano Movement is lacking.

8. See note 2 above. Ong adds that, "in lieu of more elaborate analytic categories, primary oral culture also tends to break down issues in simple polarities in terms of good and evil, 'good guys' and 'bad guys' " (p. 3).

9. The Mexican muralists also utilized clichés, stereotypes, and Manichaean simplifications in their art. Ironically, these same muralists have been utilized by the established Mexican ruling party to support and institutionalize its propaganda.

10. Luis Leal says that *I Am Joaquín* is not Manichaean in its vision. "Manichaeism, of course, can be avoided. Corky Gonzales does it by identifying the hero of his poem not only with Cuauhtémoc, Juárez, and Madero, but also with Cortés, Maximiliano, and Huerta" ("The Problem of Identifying Chicano Literature," in *The Identification and Analysis of Chicano Literature*, ed. Francisco Jiménez, p. 4). However, the fact that Gonzales uses a dialectic to synthesize the duality of good and evil into a national character does not change his simplistic vision, according to which Mexicans and Chicanos are good and Anglo Americans are bad. Synthesis is operative only when conflict is interior; when the threat is exterior, a strict Manichaeism is imposed. Manichaeism is a characteristic of primary oral cultures; see notes 2 and 8 above.

4. The Teachings of Alurista: A Chicano Way of Knowledge

1. My translation from the French.

2. Page numbers are from the 1974 Pocket Book edition.

3. Information from a conversation with José Armas, owner and head editor of Pajarito Publications, and Francisco Lomelí.

4. Alurista, "La estética indígena a través del floricanto de Nezahualcoyotl," *Revista Chicano-Requeña* 5, no. 2 (1977): 56–57. "In human beings themselves there arises this dialectic between the eternal and the ephemeral through the metaphor 'heart' and it moves us within, it is the continuum of life which transforms with death to return to its eternal divine origin; hence, 'heart' is what endures. 'Face' is what perishes, it is the personality, the body and mind, vehicle of the eternal heart of the Giver of Life. The face abandons us day by day, but the heart continues its movement inside and outside of our corporeal and intellectual presence. The 'flower' is the face and 'song,' the heart. Flower and Song will humanize, teach, and gladden the heart and face of nations, bringing them closer to creation, the Creator, and to themselves through the movement and the measure that cause harmony-periodicity, dialectic relationship among nations giving rise thusly to the unity of all beings."

5. Since the pages of *Floricanto* are not numbered, all references will be to poem numbers.

6. Mircea Eliade, *The Myth of the Eternal Return*, p. 35. "Every sacrifice repeats the initial sacrifice and coincides with it. . . . profane time and

duration are suspended. . . . insofar as an act (or object) acquires a certain reality through the repetition of certain paradigmatic gestures, and acquires it through that alone, there is an implicit abolition of profane time, of duration, of 'history'; and he who reproduces the exemplary gesture thus finds himself transported into the mythical epoch in which its revelation took place.''

7. Mixed metaphors are consonant with Alurista's vision of the world as totally interdependent, a concept possibly derived from pre-Columbian thought, as described by Jacques Soustelle, *La Pensée cosmologique des anciens mexicains*, p. 9: ''Ce qui caractérise la pensée cosmologique mexicaine, c'est précisément la liaison constante d'images traditionnellement associées. Le monde est un système de symboles qui se reflètent les uns les autres: couleurs, temps, espaces orientés, astres, dieux, phénomènes historiques se correspondent. Nous ne nous trouvons pas en présence de 'longues chaînes de raisons,' mais d'une imbrication reciproque de tout dans tout a chaque instant. . . . Et ce systeme, si étranger que nous le sentions, n'est pas anarchique. Sa cohésion est faite des attitudes traditionnelles du peuple qui l'a élaboré,—attitudes sentimentales et affectives codifiées en mythes et en rituel, non pas réflexions rationnelles sur l'expérience. Son unité, sa solidité internes, sont subjectives. L'image mexicaine de l'univers est accordée au peuple mexicain; c'est lui qu'elle reflète, et non le monde.'' [What characterizes the cosmological thought of the Mexicans is precisely the linking of images that are traditionally associated. The world is a system of mutually reflecting symbols: colors, times, oriented spaces, stars and planets, gods, historic events, they all relate to one another. We do not find ourselves in the presence of ''a long chain of rationalizations,'' but rather of a reciprocal overlapping of everything in everything else at each instant. . . . And this system, however strange it may feel to us, is not anarchical. Its cohesion comes from the traditional attitudes of the people who elaborated it—emotional and affective attitudes codified in myths and rituals, not through rational reflection on experience. Its unity, its internal solidity are subjective. The Mexican image of the universe corresponds to the Mexican people; the image reflects them, not the world.]

To construct classic, closed metaphors would create independent units within the text, denying Alurista's philosophy.

8. The expansion is metaphorical in poetic terms, but in terms of the spatial religiosity of Alurista's aesthetics, the expansion of an image is the material enlargement of the real world.

9. Alurista is visually oriented, often creating rhythmic flows of visual structures with the placement of the lines. This makes him very much a poet of the printed word, although his content and techniques derive from the oral tradition.

5. The Heroics of Self-Love: Sergio Elizondo

1. Sergio Elizondo, *Perros y antiperros: Una épica chicana*. The book was written in Spanish and translated into English by Gustavo Segade,

appearing in a bilingual edition. In the discussion I often cite the translation only, using the Spanish when it is necessary to the explanation. At times, I have taken the liberty of changing the translation to more accurately reflect the original.

2. Elizondo does not consider the work an epic and has told me that the addition of the subtitle was unauthorized.

3. There is no concise translation for *con safos*. It means something like "King's X" and "ditto" or "doubles" when dealing with a threat; "top it" or "dare you" when used as a dare; "better not touch" or "hands off" when used with a signature. It has now come to mean "written by a Chicano."

4. Garci Rodríguez de Montalvo, *Las sergas de Esplãdian* (Burgos: Juã de Jũta Florentín, 1526).

5. Gonzales, *I Am Joaquín*, p. 82.

6. The Voice of Silence: Miguel Méndez, Poet

1. Robert Graves, *The White Goddess*, Ch. 3, pp. 49–60.

2. Bruce-Novoa, "La voz del silencio: Miguel Méndez," *Diálogos* 12, no. 3 (May–June 1976): 27–30.

3. Miguel Méndez, "Tata Casehua," in *El Espejo / The Mirror*, 1st ed., ed. Octavio Romano, pp. 30–43.

4. The line numbers given are according to a count of lines in the book as a whole, for a total of 1753. *Criaderos* was written and published in Spanish; the translations provided in the text are my own.

5. "La historia en su versión escrita es una puta vulgar. Desdeña a los pueblos que no otorgan la lisonja del oro y del poder" [History, in its written version, is a common whore. It disdains nations who do not grant it the flattery of gold and power] (Méndez, "Tata Casehua," p. 41). "La historia escrita, coqueta liviana, los desdeña a los pobres como toda puta que no otorga favores si no pulsa el oro de la paga" [Written history, loose coquette, disdains the poor, as does every whore who does not grant favors if gold pay does not flow] (Méndez, *Peregrinos de Aztlán*, p. 177).

6. Bruce-Novoa, "Chicanos in the Web of Spider-Trickster," in *The Don Juan Papers: Further Castaneda Controversies*, ed. Richard de Mille, pp. 271–274. For an analysis of Castaneda's books and their contradictions, see Richard de Mille, *Castaneda's Journey*.

7. Carlos Castaneda, *A Separate Reality: Further Conversations with Don Juan*, p. 23.

7. Time, Death, and the Other Voice of Silence: Tino Villanueva

1. "The open in truth is silence / But in you it was a voice / and now it arises and sings." This poem was published as a pamphlet (Mexico City: Imprenta Madero, 1969).

2. Bruce-Novoa, "The Other Voice of Silence: Tino Villanueva," in

Modern Chicano Writers, ed. Joseph Sommers and Tomás Ybarra-Frausto, pp. 133–140 (henceforth referred to as *OVS*).

3. "Behind, dust settles surely, / and sweeps away every trace you have left. / A vague echo vibrates from the past / and announces that time quickly, / finally defeats you, flees, and does not return. / A bell tower is heard in the distance / crying a dry and now tired rhythm; / and you, with an obvious tinge of sadness, / with unsure steps toward an unknown dream / walk weakly, quiet and shrunken. / Destiny then encircles and possesses / your soul defenseless with its wounded breath; / and on shadows falls your rigid determination / not to die completely into oblivion."

Hay otra voz contains thirteen poems in English, twelve in Spanish, and five in which the Spanish and English are mixed. They will be quoted as they were written. Bracketed translations are mine.

4. Eliade, *The Myth of the Eternal Return*, p. 35. See Chapter 4, note 6.

5. Ramón Xirau, *Palabra y silencio*, p. 144; my translation.

6. Jorge Luis Borges, "The New Refutation of Time," in *Labyrinths, Selected Stories and Other Writing*, ed. Donald A. Yates and James E. Irby, pp. 233–234.

7. See Chapter 2, note 1.

8. See Chapter 2.

9. For another version of the incident, see Hunter S. Thompson, "Strange Rumblings in Aztlán," in *The Great Shark Hunt*, pp. 119–151.

10. In *OVS* I explained that the first two sections of the book are bilingual, "in that the poems are in either one language or the other, while the last section contains only one poem ("Escape") which is written only in Spanish. The mixing of two languages I call interlingualism, because the two languages are put into a state of tension which produces a third, an 'inter' possibility of language. 'Bilingualism' implies moving from one language code to another; 'interlingualism' implies the constant tension of the two at once. In truth, although the first two sections of *Hay otra voz Poems* are technically bilingual in structure, the total experience of the reading is interlingual, but only in the last section does the surface of the text itself become obviously interlingual" (p. 133).

8. A Voice against Silence: Ricardo Sánchez

1. Ricardo Sánchez, *Canto y grito mi liberación (y lloro mis desmadrazgos . . .): Pensamientos, gritos, angustias, orgullos, penumbras poéticas, ensayos, historietas, hechizos almales del son de mi existencia* [I sing and shout my liberation (and I cry my pains . . .): Thoughts, shouts, anxieties, pride, poetic shadows, essays, stories, soulful spells to the beat of my existence]. It will be referred to as *CG*. *HechizoSpells: Poetry / stories / vignettes / articles / notes on the human condition of Chicanos & picaros, words & hopes within soulmind* will be referred to as *H*.

2. Sánchez seems, at times, to be a disciple of Emile Durkheim, who used the term *anomie*, one of Sánchez' favorites, to describe alienation in modern, industrial society's chaotic overabundance of everything without

orderly control or logical connection. See Durkheim, *The Division of Labor in Society*.

3. Eliade, *The Sacred and the Profane*, p. 23.

4. See Chapter 2.

5. Eliade, *Patterns in Comparative Religion*, p. 379.

6. The titles of his books (see note 1 above), are good examples of Sánchez' filling of space in a baroque fashion. *CG* has two introductions, a preface, a poem by the illustrator, Manuel Acosta, and an explanation of sorts by the author.

9. Rituals of Devastation and Resurrection: Bernice Zamora

1. "Intimacy is violence. . . . If the individual is described in the operation of the sacrifice, he is defined by anguish."

2. Marta Weigle, *The Penitentes of the Southwest* (referred to as "Weigle"), p. 3. The Penitentes were "localized associations" of men "originally organized for pious observances involving the expiation of sin through prayer and bodily penance, and for mutual aid [who] acquired judicial and political influence. Besides functioning as an integrative social power in isolated communities, these fraternities also became a conservative cultural force—preserving language, lore, customs, and faith, especially in poorer rural and urban areas of predominately Hispanic population. Now a secret religious society of restricted membership and indeterminate influence, the *Cofradías* (Confraternities) or *Hermandades* (Brotherhoods) formerly served as the nucleus of a folk religion in the fullest sense" (p. 3). Located mostly in Northern New Mexico and Southern Colorado, the Penitentes influenced the Chicano culture in the area by preserving traditions and language. They still exist. Weigle gives a count of 135 *moradas*, or gathering centers, in 1960, with approximately two to three thousand members. Weigle's book is useful for background information.

3. Carl S. Knowlton, "Changing Spanish-American Villages of Northern New Mexico," *Sociology and Social Research* 53 (1969): 471.

4. Munro S. Edmonson, *Los Manitos*, p. 44.

5. Eliade, *The Myth of the Eternal Return*, p. 35.

6. Georges Bataille, *Théorie de la religion*, p. 67: "on sacrifie *ce qui sert*, on ne sacrifie pas des objets luxueux. Il ne pourrait y avoir sacrifice si l'offrande était à l'avance détruite. Or, privant dès l'abord d'utilité le travail de fabrication, le luxe a déjà *détruit* ce travail . . . Sacrifier un objet de luxe serait sacrifier deux fois le même objet." [One sacrifices useful objects, not objects of luxury. There could be no sacrifice if the offering had been destroyed beforehand. And, by depriving the work of fabrication of any utility from the beginning, luxury has already *destroyed* it . . . To sacrifice a luxury object would be to sacrifice the same object twice.]

7. An *alabado* "(from the opening words: *alabado sea*, praised be) is a hymn in praise of the Sacraments" (Lorenzo de Cordova, *Echoes of the Flute*).

8. Weigle, *Penitentes*, p. 25. "Women may sometimes have been members of a brotherhood; but it is more likely that they generally served

as auxiliaries—preparing meals, cleaning the morada, caring for the sick, helping at velorios (wakes or vigils) and following public processions. . . . In any case, women almost invariably played subordinate, supportive roles.''

9. Paz, *The Labyrinth of Solitude*, pp. 197–204.

10. See Guillevic, *Selected Poems*, pp. ix–x.

11. Robinson Jeffers, *The Double Axe*, p. xxi.

12. Ibid., p. 172.

13. Robinson Jeffers, *Dear Judas and Other Poems*, p. 106.

14. Robinson Jeffers, *Selected Poems*, p. 102.

15. Ibid., pp. 14–34.

16. Jeffers, *The Double Axe*, p. 117.

17. Jeffers, ''Return,'' in *Selected Poems*, p. 60; ''To Death,'' in *Selected Poems*, pp. 96–97; ''The Inquisitors,'' in *The Double Axe*, p. 147.

18. Jeffers, *The Double Axe*, p. 117.

19. Jeffers, *Selected Poems*, p. 24.

20. Ibid., p. 102.

21. Jeffers, *Dear Judas and Other Poems*, p. 104.

22. Ibid., pp. 106–107.

23. Eliade, *Patterns in Comparative Religion*, p. 164.

10. Patricide and Resurrection: Gary Soto

1. Frank Serna, ''*The Elements of San Joaquin*: A Celebration of the Spirit in a World of Decay,'' unpublished paper, Yale University, 1979.

2. Sadako is Gary Soto's wife, but she is not identified in the book, although there is an extratextual reference to the name on the back cover, where Sadako Soto receives photo credit for Gary Soto's picture. In any case, the image in the text must rely on its own power to exist, and ambiguity is part of that power.

3. Soto speaks to a *you* who is part of the middle class he is attacking in the poems. The book is written for a non-Chicano audience in great part. Soto publishes in non-Chicano magazines, addresses a non-Chicano reader; and this gives his poetry a certain tone unlike that of most of the other Chicanos, who write for a more specific, Chicano audience.

4. This same sexual frustration underlies Raúl Salinas' poem analyzed in Chapter 2.

SELECTED BIBLIOGRAPHY

Primary Sources

Alurista. *Floricanto en Aztlán*. Los Angeles: Chicano Studies Center, University of California, Los Angeles, 1971.
———. *Nationchild Plumaroja*. San Diego: Toltecas en Aztlán, 1972.
———. *Timespace Huracán*. Albuquerque: Pajarito Publications, 1976.
Delgado, Abelardo. *Chicano: 25 Pieces of a Chicano Mind*. Denver: Barrio Publications, 1969.
Elizondo, Sergio. *Perros y antiperros: una épica chicana*. With translation by Gustavo Segade. Berkeley: Quinto Sol Publications, 1972.
Gonzales, Rodolfo. *I Am Joaquín / Yo soy Joaquín*. New York: Bantam Books, 1972.
Harth, D., and L. Baldwin, eds. *Voices of Aztlán: Chicano Literature Today*. New York: Mentor Press, 1974.
Méndez M., Miguel. *Los criaderos humanos (épica de los desamparados) y Sahuaros*. Tucson: Editorial Peregrinos, 1975.
———. *Peregrinos de Aztlán*. Tucson: Editorial Peregrinos, 1974.
———. "Tata Casehua." In *El Espejo / The Mirror*, 1st ed., edited by Octavio Romano, pp. 30–43. Berkeley: Quinto Sol, 1969.
Montoya, José. "El Louie." In *Aztlán: An Anthology of Mexican American Literature*, edited by Luis Valdez and Stan Steiner, pp. 333–337. New York: Random House, Vintage Books, 1972.
Navarro, J. L. "To a Dead Lowrider." In *Aztlán: An Anthology of Mexican American Literature*, edited by Luis Valdez and Stan Steiner, pp. 337–339. New York: Random House, Vintage Books, 1972.
Ramírez, Orlando. *Speedway*. San José: Mango, 1979.
Salinas, Raúl. *Un Trip through the Mind Jail y Otras Excursions*. San Francisco: Editorial Pocho-Che, 1980.
———. *Viaje / Trip*. Providence: Hellcoal Press, 1973.
Sánchez, Ricardo. *Canto y grito mi liberación*. Garden City: Anchor Books, 1973.
———. *HechizoSpells*. Los Angeles: Chicano Studies Center, University of California, Los Angeles, 1976.

Soto, Gary. *The Elements of San Joaquín.* Pittsburgh: University of Pittsburgh Press, 1977.

Villanueva, Tino. *Hay otra voz Poems.* Staten Island: Editorial Mensaje, 1972.

Zamora, Bernice. *Restless Serpents.* Menlo Park: Diseños Literarios, 1976. (Bound jointly with José Antonio Burciaga, *Restless Serpents.*)

Secondary Sources

Alurista. "La estética indígena a través del floricanto de Nezahualcoyotl." *Revista Chicano-Riqueña* 5, no. 2 (1977): 48–62.

Arrellano, Anselmo, ed. *Los pobladores nuevo mexicanos y su poesía, 1899–1959.* Albuquerque: Pajarito Publications, 1976.

Barker, George Carpenter. *Pachuco: An American-Spanish Argot and Its Social Functions in Tucson, Arizona.* Tucson: University of Arizona, 1950.

Bataille, Georges. *Death and Sensuality: A Study of Eroticism and Taboo.* New York: Walker and Co., 1962.

———. *Théorie de la religion.* Paris: Gallimard, 1973.

Becker, Ernest. *The Denial of Death.* New York: Free Press, 1973.

———. *The Structure of Evil: An Essay on the Unification of the Science of Man.* New York: Free Press, 1976.

Blanchot, Maurice. *El espacio literario.* Translated by Vicky Palant and Jorge Jinkis. Buenos Aires: Paidos, 1964.

Borges, Jorge Luis. *Labyrinths, Selected Stories and Other Writing,* edited by Donald A. Yates and James E. Irby. New York: New Directions, 1964.

Braddy, Haldeen. "The Pachucos and Their Argot." *Southern Folklore Quarterly* 24, no. 9 (December 1960).

Brown, Norman O. *Life against Death.* Middletown: Wesleyan University Press, 1959.

Bruce-Novoa. *Chicano Authors: Inquiry by Interview.* Austin: University of Texas Press, 1980.

———. "Literatura chicana: La respuesta al caos." *Revista de la Universidad de México* 39, no. 12 (August 1975): 20–24.

———. "The Other Voice of Silence: Tino Villanueva." In *Modern Chicano Writers,* edited by Joseph Sommers and Tomás Ybarra-Frausto, pp. 133–140. New York: Prentice Hall, 1979.

———. "The Space of Chicano Literature." In *The Chicano Literary World, 1974,* pp. 22–51. Las Vegas, N.M.: New Mexico Highlands University, 1975. Reprinted in *De Colores* 1, no. 4 (1975): 22–42.

———. "La voz del silencio: Miguel Méndez." *Diálogos* 12, no. 3 (May–June 1976): 27–30.

Castaneda, Carlos. *A Separate Reality: Further Conversations with Don Juan.* New York: Pocket Books, 1972.

———. *The Teachings of Don Juan: A Yaqui Way of Knowledge.* New York: Pocket Books, 1974.

Chomsky, Noam. *Syntactic Structures.* The Hague: Mouton, 1957.

Cordova, Lorenzo de. *Echoes of the Flute*. Santa Fe: Ancient City Press, 1971.

De Mille, Richard. *Castaneda's Journey*. Santa Barbara: Capra Press, 1976.

————, ed. *The Don Juan Papers: Further Castaneda Controversies*. Santa Barbara: Ross-Erikson Publisher, 1980.

Derrida, Jacques. *Of Grammatology*, translated by Gayatri Chakravorty Spivak. Baltimore: Johns Hopkins University Press, 1976.

Durkheim, Emile. *The Division of Labor in Society*. New York: Free Press, 1947.

Edmonson, Munro S. *Los Manitos: A Study of Institutional Values*. New Orleans: Middle American Research Institute, Tulane University, 1957.

Eliade, Mircea. *The Myth of the Eternal Return*. New York: Harper and Row Torchbooks, 1959.

————. *Patterns in Comparative Religion*. Cleveland: World Publishing Company, 1970.

————. *The Sacred and the Profane: The Nature of Religion*. Translated by Willard Trask. New York: Harcourt, Brace and World, 1959.

García Ponce, Juan. *La aparición de lo invisible*. Mexico City: Siglo XXI, 1968.

González, Rafael Jesús. "Pachuco: The Birth of a Creole Language." *Arizona Quarterly* 23, no. 4 (Winter 1967).

Graves, Robert. *The White Goddess: A Historical Grammar of Poetic Myth*. New York: Noonday Press, 1969.

Griffith, Beatrice. *American Me*. Cambridge, Mass.: Riverside Press, 1947.

Guillevic. *Selected Poems*. New York: New Directions Books, 1968.

Huizinga, Johan. *Homo Ludens: A Study of the Play-Element in Culture*. Boston: Beacon Press, 1955.

Jeffers, Robinson. *Dear Judas and Other Poems*. New York: Liveright, 1977.

————. *The Double Axe*. New York: Liveright, 1977.

————. *Selected Poems*. New York: Vintage Books, 1965.

Knowlton, Carl S. "Changing Spanish-American Villages of Northern New Mexico." *Sociology and Social Research* 53 (1969): 471.

Leal, Luis. "The Problem of Identifying Chicano Literature." In *The Identification and Analysis of Chicano Literature*, edited by Francisco Jiménez. New York: Bilingual Press, 1979.

León-Portilla, Miguel. *Aztec Thought and Culture: A Study of the Ancient Nahuatl Mind*. Norman: University of Oklahoma Press, 1963.

————. *La filosofía nahuatl estudiada en sus fuentes*. Mexico City: Universidad Nacional Autónoma de México, 1966.

McWilliams, Carey. *North from Mexico*. New York: Greenwood Press, 1948.

Marcuse, Herbert. *Eros and Civilization*. Boston: Beacon Press, 1955.

Merrel, Floyd. "Toward a New Model of Narrative Structure." In *The Analysis of Hispanic Texts: Current Trends in Methodology*, edited by Mary Ann Beck et al. Jamaica, N.Y.: Bilingual Press, 1976.

Meyer, Doris. "Anonymous Poetry in Spanish Language New Mexico Newspapers (1880–1900)." *Bilingual Review* 2 (1975): 259–275.

Ong, Walter J. "Literacy and Orality in Our Times." In *Profession 79* (selected articles from the *Bulletins* of the Association of Departments of English and the Association of Departments of Foreign Languages, 1979), pp. 1–7.

Ortega, Adolfo. *Caló Tapestry*. Berkeley: Editorial Justa, 1977.

Ortego, Philip. "Backgrounds of Mexican American Literature." Ph.D. dissertation, University of New Mexico, 1971.

Paz, Octavio. *The Labyrinth of Solitude*, translated by Lysander Kemp. New York: Grove Press, 1961.

Princeton Encyclopedia of Poetry and Poetics, edited by Alex Preminger et al. Princeton: Princeton University Press, 1974.

Ramírez, Orlando. "The Myth of the Pachuco: A Chicano Reading." Senior essay, Yale University, 1977.

Ramos, Samuel. *El perfil del hombre y la cultura en México*. Mexico City: Universidad Nacional Autónoma de México, 1963.

Rivera, Tomás. "Chicano Literature: Fiesta of the Living." In *The Identification and Analysis of Chicano Literature*, edited by Francisco Jiménez. New York: Bilingual Press, 1979.

Roethke, Theodore. *The Collected Poems*. Garden City: Anchor Press / Doubleday, 1975.

Romano, Octavio. "The Historical and Intellectual Presence of Mexican-Americans." In *Voices: Readings from El Grito, 1967–1971*. Berkeley: Quinto Sol Publications, 1971.

Saldívar, José. "Anaya, Faulkner, and Borges." Senior essay, Yale University, 1977.

Serna, Frank. "*The Elements of San Joaquín*: A Celebration of the Spirit in a World of Decay." Unpublished paper, Yale University, 1979.

Soustelle, Jacques. *La Pensée cosmologique des anciens mexicains (représentation du monde et de l'espace)*. Paris: Herman et Cⁱᵉ, 1940.

Steiner, George. *After Babel: Aspects of Language and Translation*. London: Oxford University Press, 1975.

Thompson, Hunter S. "Strange Rumblings in Aztlán." In *The Great Shark Hunt*, pp. 119–151. New York: Summit Books, 1979.

Villanueva, Tino. *Chicanos: Antología histórica y literaria*. Mexico City: Fondo de Cultura Económica, 1980.

———. "Sobre el término 'Chicano.' " *Cuadernos Hispanoamericanos*, no. 336 (June 1978): 378–410.

Weigle, Marta. *The Penitentes of the Southwest*. Santa Fe: Ancient City Press, 1970.

Xirau, Ramón. *Palabra y silencio*. Mexico City: Siglo XXI, 1971.

Ybarra-Frausto, Tomás. "The Chicano Movement and the Emergence of a Chicano Poetic Consciousness." *New Scholar* 6 (1977): 81–109.

INDEX

Abelardo. *See* Delgado, Abelardo

Alienation, 9–10, 70, 83, 111–112, 151, 161, 187, 189, 193, 201, 209

Alurista (Urista, Alberto), 3, 96, 212–214; *Floricanto en Aztlán*, 69–95; *Nationchild Plumaroja*, 69, 70; *Timespace Huracán*, 69

Anti-heroes, 15, 17, 25

Art, 10, 16, 23–24, 33, 43, 63; 140, 142, 144, 162, 182; academic, 32; graffiti as, 43, 45, 103, 157–158; of synthesis, 32; religious, 32
—genres of: muralism, 61, 64, 181; painting, 31–32, 64, 78; sculpture, 31–32, 120, 128

Assimilation, 8, 11, 13, 51, 60, 62, 64, 116, 122, 145–146; as death, 8, 11. *See also* Melting pot

Axis mundi, 5–8, 15, 44–45, 153, 155–156, 158, 161, 163, 165, 170, 173, 178, 186–188, 204, 206, 213–215; definition of, 217n.5

Aztecs. *See* Native Americans

Aztec Thought and Culture (León-Portilla), 71, 86

Aztlán, 3, 98–99, 101, 106, 128, 162–163, 168–169, 178

Barrio, 9, 14, 34–47, 79, 84, 89, 91, 99, 103, 107, 152–153, 155–158, 213–214

Becker, Ernest, 10–12, 212–213; *The Denial of Death*, 11–12; *The Structure of Evil*, 10

Blacks, 19, 44, 104, 121

Blood, 49, 52–55, 59, 61–63, 65–66, 68, 73, 75, 77, 79, 82–83, 85–87, 110, 114, 117, 119, 121–122, 163–164, 166–167, 169, 173, 175–176, 178, 181–182, 196; and bleeding, 53, 61, 82, 121–122, 166, 178, 182; pure, 61–62, 66; as sacrifice, 49–50, 52–53, 61–63, 66, 68, 110, 163, 165, 166, 178, 213–214

Bogart, Humphrey, 17, 19, 22–23, 220n.9

Borges, Jorge Luis, 143

Canto y grito mi liberación (Sánchez), 151–152, 157–158

Castaneda, Carlos, 69–71, 82, 92–93

Chaos, 5, 8–12, 34–35, 40, 44–46, 49, 57, 60, 65, 72, 74, 80, 129, 152–154, 156, 158, 160, 164, 175, 185–186, 195, 206, 212–213, 215; death as, 11, 35; modern society as, 9, 51–52, 59, 68

Chávez, César, 58, 147, 170

Chicano literature, 3, 30, 33, 47–48, 54, 110, 129, 152, 190, 192, 211–212, 214; elegy as, 7, 12–14; paradigm of, 5–13, 14, 48, 96

Chicano Movement, 3, 48, 50, 54–56, 58–59, 67–68, 84–85, 100–102, 106–107, 109–111, 114, 145–147, 157

Chicanos: definition of, 12

Cortés, Hernán, 40, 48, 53, 55, 104

Cosmicization, 8, 10, 45, 49, 52, 56, 74, 80, 129, 156, 158, 212; definition of, 218n.12

Cuautémoc, 48, 53, 128

Death, 5-12, 14-16, 18, 21-23, 25-28, 32, 34-36, 40, 44, 49, 52, 59, 61-66, 75, 77-79, 82, 85, 91-93, 98, 106-112, 117-120, 122, 124-129, 131-145, 148, 153-155, 157, 166, 171, 175-177, 179, 187-196, 198-209, 211-212, 214; assimilation as, 8, 11, 65; life and, 5-8, 12, 28, 52, 92, 108, 136, 195; suicide, 82-83, 84, 110, 167
Denial of Death, The (Becker), 10-12
Derrida, Jacques, 6, 8
Delgado, Abelardo (Lalo), 14, 35, 212, 214; "Stupid America," 30-34
Drugs, 22, 35, 188, 194; beer, 155; cocaine, 191; heroin, 22-23, 153-154; marijuana, 41, 43-44, 154

Eagle and serpent, as symbol of Mexico, 53, 83, 85, 108
Elegy, 7-10, 12, 14, 25, 27; definition of, 7; origin of, 8, 25; as paradigm of Chicano literature, 7-10
Elements of San Joaquin, The (Soto), 185-211
Eliade, Mircea, 8-9, 49, 51, 213
Eliot, T. S., 186; *The Waste Land*, 186-187, 206-207
Elizondo, Sergio, 147, 212-214; *Perros y antiperros*, 96-115
"El Louie" (Montoya), 3, 14-25, 26-28, 35-36, 212-214
Epic, 7, 96, 118

Floricanto en Aztlán (Alurista), 69-95

Games, 21, 41, 43, 80; circular, 36-38; customs as, 39; drugs as, 41; macho, 37-39; murder as, 44; mimetic, 23; story telling as, 40; writing as, 45
—specific: bingo, 39; boxing, 62, 173; cake-walk, 39; cops-and-robbers, 38; marbles, 35-37, 40-41, 44, 85-87; poker, 16; pool, 21-22; spin-the-wheel, 39
Gonzales, Rodolfo "Corky," 96, 114; *I Am Joaquín*, 3, 48-68, 69, 110, 212-214
Graves, Robert: *The White Goddess*, 117
Guillevic, 168-169

Hay otra voz Poems (Villanueva), 131-150
HechizoSpells (Sánchez), 152-157
Hero (heroic systems), 8, 10-13, 14, 19-20, 23-25, 28, 29, 34-35, 37, 46-47, 52, 54-59, 61, 64-65, 66, 69, 103, 110, 117, 126, 129, 170, 212, 215
Hidalgo, 55, 59
Hierophanies, 11, 35-36, 49, 74, 80-81, 90-91, 114, 163, 178-179, 212, 213; definition of, 11; poetry as, 81; sun as, 80, 90-91. *See also* Sacred; Solarcentrism
History, 7, 11, 17-18, 27, 32, 33, 37, 49-52, 57-66, 74, 76, 88, 97-98, 103-105, 109, 113, 114, 116, 120-123, 129, 141, 158, 182, 201, 208, 213; as communal knowledge, 27, 49, 74, 79; as historical figures, 27, 31, 48, 52; perspective of, 50, 60, 64-65, 73, 79, 104; poetry as, 82. *See also* Oral history; Oral tradition
Home space, 8, 14, 20, 22, 34, 35-36, 41, 56, 190, 199
"Homing" (Sánchez), 152-157
Homo poeta, 8, 10-12, 171, 213; definition of, 10

I Am Joaquín (Gonzales), 3, 48-68, 69, 110, 212-214
Imago mundi, 34-35, 45-46, 155
Inhumanism, 174-176
Interlingualism, 12-13, 18, 28, 38, 42, 80, 149, 156; definition of, 226n.10

Jail (prison, *pinta*), 37, 42-43, 44-46, 62, 143, 151-152, 157
Jeffers, Robinson, 162, 170, 174-177, 181-182
Jews, 55-56, 104
Juárez, Benito, 48, 55-56

Killing, 28, 36, 44, 49, 52, 55, 58, 63, 66, 75, 82, 107, 110, 122, 124, 175, 181, 190, 198, 200, 213

Land (property), 49, 52-54, 56-57, 62, 97, 100-101, 105, 107-108, 110-114, 119-121, 127, 153-154, 160, 162; loss of, 49, 58, 63, 98-99, 101, 103, 105-106, 111, 121

Lawrence, D. H., 139
León-Portilla, Miguel: *Aztec Thought and Culture*, 71, 86
Lévi-Strauss, Claude, 4
Llorona, 39–40, 44, 153–154, 156; definition of, 39–40; as police car siren, 42
Los criaderos humanos (Méndez), 116–130, 212
Love, 63–64, 84, 96–103, 105–109, 111–112, 114, 119, 125–127, 132, 137–139, 141, 151, 156, 167–170, 172–175, 183, 205, 207, 209, 212–215
Lowrider, 25–27; definition of, 220n.12

Machismo, 21, 36–37, 39, 42, 45, 63, 101–105, 120, 123, 167, 169, 173, 181, 205, 209, 211, 214
Malinche, 40, 104, 110, 113, 207
Marbles. *See* Games
Marijuana. *See* Drugs
Mayans. *See* Native Americans
Melting-pot, 9, 60, 88. *See also* Assimilation
Méndez, Miguel, 147; *Los criaderos humanos*, 116–130, 212; *Peregrinos de Aztlán*, 117; "Tata Casehua," 117, 126
Merrel, Floyd, 4–5
Mestizaje (mestizo), 31, 49, 50, 52–55, 57, 60, 62–66, 100, 101, 106, 110, 175, 178
Mexican Revolution, 37, 56–57, 61, 64, 84; failed, 57, 100, 106, 108, 111
Migrant workers, 99, 119, 144, 147, 185, 187, 196–198, 201, 208
Miscegenation, 49, 53, 61, 87, 104–105; rejected in the U.S.A., 52, 54, 60, 63–64
Misogyny, 186, 193–194, 204–206, 209
Modern society, 8–9, 69, 74, 160; as chaos, 51–52, 59, 68; as death, 65; as dehumanizing, 54; as insanity, 65, 162; as threat, 50; in disintegration, 9, 152
Montoya, José, 30, 96, 211; "El Louie," 3, 14–25, 26–28, 35–36, 212–214

Moon landing, U.S., 97, 99, 122, 127, 141
Murrieta, Joaquín, 58, 63, 109–110
Music, 17–19, 44, 64, 68, 84, 87, 100–103, 106, 116, 120, 122, 142, 153–155, 207
Myth and mythology, 11, 34, 66, 111, 116, 127–128, 156, 169, 183, 207; allegorical, 128; Aztec, 127; of Aztlán, 3; beasts of, 160; of garden, 206; Greek, 89, 90, 170; structure of, 4; time as, 39, 69, 74, 81, 140; of woman's presence, 57

Nationchild Plumaroja (Alurista), 69–70
Native Americans, 31, 32, 55, 56–57, 60, 70, 102, 104, 106, 117, 128, 154, 177; Aztecs, 53, 56–57, 66, 76, 85, 89, 127, 154, 177; Chamulas, 57; Chichimecs, 53; Mayans, 53, 57, 154, 177; Nahuas, 69, 17–71, 74, 77, 80–81, 85–86, 164; pre-Columbian, 53–54, 81, 83, 85, 91, 93, 110–111, 127, 169; Tarahumaras, 57; Yaquis, 57, 117, 125; Zapotecs, 57
Navarro, J. L., 30, 145; "To a Dead Lowrider," 25–29, 145–146, 212, 220n.12
Nezahualcoyotl, 48, 53

Ong, Walter J., 222n.2
Oral history, 29, 64, 96, 110, 122, 125, 129, 197
Oral tradition, 34, 46, 48, 49, 56, 64, 71, 93, 96, 98–99, 103, 108–109, 116–117, 122, 128, 146, 212–213, 222n.2; writing the, 32–34, 46, 64, 103, 116, 129, 147
Order, 5–6, 38, 47, 52, 54, 65, 74, 157, 170, 186, 192, 199–202, 208; as chaos, 45–46; cosmic, 11, 160, 178

Pachuco, 14, 17–18, 22, 25–29, 42–44, 46–47, 144–147, 149, 157–158, 213; baby chukes, 21; cities of, 18; definition of, 218–219n.2
Paradigm charts of works: abstract, 5; *The Elements of San Joaquin*, 210; "El Louie," 24–25; *Floricanto en Aztlán*, 94–95; *Hay otra voz Poems*, 150; *I Am*

Joaquín, 66–68; *Los criaderos humanos*, 129–130; *Perros y antiperros*, 114–115; *Restless Serpents*, 183–184; Sánchez' works, 158–159; "Stupid America," 33–34; "To a Dead Lowrider," 29; "A Trip through the Mind Jail," 46–47
Paradigm of Chicano literature, 5–13, 14, 48, 96
Paz, Octavio, 104, 207, 219n.4, 220n.7
Penitentes, 160–166, 171, 173, 178–180, 182, 227n.2, 228n.8
Peregrinos de Aztlán (Méndez), 117
Perros y antiperros (Elizondo), 96–115
Picasso, Pablo, 31–32
Pilgrimage, 6, 53, 56, 76, 85, 89–90, 119, 187, 196
Play, 10, 20–21, 37–40, 43, 88; crime as, 38; writing as, 36, 45, 88. *See also* Games

Quetzalcóatl, 110

Ramírez, Orlando, 18, 211, 219–220n.5
Raza, 49–50, 53, 56, 63, 66, 73–74, 76, 78, 83–84, 88–91, 93, 144, 149, 157, 214
Restless Serpents (Zamora), 160–184
Rite of passage, 7, 9, 35, 43, 70, 102, 142, 167, 217
Ritual, 8, 10–11, 28, 36–38, 63, 74, 80, 90, 95, 117, 119, 139–140, 142–144, 148, 160–162, 165–170, 174–177, 181–182, 213–215; dancing as, 37, 167; death as, 91, 93; eating as, 99; funeral, 8, 171; heroics as, 11; love as, 169; macho, 173; male, 165; paradigmatic process of, 49, 56, 62, 66; Penitente, 160, 163–164, 171, 173; poem as, 91, 179; sex as, 37–38, 166–167, 181; women's, 168; writing as, 164, 169, 173, 182
Rivera, Tomás, 47, 218n.10

Sacred, 5, 8, 11, 117, 140, 160–161, 162–164, 166, 171, 180–182, 187, 192, 198, 201, 213; act, 72, 215; altars, 62; bard, 71; center, 6, 40, 165–166; erotic act, 179; harmony,

90; invocation, 8; land, 160; nature, 174, 177, 208; play, 164; power, 82, 165, 167, 173; right, 56; silence, 128; space, 6, 10–11, 34–35, 165; spot, 205; time, 74, 165, 171; word, 72. *See also* Hierophanies; Solarcentrism
Sacrifice, 28, 48, 55, 61, 62, 90, 93–94, 140, 161, 182–183, 223–224n.6; and blood spilling, 49–50, 52–53, 57, 59, 61–63, 66, 68, 110, 163, 165, 166, 178, 213–214
Salinas, Raúl, 14, 214; "A Trip through the Mind Jail," 34–47, 152–153
Sánchez, Ricardo, 211, 213–214; *Canto y grito mi liberación*, 151–152, 157–158; *HechizoSpells*, 152–157; "Homing," 152–157
Santeros, 31–32
School, 43–44, 46, 86, 114, 146–147; as death, 8; as threat, 9; rejection of Chicanos by, 39, 41, 145, 152
Shakespeare, William, 172–173
Silence, 21, 28, 55, 102, 104, 116–117, 120, 122–123, 127–128, 131, 142–145, 147–149, 151, 154, 157–158, 185, 194–195, 204
Solarcentrism, 74, 77, 83, 87, 89
Soto, Gary, 214; *The Elements of San Joaquin*, 185–211
Space (literary), 14, 16, 28–29, 45, 51, 56, 78, 80–81, 84, 88, 93, 117, 129, 143–144, 146, 149, 157, 161, 178, 179, 195–196, 211
Structure of Evil, The (Becker), 10
"Stupid America" (Delgado), 30–34
Sun, 73, 75, 76, 77, 79–80, 83, 90–92, 97–103, 105, 107–108, 111, 127, 134–137, 141, 143–144, 147, 167–168, 177, 200; Chicanos as, 91; poet as, 90. *See also* Solarcentrism

"Tata Casehua" (Méndez), 117, 126
Thomas, Dylan, 140, 148
Time, 7, 73, 92, 96, 155, 157, 165, 172, 173; of the barrio, 37; corrosive, 35; mythical, 69, 74; oppressive, 131–133, 135–145, 147–148; as society's regulator, 74. *See also* Time-space

Time-space, 39, 74, 80, 91, 93, 148, 165, 208

Timespace Huracán (Alurista), 69

Tlamatini, 69, 71-72, 81-82, 89, 93; definition of, 71

"To a Dead Lowrider" (Navarro), 25-29, 145-146, 212, 220n.12

Tonantzin, 57, 76, 85. *See also* Virgin of Guadalupe

"Trip through the Mind Jail, A" (Salinas), 34-37, 152-153

United Farm Workers Union, 98, 100-103, 105-107, 110, 114, 127, 147

United States western conquest, 31, 50, 63-64, 81, 98-99, 103, 111

Villa, Francisco "Pancho," 48, 56-57, 108

Villanueva, Tino, 12, 151, 212, 214; *Hay otra voz Poems*, 131-150

Virgin of Guadalupe, 48, 57, 76, 84-85, 98, 102-103, 105-106

Waste Land, The (T. S. Eliot), 186-187, 206-207

White Goddess, The (Graves), 117

Woman, image of, 17-18, 37-42, 44, 57-58, 63-65, 68, 75-76, 97-98, 100-110, 114, 119-120, 122-123, 127, 145, 151, 154, 160-161, 165-168, 172-173, 175-187, 193-194, 198-199, 201-205, 208-209, 214; as culture, 63; as death, 40, 108; exclusion of, 160, 165, 166, 173; as Mother Earth, 119, 121, 127; as passive, 58, 64, 181; as receptacle of tradition, 57-58, 64, 97, 107, 109-110; as sacred voice, 198; as sex object, 37, 38, 39, 42, 175, 193

Work, 10-11, 53-56, 62, 63, 73-75, 77, 79, 82-86, 89, 91, 96, 98-100, 102-103, 106, 108-112, 119, 134, 151, 155, 166, 181, 185, 188-191, 195-198, 201, 205, 208, 212

Yaquis. *See* Native Americans

Zamora, Bernice, 3, 211-212, 214; *Restless Serpents*, 160-184

Zapata, Emiliano, 48, 56-57, 59

Grateful acknowledgment is made to the following for permission to reprint previously published material:

Abelardo Delgado, for "Stupid America."

Alurista, Aztlán Publications/UCLA, and Chicano Studies Center, UCLA, for poems and excerpts from *Floricanto en Aztlán*.

Sergio Elizondo, for excerpts from *Perros y antiperros*.

Rodolfo Gonzales, for excerpts from *Yo soy Joaquín / I Am Joaquín*.

Miguel Méndez M., for excerpts from *Los criaderos humanos (épica de los desamparados) y Sahuaros*.

José Montoya, for excerpts from "El Louie," previously published in *Aztlán: An Anthology of Mexican American Literature*, ed. Luis Valdez and Stan Steiner (Vintage Books, 1972).

J. L. Navarro, for excerpts from "To a Dead Lowrider," previously published in ibid.

Raúl Salinas, for excerpts from "A Trip through the Mind Jail," previously published in ibid.

Ricardo Sánchez and Chicano Studies Center, UCLA, for excerpts from *HechizoSpells*, ©Ricardo Sánchez, Ph.D., 1976; Ricardo Sánchez for excerpts from *Canto y grito*, ©Ricardo Sánchez, 1971 & 1973.

Black Warrior Review, for excerpts from "In December" by Gary Soto.

Graham House Review, for excerpts from "County Ward" by Gary Soto.

"Copper" by Gary Soto is reprinted with permission from *The North American Review*, copyright ©1976 by the University of Northern Iowa.

Gary Soto and *Partisan Review*, for quotations from the poem "Spirit," first published in *Partisan Review*, vol. 43, no. 2 (1976); first published in book form in *The Elements of San Joaquin* (University of Pittsburgh Press, 1977).

Poetry Now, for quotations from the poems "Summer" and "History" by Gary Soto, first published in *Poetry Now*.

Excerpts from other poems by Gary Soto reprinted from THE ELEMENTS OF SAN JOAQUIN by Gary Soto by permission of the University of Pittsburgh Press. ©1977 by Gary Soto.

Tino Villanueva and Editorial Mensaje, for poems and excerpts from *Hay otra voz Poems*.

Bernice Zamora, for poems and excerpts from *Restless Serpents*.